Music Technology and Education

Amplifying Musicality

Second Edition

ANDREW R. BROWN
GRIFFITH UNIVERSITY,
BRISBANE, AUSTRALIA

Routledge
Taylor & Francis Group

NEW YORK AND LONDON

Second edition published 2015
by Routledge
711 Third Avenue, New York, NY 10017

and by Routledge
2 Park Square, Milton Park, Abingdon, Oxon, OX14 4RN

Routledge is an imprint of the Taylor & Francis Group, an informa business

© 2007, 2015 Taylor & Francis

Library of Congress Cataloging-in-Publication Data
    Brown, Andrew R., author.
Music technology and education : amplifying musicality / Andrew R. Brown. — Second edition.
        pages cm
    Includes bibliographical references and index.
    1. Music—Instruction and study—Technological innovations.   2. Computer music—Instruction and study.   3. Music and technology.   I. Title.
    MT1.B789 2015
    780.7—dc23
    2014022218

ISBN: 978-0-415-72313-8 (hbk)
ISBN: 978-0-415-72314-5 (pbk)
ISBN: 978-1-315-85786-2 (ebk)

Typeset in Sabon
by Apex CoVantage, LLC

Printed and bound in Great Britain by
TJ International Ltd, Padstow, Cornwall

Contents

Preface

This book is about amplifying musicality with technologies. In particular it is about how the technologies of our time—electronic and digital devices and the software and infrastructure they employ—can enhance music making, learning and teaching. The book describes the variety of roles that technology can play in music education and includes information about a broad range of music technologies and their educational applications. The book provides the reader with an overview of the field and sufficient detail to extend their knowledge of, and engagement with, music technology in a variety of ways. It outlines how music technologies can assist learning and teaching across a wide range of musical activities.

The topics covered are diverse and therefore chapters are organized into five sections: concepts, creation, presentation, reflection, and implementation. The book begins by discussing relevant educational and philosophical concepts that guide the use of music technologies in education and these provide a framework for the remaining chapters. The next several chapters focus on creative activities using music technologies, including the recording, production, and publishing of music. The discussion moves on to the use of music technologies for presentations and performances, covering sound reinforcement, performing with technologies, and preparing audio visual presentations. Following this is an exploration of reflective practices facilitated and enhanced using media technologies and the Internet. This includes approaches to music research, skills training, and online learning and assessment. Finally, the book deals with implementing, integrating, and managing music technologies in schools and colleges and considers how digital technologies can assist with educational administration.

Each chapter provides information and practical advice about the topic under discussion, and explores its application in educational contexts. Chapters include a concise summary, questions for reflection on the topic, teaching tips, and suggested tasks. The content is designed to be applicable to a broad range of circumstances and equipment, and there are frequent real-world examples that help to ground the material. While topics are focused on music technology, they are related to common music activities, such as composing, performing, listening, and evaluating. This allows easy correlation with educational frameworks such as the standards advocated by the National Association for Music Education (NAfME) in the United States and proposed ICT-enabled practices in the European Commission's 'creative classrooms' (CCR) initiative.

Music technologies have changed considerably since the first edition of this book was published, just months before the launch of Apple's iPhone in early 2007 and a year before the term MOOC was coined in 2008. Somewhat prophetically, in the final chapter of the first edition I wrote, "As computing power grows, smaller battery-powered devices will replace desktop computers. The student's mobile phone will be their main computing device" (p. 311). As this edition is released we find ourselves in the age of the tablet computer, a wave that began as a ripple with the iPhone's introduction and gathered momentum with the launch of the iPad in 2010. Tablet computers today are smaller, more tactile, more powerful, and more connected than personal computers were almost a decade ago. These devices have combined with developments in interactive web technologies to start a revolution in the delivery of education online.

The term computer, therefore, has been displaced from the book's title; it is now too narrowly defined. This is somewhat ironic, given that computing technologies are more pervasive than ever. But it is just this ubiquity that masks the shared computational nature of digital technologies. We now distinguish between computers, tablets, smartphones, and the many specialized music technologies such as digital pianos and electronic tuners. This second edition embraces these developments and has been updated and revised to reflect contemporary circumstances: mobile devices and their apps, wireless technologies and networks, and trends in music distribution and social media.

Music technologies are increasingly a part of our music making, sharing, and learning. This book provides information and guidance to help explore the creative and educational possibilities that music technologies present, perhaps the most significant of which is leveraging technologies to develop and amplify musicality.

Andrew R. Brown, 2014.

Preface to the First Edition

This book is concerned with the use of the computer for educational activities that lead to enhanced music making and the development of musical intelligence. It is a practical and philosophical guide for teachers, trainee teachers, and interested parents in the use of the computer for music education, and provides valuable information on specific topics for students and musicians generally. The material covers topics ranging in sophistication from musical games for young children, through audio recording and musicianship applications for the middle school, to analytical, algorithmic, and interactive music activities suitable for senior students. The broad range of included material reflects the fact that a meaningful music education involves experiencing music making, reflecting upon that experience, and sharing music within a community. The book outlines how computers can play a role in facilitating and enhancing musical experiences and understandings and is applicable across all facets of music education.

This book is not a step-by-step guide to software usage that would replace an equipment manual, nor does it provide prescriptive lesson plans that would (more than likely) suit only a small range of educational circumstances. Instead, it paints a broad picture of the role the computer can play in areas including music publishing, sound recording, music distribution in the age of the Internet, music and sound analysis, and educational administration (to name a few areas). Each chapter outlines how computers can contribute to music education in a particular way, discusses relevant software applications including their strengths and weaknesses, and provides advice on effective usage and teaching strategies. Each chapter includes reflection questions, teaching tips, and suggested activities for teachers, as well as a chapter summary. References are provided to allow the reader to follow up on resources mentioned in the text and for further investigation by the curious reader.

A number of conceptual frameworks are outlined in the earlier chapters to provide a context for the book's practical discussions. These frameworks are provided to support effective understanding of the role of the computer in music education programs. In particular, a dominant theme is to understand the computer as a musical instrument.

When approached in this way the computer can be as integrated into music education as any other musical instrument. A more detailed examination of the role of musical technologies, particularly the computer, shows that they can act as a tool, medium, or instrument. The computer can be a tool but its function is more than utilitarian, it can be a medium for musical investigation but its influence is not only on data, and it can be an instrument for expression where it facilitates both music and musical intelligence. A second conceptual framework important to this book is the notion of a student's meaningful engagement with music making. Through this lens, musical activities and experiences are characterized as providing different modes of engagement and different contexts for meaning. These each have a particular impact on students' enjoyment and motivation. This book outlines how the computer provides opportunities for meaningful engagement that can lead to a balanced and effective music education program.

The majority of the book focuses on providing practical advice and information across the areas in which computers are used in music education. These areas are categorized as music creation, presentation, reflection, and implementation. The chapters on music production provide information on how the computer is used to produce music as scores and audio recordings. They examine the way a computer supports arranging, recording, song writing, remixing, record production, and so on. The chapters on music presentation are concerned with the use of the computer in live performance and in the preparation and display of documents, web pages, and so on. The chapters on reflection outline how computers can assist musical understanding through study and investigation. Topics include music research and analysis, how the computer can support musicianship and aural training activities, and how it can be used for assessment and administrative tasks. The chapters on implementation discuss the ways in which computers can be integrated into existing music education programs, including the pragmatics of funding, purchasing, and accessing computing resources. A glossary of terms is provided to assist with understanding and clarifying the text.

It is appropriate at the beginning of any book to acknowledge those who have influenced and assisted with its creation. There have been numerous colleagues and students who have informed my understanding of both music education and computers and their assistance and tolerance is much appreciated. In particular, I would like to acknowledge [the late] Steve Dillon and Kevin Purcell, two longtime collaborators in the use of music technologies in education. Their input and contribution to the ideas in this book are at times direct and always indirect. Most importantly, I would like to thank Lenore Keough who supported and guided me through the development of this work.

Music making is an experience derived from an aesthetic involvement with creative activities around sound production and representation. The computer is a capable sound-making device and an efficient manipulator of musical symbols, thus its appropriateness for music making seems clear. This book explores the possibilities of computer-assisted music making within a learning context, and reveals ways in which the computer can be an instrument for amplifying musicality.

Andrew R. Brown, 2006.

section I
Concepts

one
Ways of Making Music with Technology

Although sound recording technologies (the tape recorder, in particular) may have been the biggest technological change affecting music education over the past 100 years, digital technologies (including computers, mobile devices, and the Internet) are currently making the most obvious impact. Technologies are ubiquitous in music today, deeply integrated into the way it is created, performed, distributed, critiqued, and preserved. The full effect of technology's influence is yet to be felt. This book explores the implications and opportunities presented to music education by electronic and digital music technologies. In order to understand how music technologies can best serve music education, we need to be clear about the ways in which those technologies affect how we think about and interact with music in the classroom. We can then design learning environments better suited to helping students develop their musicality.

The history of music education is littered with changing technologies, and this seems set to continue in the future. Maintaining the quality and relevance of music education involves understanding the ways in which technologies affect students' relationships to music. A variety of technological resources—whether paper and pencil, or acoustic or digital instruments—can be used to alter students' experiences with music. Digital technologies are the most recent to have an impact and educators are still coming to terms with the full implications of their usage.

However, turning musical ideas into musical realities depends as much on our *attitudes* as it does on our *equipment*. This chapter outlines three approaches aimed at developing a more productive use of music technology in music education. In particular, this chapter examines how digital technology can be viewed as a tool, a medium, and a musical instrument. Certainly both old and new technologies can be used in this way, but the unique ways in which computers are able to process sound and musical symbols exposes new ways of thinking and acting. Minds are, in fact, transformed by changing technologies, and relationships to those technologies shifts over time. Therefore, it is important to understand the influential partnerships people develop with technologies.

The technologies available to the music educator include printed documents, musical instruments, mechanical tools (such as metronomes), electronic and digital audio devices, MIDI (Musical Instrument Digital Interface) sequencers, computers, printers, mobile phones, Internet communications, and the like. In effect, a book is a technology, a trumpet is a technology, and a computer is a technology. Although the focus of this book will be on digital technologies, it is crucial to draw parallels between older and newer technologies as a way of illuminating the pathway to a positive working relationship with them. Creative partnerships with music technologies can assist the musician in developing musical skills, creating and transforming music and sound, and amplifying their musical expression.

Changing Technologies

Educational delivery and assessment are being transformed with the use of digital music technologies for capturing and presenting student activities. There are many ways to produce and integrate audio and video outputs, and it is now common practice to video- or webcast a music lesson, audition, or examination. Research assignments can include integrated sound and video materials, providing a rich learning platform through which both verbally and visually oriented students can express themselves. For example, in a media-rich project report a student could draw on examples of both sequenced and live versions of an arrangement, in order to illustrate changes in timbral expectations and results (see Figure 1.1).

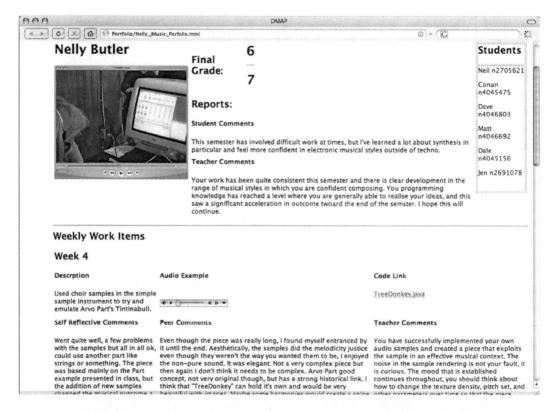

FIGURE 1.1 A rich media document can combine text, video, and audio materials.

In addition to incorporating new technologies into student assignments and activities, the inclusion of digital music technologies may also require changes in the curriculum itself. In particular, it may be necessary to broaden the definition of 'music' and the range of activities considered to be 'musical'. Educators need to accept contemporary musical practices, such as being a DJ, record producer, or app developer as valid, and teach the associated skills. There are many new opportunities available as a result of new technologies—and now education has to adapt to these new parameters. In his book *Smarter Than You Think*, Clive Thompson makes a similar comment about digital media's impact on written language skills: "Computational Power isn't just changing the old literacies of reading and writing. It's creating *new* ones. This includes literacies in video, images, and data sets, forms of information that are becoming newly plastic."[1] Other technology-driven changes to educational practices might include revising the criteria that guide the critical evaluation of music in digital formats and, of course, providing adequate infrastructure and resources.

The advantages stemming from these changes are likely to include the music program's greater relevance in students' lives, and their enhanced engagement and enthusiasm as a result. Such changes will also open up many new opportunities for music making and creative expression. These and other benefits will arise once digital technologies are used to expand musical opportunities in the classroom. There is little point in simply replacing old technologies with new ones and continuing to implement the same practices and activities. Rather, the educator must embrace new technologies and the new opportunities they bring. This shift involves transforming the ways in which we think about music and music education.

Changing Minds

While changes in technological resources can make a significant difference in how a music curriculum manifests itself, changing people's minds requires a more pervasive shift than the mere substitution of resources (e.g., musical notation presented on a computer screen rather than on paper). Changing minds is about changing metaphors; it is about the very ways in which we represent musical knowledge. For example, there is a big difference between understanding audio software as a linear 'tape recorder' and understanding it as an 'instrument' that responds dynamically to performance gestures.

The substitution of technologies, although challenging in itself, may not lead to significant changes in thinking if the same metaphors are simply applied to new technologies. There may be value in changing technologies without shifting metaphors, including greater efficiency, lower cost, and the increased integration of media systems. It certainly can be more efficient to write out a score using music publishing software. But, some substitutions may be expensive time-savers that do not necessarily result in improved musical understanding or skill level. Changes in metaphor, however, frequently result in significant changes in thinking and new potentialities for understanding the world of music.

Conceptual insights occur with new technology, but such insights are often subtle and insufficiently considered.[2] For example, the shift from using the recorder to using the electronic piano in group music performances involves a shift from monophonic to polyphonic and homophonic thinking, from vertical to horizontal pitch orientation, and from abstract octave shifts to concrete octave differences. While these changes are substantial, the shift from using the electronic piano to using the laptop computer in performance involves an even greater reconceptualization, or at least the possibility of one. The laptop computer shifts the student's focus from pitch and rhythm to timbre, time, and space. There is no longer a one-to-one correspondence between gesture and sound event, but a one-to-many possibility using complex sounds, arpeggiators, and algorithmic performance options. Laptop performance can develop the student's ability to determine sonic parameters beyond the fixed design of a given instrument, and foster radical changes in repertoire and musical style. Curriculum designers should carefully consider the metaphorical and cultural implications introduced by new music technologies, for it is these shifts that most significantly influence the minds of students.

Technological Metaphors

There are three metaphorical perspectives that inform the use of digital music technologies: the computer as musical tool, the computer as musical medium, and the computer as musical instrument. These perspectives are shown diagrammatically in Figure 1.2. Digital technologies are, to varying degrees, all of these things and more. Seeing computational devices from multiple perspectives, rather than from a single perspective, opens up a broader range of musical applications. When viewed as tools, they are seen as devices to be controlled; when understood as media, they become conduits for artistic communication; and when approached as instruments, they can be amplifiers of musical expression.

Technology as a Musical Tool

Digital technologies can be used as musical tools, and, like other tools, they can make jobs easier, tasks more efficient, and what was previously impossible possible. Tools amplify skills by providing leverage and extension. Just as an audio amplifier can make music louder, a music technology can be an amplifier of one's musicianship, enhancing musical skills and increasing musical intelligence. Tools can be quite utilitarian, that is, employed simply to get a job done. For example, the piano can act as a tool for ear training by using such musical features as intervals, chords, or rhythms for identification. In such tasks, there need not be any attempt at musical expression. Similarly, a smartphone with an appropriate app can be used as a tool for aural training, and a computer with software such as *Auralia*[3] or *Musition*[4] can provide endless practice exercises.

Technologies, when used as tools, have been characterized by media theorist Marshall McLuhan as *extensions* of human capacities.[5] For example, a person can extend

FIGURE 1.2 **Metaphors for understanding computers as music-making devices.**

their reach for hunting by using a spear, travel faster and further by using a bicycle or airplane, see further by using a telescope, and hear more clearly by using a microphone and audio amplifier. Tools can also extend intellectual abilities, not just physical ones. We can do math faster with calculators, express our ideas more clearly with languages, and understand weather patterns more thoroughly by using big data simulations.

Musical tools can range from simple physical devices, such as tuning forks, to complex devices, such as electronic tuners. They can include symbolic tools, such as common practice notation, and intellectual tools, such as metrical rhythmic grouping. The list of physical musical tools includes horns, quills, metronomes, music stands, and player pianos, while intellectual musical tools include the harmonic series, musical notation, rules of species counterpoint, and Fourier transforms.

The piano has long been used as a tool for composition. Characteristically, the composer sits at the piano with manuscript and pencil in hand and uses the piano to test ideas, confirm note choices, and play back compositional fragments. The computer, with a keyboard controller attached, can mimic this compositional practice using music publishing software such as *Finale*[6] and *Sibelius*[7] and using a mouse instead of a pencil. Tablet computers with touch screens are even better at simulating pencil and paper notational practices. However, digital technologies provide a rich array of tools that can be used for composition that go beyond the imitation of a manuscript. In particular, digital audio workstation (DAW) software provides the ability to record and layer parts, and hear them back with a variety of synthetic or imitative acoustic sounds. In this way a composition can be painted and modified with rapid aural and visual feedback. Importantly, a computer can be used recursively as a tool to develop other tools that can extend our musical reach. Software application development is becoming an increasingly valuable musical skill.

When using a tool there is an expectation that you have a task clearly in mind. For example, in order to paint a house, a painter chooses different tools that he knows will be required for that specific house; he may choose brushes, rollers, spray guns, ladders, and so on, depending upon the circumstances. Music technologies also have different strengths and weaknesses that influence how appropriate they are for the musical task at hand. It is important for a musician to understand the digital technologies available and how best to use them in conjunction with each other as a digital tool kit.

When using music technologies as tools, a musician typically acts as a *director* of proceedings, controlling the technologies in order to efficiently achieve his or her musical goals. It is important to know the scope of the musical job, to be familiar with how the particular features of each piece of software and hardware might help to get the job done, and then to maximize their musical potential. This tool-use relationship is common in human cultures, and so it should be quite clear how digital music technologies, when used as tools, can be valuable musical assistants. But, perhaps, the way in which the computer can be considered to be a musical medium is a little less straightforward.

Technology as a Musical Medium

A medium is a vehicle for transmission. With music, this is often sound, gesture, or notation. Acoustic instruments, for example, are vehicles for turning gestural energy into sound. Each instrument is made from some physical material. As vibrations pass through the material, they manifest as sounds. For example, in an acoustic guitar sound begins as vibrations in the strings after they are struck. As the strings vibrate, energy is transferred to a wooden soundboard that, in turn, resonates to amplify the sound. The sound quality of the guitar, therefore, depends on the type of material used in the strings, the manner in which they are struck, and, importantly, the properties of the soundboard. Steel and wood are the media of the guitar; they constrain its design and provide its characteristic sound.

Manuscript paper is also an example of a medium—one used for symbolic music representation through common practice notation. The properties of paper are well understood; these include being two dimensional, able to 'store' writing, persistent over time, easily transportable, and somewhat fragile.

The properties of such media can have a dramatic effect on the musical potential of objects made from those media. This potential is one of the reasons why the introduction of new media is so significant for music making, and therefore for music education. For example, when making trumpets, brass proved to be more flexible than animal horns or wood; the printing press enabled the wide distribution of written music; the introduction of electronic oscillators and filters enabled the creation of a new timbral palette able to augment acoustic sound sources. In the early twentieth century, the magnetic tape recorder emerged as a new medium capable of capturing and storing sound. The ability to record sound revolutionized music making and distribution throughout the twentieth century.

Computing technologies are able to present both sonic and symbolic information. They differ from previous music technologies because they are based on numbers; they are digital. To capture sound they use an analog-to-digital converter (ADC) and then the inverse to play it back, as depicted in Figure 1.3. They can capture light, temperature, gestures, and more with various sensors. Symbolic data can be entered directly from a QWERTY keyboard or MIDI instrument.

Digital media have a number of unique features. In particular, they can simulate or model both existing and imagined systems, they can manipulate and copy data without degradation, and they can complete these tasks at incredible speeds. Since the 1950s,

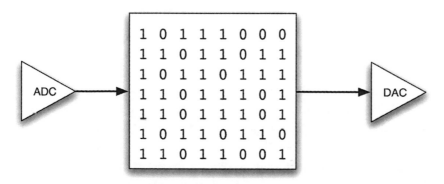

FIGURE 1.3 **Sound is converted to and from binary numbers for representation in a digital device.**

musicians from Risset and Xenakis to Eno and Eminem have been exploring the musical potential of digital machines, and the journey has only just begun.

Digital representation always involves a process of translation. For example, sound converted to electricity via microphone and then to numbers in the computer. Or compositional imagination, converted to notation and then to numbers in the computer. Through these representational and translational processes, McLuhan argues, media become metaphors that convert experience into new forms.[8] These processes can have an effect on the information being transmitted (e.g., sound or symbol), and in this way media are not neutral; they have an influence on, and contribute to, the nature of our experiences. When we are aware of this transformative capability of media and the interoperability between them, we can either compensate for it or utilize it. It is only when we ignore it or deny it that we risk having the transformational change take us by surprise or undermine our true intentions.

Digital technologies, like audio files (MP3, WAV, etc.) or streaming music services (*Spotify*, *iTunes Radio*, etc.) enable the transmission of music in digital form. In this way, digital technologies display properties of previous media like music albums, radio, and television in their serial transmission of sound. Yet they have unique features like customized streams for each listener. The digital distribution of music, in a world of ubiquitous mobile devices and the Internet, has had a massive influence on the access to and distribution of music. This shift, in turn, has had an impact on music education, particularly on how students listen to music and how they might produce, share, and commercialize their own music.

Another property of a medium is its persistence. When music is written on paper as a score, it becomes more permanent than if it were improvised. The score then takes on the life span of the medium; as long as the paper survives, so does the written music. However, the persistent aspects of notated music are only partial. Writing music in common practice notation cannot fully capture all of the qualities inherent in music. Rhythm values are quantized to the closest rhythmic value (quarter note, eighth note, etc.), pitch is quantized to the closest semitone, and dynamics are reduced to general statements, such as mezzo forte and crescendo. Therefore, the medium through which a musical manuscript is transmitted and the conventions of notation influence which aspects of the music are preserved and which are discarded.

Digital representation and storage is no different. Ultimately, data is quantized to values of 1 or 0. However, in practice, the resolution is often so high that any numerical imprecision is imperceptible. Music is represented as numbers inside a computing device, and when musical data is processed with software, it is these numbers that are adjusted. Importantly, these numbers do not degrade with any changes (addition, subtraction, and so on), so the data inside the computer is robust and persistent. As a consequence, the computer can process and copy music in a nondestructive way, allowing a musician to try different ideas and endlessly explore a vast range of musical possibilities.

How does a digital medium affect the music itself? A digital representation of music has particular characteristics that include the quantized nature of musical attributes such as loudness, pitch, and so on. In practice, the resolution of modern computers is so high that quantization is unproblematic, but there are occasions where its effects can be observed, for example, in the aliasing of waveforms with spectra above the Nyquist frequency. The digital nature of the computer makes many processes easier than they would be in analog form (time stretching, for example). Some processes sound similar, but are fundamentally different, such as equalization or filtering. Of course, recording music through microphones and playing it back through loud speakers is likely to have an even greater unintended impact on the sonic qualities of the music than the digitization process.

Computer usage expert Alan Kay famously pointed out that musical representation as digital media adds more capability for users than simply storage and recording.

> In a book you can print a score, and that's good. But on a computer, you not only can print the score, but you can start moving things around and experimenting with whole sets of musical languages. I've used the term 'metamedia' to describe the computer, and what I mean is that it is a holder of all the media you can think of, as well as ones you haven't thought of yet. The computer allows you to capture important ideas, whatever the form of their expression, and convey them in a way that will help other people understand them, and maybe even add to them.[9]

It is these enhanced capacities to store, manipulate, and communicate data that are at the heart of the digital revolution and the increasing ubiquity of digital media in our lives.

Digital media create a vast landscape of possibilities for musical and sonic transformation. Therefore, when using digital technologies as musical media, the musician often acts as an *explorer*. As a medium, the computer becomes the terrain that can be navigated using various software applications. The destination of the journey through musical space is not always predetermined. Rather, musicians who are aesthetically attuned are able to discover interesting features of that landscape, and skilled musicians are able to seek out and exploit these discoveries using the special characteristics of the medium to productive ends. Those who become even more fluent in digital technologies find that they can interact with them as expressively as with other musical instruments.

Technology as a Musical Instrument

Musical instruments such as the piano and guitar can be more than convenient tools or useful media for communication. When played well, these instruments become a means of musical expression. Ideally, a close bond is established between a performer and his or her instrument. In terms of digital technologies, it is possible, and even desirable, to have a similar kind of relationship. Any musical instrument, including a computer, MIDI control surface, mixing desk, or smartphone, amplifies your musical abilities. As Alan Kay suggests,

> You don't need technology to learn science and math. You just absolutely don't need it. What you need to have are the right conditions. In music, if you've got the right conditions and you've got music happening, then the instruments amplify what you've got like mad. The best thing a teacher can do is to set up the best conditions for each kid to learn. Once you have that, then the computer can help immeasurably.[10]

The trick to unlocking this expressive potential is to approach the device as a musical instrument. It is this metaphor of the digital device as musical instrument that can be the most powerful in helping the music educator to decide how best to use these new digital technologies. When presented with such a decision, we simply need to ask, "what would we do if it were a clarinet, piano, recorder, or xylophone?" This approach will usually yield an appropriate answer. In addition, when deciding what musical instruments to use for an educational activity, digital devices should be considered to be viable options.

The most common context in which a piece of musical equipment becomes an *instrument* is in live performance. Playing the piano is generally associated with real-time performance; music technologies are also increasingly being played in real time. For example, laptop computers and apps for mobile devices are used to produce electronic music live. The *Ocarina* app from Smule, for instance, turns the iPhone into a wind instrument.[11] One big difference with electronic music performances is that the gestural relationship to the sound is sometimes less direct than with acoustic instruments. Acoustic instruments typically have a one-to-one gesture-to-sound relationship. In other words, pressing the finger down on the piano key or sliding the finger along the fretboard of a guitar has directly audible results. This one-to-one relationship can also be true for electronic and digital instruments. For example, turning the filter cutoff dial on a synthesizer will change the timbre of the sound, while hitting a pad on an MPC (music production controller) device can trigger a sound. With computers, we find this relationship when a mouse click starts a multipart music clip, or a parameter movement changes the complexity of a rhythmic part.

While performance is the most obvious context for using technologies as musical instruments, it is also possible to approach digital technologies in this way in non-real-time contexts where they act as amplifiers of ideas rather than gestures. Most musical tasks involve a degree of real-time manipulation or improvisation, as well as some preparation of musical materials. The composer Paul Lansky described his computer-assisted compositional process as "improvisation in really slow time" (personal communication, January 23, 1998). This characterization underscores the fact that the experiences of performance and composition can be similar under the right circumstances. Those conditions are determined by software and hardware design, but predominantly by the attitude and skills with which the musician approaches music technologies. Perhaps most importantly, the musician needs to be fluent in the use of the technologies and willing to be influenced by his or her interaction with them, approaching the relationship more as a partnership. Indeed, using digital technologies as musical instruments is as much about attitude as it is about action.

Using technologies effectively as instruments for musical expression requires a fluency and familiarity with the instrument that enables direct expression with little need for conscious reflection. The demands of real-time expression, in particular, require this familiarity, just like the ability to speak fluently without conscious effort. This is the kind of musicianship David Borgo describes as embodied, situated and distributed.[12] This relationship to music technologies can exist in a composition or production context, as well as in performance. Both contexts require an intense involvement that emerges from familiarity through practice. The metaphor of technology as musical instrument becomes possible only when a person is musically articulate and fluent in the representational system of the technology. Often, in this situation, the digital musician can express himself or herself more clearly with a computer than with any other instrument. Engagement with a digital system as a musical instrument is characterized by intuitive action that arises through practice, just like riding a bicycle. As an example of this level of digital music fluency at its rawest, we can look at examples of live coding practices by artists such as Andrew Sorensen.[13] As a musician begins to work closely with an instrument, even a computer, they begin to understand the musical world from the perspective of that instrument. The visual layout of the piano keyboard is a good example of how the physical instrument can provide a useful way of conceptualizing frequency as a stepped series of pitches from low on the left to high on the right. This type of understanding, inherited from instrument design, can be so deeply ingrained that it is often hard to see its influence. The computer scientist and educator Seymour Papert emphasizes this point in his writings, noting that the "computer presence [can] contribute to mental processes not only instrumentally but in more essential, conceptual ways, influencing how people think even when they are far removed from the physical contact with a computer."[14]

It is clear that adopting the metaphor of technology as musical instrument can lead to a deep engagement with the technology, just like that required by any other musical instrument. As a result, the musical learning stimulated by such an interaction with digital technologies can be every bit as authentic and rewarding as that available from more traditional musical instruments.

Despite the potential for such a close relationship, at the end of the day music technology is simply equipment, and this can lead to an uneven partnership wherein the musician's skill level and attitude make a bigger difference than the equipment design or construction. For example, while a better piano might make some improvement to the sound of the instrument being played, and a faster, more fully loaded digital device or software might also make some improvement to the music it produces, in both cases a better-skilled musician—one who can learn to harness the technology for musical expression—will make a much more significant impact on the music than better equipment alone.

Learning how to use computing devices for music making is best approached like learning any other musical instrument: it requires regular and focused practice, but it can be very rewarding. While music technologies can provide some immediate gratification with little effort, realizing their full expressive potential involves developing understanding and fluency. By embracing positive attitudes toward technology and approaching it as a musical partner, musicians can develop deeper relationships with music from which they will gain much insight and enjoyment.

Conclusion

Music educators can influence student learning by controlling the technological environment in which they operate and the attitudes they promote. The computer can amplify musicianship by being considered broadly as a tool, a medium, and an instrument. The technological environment, including the stance towards it as a tool, medium, or instrument, comes together for the music educator with content knowledge and pedagogical approaches to managing learning. These three aspects come together within an educator as a contextualized, or situated, form of knowledge Mishra and Koehler call Technological Pedagogical Content Knowledge (TPCK).[15] In order to maximize student learning through computer-based musical experiences, educators need to consciously contextualize technological changes, develop appropriate music making activities, and provide adequate opportunities for reflection. We can change minds and change music by changing technologies and the way we use them.

Reflection Questions

1. What are the metaphorical perspectives from which technologies can be viewed as music equipment?
2. What is the role of the teacher in changing technologies in a learning environment?
3. Which is more critical for making music effectively with technology: attitudes or equipment?
4. In what ways can a computer assist a musician?
5. To what degree can technological skills be considered musical skills?
6. Name some digital musical tools and describe how they can be used as tools.
7. Which musical media are commonly used in the classroom?
8. Is the effect of media neutral when they are used to make music?
9. Is the computer a single piece of equipment or a toolkit?
10. What are the differences in approaching technologies as tools, media, and instruments?

Teaching Tips

1. Document performances as audio and video recordings to assist in reflection and assessment.
2. Use the computer to present music information in media-rich ways that integrate text, image, and sound.
3. Encourage students to use audio and video materials for assignments so that they can demonstrate their understanding of different media.
4. Use a variety of music representation systems to provide a richer understanding of abstract musical concepts.
5. Remember that changing metaphors requires a change in thinking; simply changing technologies is not necessarily sufficient.
6. Look for opportunities to include music technologies in musical performances.
7. Maximize student learning by using the most appropriate technology for the job, not simply the most available.
8. Match the characteristics of technologies with desired learning outcomes.
9. When undecided about how best to use music technologies, rethink the problem using an acoustic instrument substitute.
10. Like any other instrument, digital technologies need to be practiced, so support that need with appropriate student access and time.

Suggested Tasks for Educators

1. Attempt the same musical task using a variety of software applications to reveal some of the comparative strengths and weaknesses of each.
2. Audit your uses of music technologies to see how much you are using them as tools, media, or instruments.

3. Make a list of the technologies used in your music teaching or learning and describe your use of each as a tool, medium, and instrument.
4. Identify opportunities in the music curriculum where music technologies could be used as a tool, medium, and instrument.
5. Experiment with ways that you can include digital technologies in your musical performances.

Chapter Summary

Technologies assist in transforming musical ideas into musical realities. Understanding the non-neutral partnership with technology is important in managing that influence. Making music with technologies can be made more effective by considering different approaches to the use of technology. In particular, we should consider music technologies as tools, media, and instruments. When understood as a tool, the role of technology is to assist us in efficiently achieving our goals; our approach can be characterized as that of director. When understood as a medium, technology can capture, transform, and communicate music; our approach is one of exploring the opportunities they present. When understood as a musical instrument, technology can be used as a sounding board that reflects and amplifies our musicality; our approach is to focus on musical expressiveness in partnership with technology. Using digital technologies can lead to novel experiences that expose us to new ways of thinking. We can, in fact, change minds by changing technologies and our relationship to them.

Notes

1. Thompson, C. (2013). *Smarter than you think: How technology is changing our minds for the better.* New York: Penguin Press, p. 87.
2. Brown, A. R., & Purcell, K. (1988). *Music technology: A transparent integration.* Paper presented at the XVIII ISME International Conference: A world view of music education, Canberra, Australia.
3. *Auralia*, ear training software from Rising Software: www.risingsoftware.com/auralia/.
4. *Musition*, music theory software from Rising Software: www.risingsoftware.com/musition/.
5. McLuhan, M. (1964). *Understanding media: The extensions of man.* London: Sphere Books.
6. *Finale*, music notation software: www.finalemusic.com/.
7. *Sibelius*, music notation software: www.sibelius.com.
8. McLuhan, *Understanding media*, 67.
9. Kay, A. (n.d.). "The Dynabook Revisited." Interview by *The Book & The Computer*. www.squeakland.org/resources/articles/article.jsp?id=1007 (accessed January 2014).
10. Ibid.
11. *Ocarina*, a woodwind-like app for the iPhone: www.smule.com/apps.
12. Borgo, D. (2012). Embodied, situated and distributed musicianship. In A. R. Brown (Ed.), *Sound musicianship: Understanding the crafts of music* (pp. 202–212). Newcastle upon Tyne, UK: Cambridge Scholars.
13. Live coding videos by Andrew Sorensen: http://vimeo.com/andrewsorensen.
14. Papert, S. (1980). *Mindstorms: Children, computers, and powerful ideas.* New York: Basic Books, p. 4.
15. Mishra, P., & Koehler, M. (2006). Technological pedagogical content knowledge: A framework for teacher knowledge. *Teachers College Record, 108*(6), 1017–1054.

two
Principles of Learning Music with Technology

There is a range of issues that inform the use of technologies for music making. This chapter considers a few of these issues—some that are well documented and others that are more novel. Exploring these matters can help to reveal our assumptions, just as working with new technologies can expose our habits and preferences. This chapter explores the ways in which technologies amplify our decisions; why technologies cannot be invisible in the music-making process; the impact of cultural and environmental contexts on technological design and use; the importance of analogy for assisting in and directing our activities involving technology; the impact of music technologies on our notions of musicianship; how technologies can act as a scaffold and support in music making; the importance of motivation in music learning and how technology does not fundamentally change this fact; and how a matrix of meaningful engagement can help to frame musical activities and interaction with technologies. Even though this is an extensive list of topics, the chapter's overall message is a simple one: the application of new music technologies in an educational setting has benefits beyond simply influencing the practical activities undertaken by teachers and students. Rather, harnessing these new technologies facilitates the reevaluation and clarification of creative and educational principles.

Amplification

There is a saying that "to err is human but to really screw up you need a computer." The reality behind this witticism is that computers have the capacity to exaggerate our actions. With computers we are able to achieve more things, of greater scope, in less time, and with less effort. The difficulty posed by this enhancement is that we need to make sure we are doing the appropriate thing in the first place, lest we amplify our mistakes or misdirection. Put more simply, "garbage in, garbage out." For instance, we can use the Internet to search for a lot of information, but it is crucial to ask the right questions. As an example from music making, we can easily generate thousands of notes in an algorithmic composition, but is that algorithm going to produce notes that we will find aesthetically pleasing?

In the 1960s, Marshall McLuhan championed the notion that technologies extend human capacities.[1] He pointed out that telescopes enhance eyesight, bicycles extend our capacity for travel, cranes increase our ability to lift, and so on. He was particularly interested in media as intellectual and cultural amplifiers. As outlined in Chapter 1, digital technologies are powerful as media. Technologies can extend our ability to solve mathematical formulae, articulate our thoughts using word processors or social media, and manage compositional tasks using sequencers and music publishing software.

There is some debate about the degree to which computers should be used to enhance our creative abilities and not just to achieve efficient production (making certain jobs obsolete in the process). The core of this debate corresponds to the conceptualization of music technologies as either tools, media, or instruments, as discussed in Chapter 1. While technologies can clearly act as either, the computer is quite often relegated to being a tool for drill-and-practice skill development or the printing of neat musical scores. Meanwhile, the computer's ability to amplify musical creativity through, for example, experimentation with compositional structures, sound design through digital synthesis, or creative expression via interactive performance, is overlooked.

We miss a significant opportunity if we fail to maintain a focus on the aspects of music that can lead to meaningful experiences and rich cultural outcomes for communities. As we embrace new technologies, we limit this opportunity if we only utilize them for the superficial and utilitarian aspects of musical practice. According to John Dewey, "The abiding struggle of art is thus to convert materials that are stammering or dumb in ordinary experience into eloquent media,"[2] and he may as well have been talking about digital technologies today. Exploring the use of music technologies in education in particular, we are drawn to thinking more about the fundamental relationships between creativity and technology. Indeed, the more philosophical aspects of using technologies point in the direction of artistic creativity. As Heidegger suggested, "The more questioningly we ponder the essence of technology, the more mysterious the essence of art becomes."[3] In order to get the most out of our consideration of the role played by music technology in education, we need to reevaluate our approaches to music, learning, and technology. In struggling to understand the educational uses of technology, we indirectly reveal and amplify other fundamental assumptions.

Invisibility

An acoustic musical instrument mediates our interaction with music. The instrument enables and constrains the kind of music we can make according to its design and material properties. For example, a snare drum has limited pitch variation, a flute can only play one note at a time, and a piano cannot control the dynamic of a sound after the key has been struck. These characteristics are determined by the design features of each instrument. Similarly, digital technologies have their own design characteristics that determine a particular set of musical possibilities, some that are obvious and others that are less so. As such, technologies, old and new, are never neutral or invisible in the music-making process.

The influence of technology on human affairs has long concerned sociologists and designers. In his writings on technology and culture, Neil Postman argues that language is a technology. Even though it is often considered invisible, language is embedded in ideological assumptions and can structure and direct thinking.[4] Postman also suggests that educational curricula and the institutional organization of education are also human constructions—technologies—although we often overlook the significant influence they have on student learning. It may appear, therefore, that it is desirable to be more aware of the impacts of inbuilt biases in technologies on outcomes. But this is not always the case; at times we simply want technologies to get out of our way.

Donald Norman, an expert on technology design, directly addresses this duality in his book *The Invisible Computer*, in which he argues for the increased invisibility of the computer and an augmented focus on human needs and capacities.[5] Like Postman, Norman is aware that technologies can have a strong influence and proposes to redesign them with the aim of nudging user actions in a preferred direction. Norman is keenly aware that designing technologies to appropriately direct human activity can be a challenge. For this reason, it is critical to make smart choices about music software and hardware. The outcomes of specific systems are influenced by the designer's cognitive or physical preferences and understandings. When we choose a piece of music software, or other technology, we are essentially deciding, in part, whether or not our priorities align with those of the designer.

Because so much depends on the designer's choices, some musicians choose to take on the role of designer and build their own software. Designing your own software does not generally make that software invisible, but rather reinforces your own habits. In a way, self-designed technologies are mirrors rather than pathways to musical understanding. There are a number of tool kits for building your own music software, the most common being *Max* by Cycling '74.[6] The design of music software is seen as advanced musicianship, and most people will choose to use software that has been designed by others, although it is becoming more accessible. In any case, whether building your own music technology or using one created by others, it is useful to be aware of what is made visible or invisible as a result of the choices made during its development.

Even if technologies are well designed, Norman suggests that the task of shifting people's habits and conventions towards the use of new technologies is the largest challenge. "The problem is," he states, "that whether it be a phonograph or computer, the technology is the easy part to change. The difficult aspects are social, organizational, and cultural."[7] Educational culture can be particularly slow to evolve. However, educationalists do understand the influence of social and environmental conditions on behavioral change and can take these into account alongside considerations of technological invisibility when designing educational experiences that include music technologies.

Context

It is a truism that no person is an island; we are the products of our physical and social surroundings. The impact of these contexts is no less critical in terms of music technologies than other areas of our cultural lives.

Often digital technologies used for music are also telecommunications devices and intimate agents of our social contexts. However, before looking further at our social contexts, there are important issues of physical context to be considered. As with other educational resources, music technologies are best used in resource-rich learning environments. Such an environment might include a spacious room, high-quality audio playback, a library of books and recorded music, acoustic instruments, and so on. The importance of one's physical surroundings is often overlooked at educational institutions, where computer laboratories, (just) adequate for word processing, are often unthinkingly adapted for musical tasks and then squeezed into unsuitable spaces. It is not a pretty sight to see a clarinet player in a computer lab trying to record a track with audio recording software, crammed between rows of tightly packed desks amidst the chatter of others and the noise from the sports field coming through the window.

Mobile technologies, such as tablet computers and smartphones, have made it more convenient to integrate music technologies into existing music teaching spaces. These technologies have also become assimilated into students' musical practices and leisure activities as well. Chapter 17 discusses this integration of music technologies in more detail.

Technology has played an increasingly important role in supporting the social context for musicians. The Internet and other telecommunication devices link people together via instant messaging, voice chat, e-mail, discussion forums, blogs, podcasts, and network jamming. Social media, such as Facebook and Twitter, have become important tools in the sharing of information, discussion of issues, organization of rehearsals, and publicity of concerts. This virtual social context, in many cases, has become as prominent in people's lives as their physical social interactions. In education, online learning systems, such as massive open online courses (MOOCs), demonstrate the value of these technological networks in transcending geographic boundaries, and suggest that online communication between students can be as important for student achievement as content delivery.[8]

Analogy

Digital technology is a chameleon; it can change its appearance with the launch of a new software application. When we contemplate this characteristic, it seems like magic, as if there must be some mysterious and unfathomable trick. Under normal circumstances, however, we do not give it a second thought—*of course* my phone can also be a guitar tuner.

While computational processes are indeed complex, they are made up of simple building blocks. The computer, in essence, only understands numbers—0s and 1s, to be precise. The computer's complexity, however, derives from its layer upon layer of abstraction and functionality. In each new layer, new conceptualizations and analogies are used.

The 'skin' of the computer software is the graphical user interface (GUI), and it is here that the most blatant mimicry occurs. We can make the computer screen look like a piece of manuscript paper with its characteristic texture and smudges, or we can make a reverb or synthesizer plug-in look like a physical device made of steel and wood. At all times, we should keep in mind that these illusions, while often useful or 'friendly', can obscure as much as they reveal about the operation of the software.

Despite the potential for obfuscation, analogy can be very useful in providing ways in which to understand complex phenomena. Musical knowledge is often represented through different analogies, as in, for example, the description of a timbre based on an instrument's design or acoustic attributes. A sound may be described as woodwind-like, or brass-like, with reference to the design of the instrument. A sound object[9] can alternatively be described according to its spectral distribution, amplitude envelope, and other acoustic properties, as in the electroacoustic musical tradition.

Both the notable researcher Douglas Hofstadter and the psychologist Emmanuel Sander make great claims about analogy being "the core of all thinking."[10] They suggest that analogies are the basis for the ways in which we categorize elements according to their similarities and differences, as well as the basis for insight through new conceptual organization or inference. They also suggest that analogies operate at all levels of the conceptual hierarchy. Musical examples might include basic principles, like higher and lower pitch, or the genealogy of musical styles that draw on each other as influences and combine elements and practices as a form of syncretism. Analogy may also assist in the temporal aspects of learning, building new concepts as elaborations of or deviations from previous experiences.

Analogy is employed in the design of music technologies to highlight the similarity between them and previous (more familiar) media; for example, in the use of a tape-recorder interface in digital recording systems. If expectations inherent in the analogy are maintained, then there should be a smooth transfer from the use of analog to digital media formats. One challenge inherent in the tape-recorder analogy is the effect of playback speed on pitch. Maintaining the analogy of a tape machine would involve increasing and decreasing the pitch with speed, but most system designers (and users) consider it more useful to separate speed and pitch change in digital audio systems.

The benefits of using analogies when shifting between technologies include a simpler transition and more obvious integration with existing practices, as in substituting manuscript paper with computer notational packages. But, on the other hand, we risk limiting innovation by constraining imagination, or by misunderstanding and obscuring how things really work.

Analogies, therefore, can be both limiting and misleading. When one has a hammer, the world looks like a nail. If we rigidly adhere to concepts drawn from previous media and their contexts, we might limit the new opportunities that new technologies provide. For example, the interface of previous versions of Apple's iPhone used skeuomorphic design elements where calendars had faux leather trim or ripped pages. Over the years, these design elements were increasingly criticized as being irrelevant and misleading, and they were largely removed in version 7 of the phone's operating system.

Being aware of the analogies that are employed in technologies can help us to understand them more thoroughly and appreciate why they behave as they do. Being aware of how digital technologics operate beneath their analogical surface, however, will enable greater appreciation of how they might be used.

Musicianship

What are the skills and understandings necessary to operate effectively as a musician? The answers to this question are as varied as the musical practices and cultures present throughout the world, underscoring the provisional and contextual nature of musicianship. A changing technological landscape has an impact on any contemporary definition of musicianship, but in what ways?

In the book *Sound Musicianship: Understanding the Crafts of Music*,[11] edited by this author, a variety of contributors addressed the question of what constitutes twenty-first-century musicianship from a range of perspectives including music as sound, perception, embodiment, and culture. Music technologies have an impact on each of these perspectives. As sound-making devices, digital technologies are tightly integrated in contemporary practices. These devices affect the ways in which we access and appreciate music, and provide important insights into the connections between music and our brains. Our interactions with music technologies have introduced performance techniques using new instruments and interfaces. Mobile technologies have reignited interest in the gestural control of sound. Cultural changes brought about by digital technologies include the development of new musical styles based on electronic and digital tools, the disruption of models of commercialization and distribution, and shifts in music commentary and critique as a result of social media.

Insights into digital musicianship can arise when looking at how experienced computer musicians and electronic music producers develop skills. Their common learning strategies include asking questions of their colleagues, reading software manuals, listening to music, searching Internet discussion boards, experimenting with equipment, and learning a computer programming language. They seek out knowledge that includes information about the physics of sound, basic electronics, digital audio principles, and software algorithms. They constantly seek new information sources on the Internet where they can further their knowledge and converse with like-minded artists.

These approaches to knowledge acquisition can be categorized as those concerning the nature of music and digital sound representation, those concerning the technology itself, those concerning music creation strategies, and those concerning the communication of ideas with others. These learning strategies are largely informal, and incorporate a lot of exploration and investigation. Information is accessed on a need-to-know basis, rather than deliberately organized or following a set curriculum. Learning conforms to individual needs, and success relies on the development of effective search and discovery methods. The experiences of such musicians resemble a pedagogy that is based more on creativity than on repertoire. Studies of contemporary musicianship that wish to embrace the use of music technologies will benefit from an examination of these areas of understanding and ways of acquiring skills and knowledge.

Scaffolding

Digital technologies are well placed to provide learning support. They can mimic the characteristics of many other educational media, and they can be automated through programming to take a somewhat active role in supporting students' musical activities. Notions of scaffolding are premised on the understanding that students build their own knowledge through experience and that supported (scaffolded) activities can enable experiences that would otherwise remain inaccessible. This constructivist approach was strongly argued in the writings of John Dewey and was one of the significant findings to emerge in the experimental psychology of Jean Piaget.[12]

One area where the computer can become a scaffold to music learning experiences is in the use of auto-accompaniment and backing tracks in performance. The use of such tools enhances motivation by filling out the sound, providing stability, and keeping the student in time and in tune. The accompaniment can be layered so that aspects of the scaffold may be removed as the student gains more skill and confidence. In more sophisticated programs, such as *SmartMusic*, the system can listen to the student's performance and adjust its performance accordingly, in order to compensate for the student's variations or errors.[13] Some systems can analyze the performance and provide feedback on how it might be improved. These accompaniment systems are discussed further in Chapter 11.

Network improvisation environments can provide scaffolding by using algorithmic processes to generate surface-level details of performances while students control the meta-level arranging and conducting parameters. Thus, students can develop collaborative and ensemble skills through real-time networking between devices, either locally or at distributed sites. Programs such as *jam2jam* provide scaffolded performance environments in which students control meta-level musical intensities and arrangements.[14] Some programs, such as *GarageBand*[15] or *iKaossilator*[16] for the iPad, allow devices to be synchronized so that music plays at the same tempo and remains in time with each other device. Some programs also allow for the recording of a distributed performance on a single device.

Music clip libraries and generative compositional processes are often embedded in music production software, in order to provide material that can be collated, tweaked, and assembled into an arrangement. Employing prepared music clips allows the user to focus on form and arrangement without having mastered lower-level compositional techniques, and provide the user with the freedom to learn by proceeding from macro-structure to microstructure, rather than by a traditional bottom-up approach.

Software Programming enables digital technologies to be more interactive and automated, greatly enhancing their capacity to scaffold student learning. They can act as performance accompanists, compositional assistants, reviewers, and critics, as well as resource libraries. Learning is often more fun when progress is enhanced through either real or virtual collaboration and support.

Motivation

The reason for undertaking an activity is distinct from the method used to achieve the outcome. Often educational objectives relate to skills and knowledge to be acquired, and activities and processes are designed to enhance these objectives. However, goal-oriented approaches are not always sufficient for engaging students in the learning process. Musicians' motivations often revolve around the desire to express themselves, have fun, develop social relationships, be curious and inquisitive, gain economic benefit, solve puzzles, and so on. Even while technologies may change, these fundamental human drives do not. As the educationalists Ken Robinson and Lou Aronica emphasize, the means for education to manage the "driving cultural and technological forces" is to focus on "[t]he features of aptitude and passion [and] the conditions [of] attitude and opportunity."[17] Therefore, many common motivational techniques used in music education, such as music camps and public performances, are just as applicable when learning with new music technologies. However, technology-based activities have their own cache of attractive motivational features that can help to keep people engaged in learning and making music.

For many students, digital technologies have some inherent motivational qualities. The most obvious of these is the dominant role they play in contemporary culture. The computer is associated with contemporary musical styles (rock, dance, and electronic music, in particular) that are likely to appeal to students. Musically, computers are used for recording and production, and increasingly as tools in the live performance of popular music. Digital technologies play a dominant role in accessing and distributing music through audio file sharing, downloading, and streaming. They also play a central role in social media communications. Because games are the category of mobile apps most often downloaded from the Internet, mobile devices have become associated with fun and play. Collectively, these activities link digital technologies to everyday cultural experiences more closely than ever before, especially for teenagers.

Many students relate to the technical or scientific aspects of the computer and are interested in how the technology works. Often, this is a different kind of student than the one who might normally be drawn to the artistic or social aspects of music. Meanwhile, the 'maker' movement and do-it-yourself (DIY) culture have embraced computing, and the construction of simple music devices and software has become increasingly popular. Some more musically sophisticated students may be interested in digital technologies because they can see the potential for musical exploration through the development of new techniques and musical forms.

As a result of this array of motivational forces, new technologies are sometimes used almost exclusively for their ability to entice students to participate in musical activities. Computing has become so widespread, however, that this ploy is rapidly losing its potency. The use of technology needs to be integrated with the constructive and communicative motivations (as outlined above) that remain inherently interesting, rather than relegated to less motivating tasks such as theory drills and aural training, Internet research for assignments, or administrative tasks.

Motivation is complex and multilayered. The attractiveness of digital technologies as contemporary devices is only a superficial attractor, and therefore music programs would benefit from positioning their use-value within some larger motivational frameworks. These frameworks might include career ambitions, the need for social acceptance, personal satisfaction through progressive skill enhancement, and so on. Effective learning plans will take account of individual and immediate goals, as well as overarching motivations that might span many projects and often last for many years. Sometimes, the very large-scale goals set and managed by teachers may not be immediately apparent to the student; emergent connections between projects often only become evident over time.

An important guiding principle when trying to maximize student interest in music technology is to provide them with appropriate challenges. Challenging projects are ones in which students move into unfamiliar territory or must learn new techniques and processes. Challenging music technology tasks include working with unfamiliar software or hardware, developing new tools, and applying existing software to new musical processes or outcomes. Mihaly Csikszentmihalyi's research into optimal experience has found that a task is more likely to be engaging if it is complex enough to require a person to focus all of his or her energies and skills, but not so complex as to become frustrating.

Csikszentmihalyi discovered that people were happiest when undertaking an appropriately difficult challenge. As he argues, "The best moments usually occur when a person's body or mind is stretched to its limits in a voluntary effort to accomplish something difficult and worthwhile. Optimal experience is thus something we *make* happen."[18] Therefore, as an effective strategy to maximize both satisfaction and learning, educators should involve students in the setting of targets and milestones related to their musical activities, with a deliberate view to extending their abilities in the process. When interacting with new technologies, keeping the focus on an incremental rebalancing of skills and challenges will help to foster motivation and engagement.

Meaningful Engagement

The capacity of music technologies to enhance students' engagement with music is a key measure of their likely impact on learning. Research by this author suggests that there are a number of different modes of engaging with music that can be accessed through technologies and the ways in which they are used.[19] There is good reason to think that both music making and the interaction with technologies are inherently engaging, especially given the amount of time people spend carrying out these activities. However, it is also possible for each to be boring or frustrating, so attention needs to be paid to the modes of creative engagement fostered by different activities and technologies, and how these can lead to more meaningful experiences through music.

The significance of musical activities can vary depending on their relevance to the student and their connection with the broader value systems of the school and the community.[20] Music technologies have the potential to be seen as relevant to students' lives given that those technologies are essential in the production and consumption of the popular and commercial music that students are exposed to. If students can use the techniques and processes of the music makers they admire, and achieve tangibly similar results, then they will be very pleased and engaged. Meaning can also be enhanced by connecting technology-based activities with other musical activities in students' lives. In this way music technologies are normalized as part of an overall music learning strategy, rather than seen as a separate or special component.

In a well-rounded music education there are different modes of creative engagement that educators should facilitate their students to encounter through their musical experiences. A student can be engaged with music by:

- Appreciating—paying careful attention to creative works and analyzing their representations
- Evaluating—judging aesthetic value and cultural appropriateness
- Directing—crafting creative outcomes and leading creative activities
- Exploring—searching through artistic possibilities
- Embodying—being engrossed in fluent creative expression

The modes of engagement frame music as an activity and student experience as participation in these types of activities. Understanding music as an activity has been a dominant theme in twentieth-century music educational theory. Keith Swanwick established an influential taxonomy of musical activities known as CLASP (Composing, Literature studies, Audition, Skill acquisition, and Performance)[21] which was carried forward as a guiding principle for many music curricula in their focus on composing, performing, and listening as core competencies. The activity-oriented emphasis in music education was taken further by David Elliot, who developed what he termed a "paraxial" philosophy of music education that emphasized music as action in a sociocultural context. He argued, "Musicianship is demonstrated in actions, not words."[22] Christopher Small was particularly direct about characterizing music as an activity, in contrast to it being understood as a sonic or notated artifact. He used the term 'musicking' to encompass all musical actions; including composing, performing, and listening.[23]

The modes of engagement build on this heritage, and they attempt, like Swanwick's CLASP, to outline a clear set of musical activities that can help guide discussions about both a child's musical activities and their musicianship. As a framework, the modes of engagement are less embedded in traditional Western music practices than previous examples. This allows it to be applied across a diverse array of music styles and cultures. It can even be applied beyond the sonic arts to practices like computer games, film, dance, and visual arts, and to various inter-arts practices in which even these disciplinary boundaries are blurred. Therefore, the modes of engagement articulate ways of being involved with creative practices quite broadly.

Furthermore, a student can find creative meaning in the following contexts:[24]

- Personal—the intrinsic enjoyment of creative activities
- Social—the development of artistic relationships with others
- Cultural—the feeling that one's creative actions are valued by the community

These modes of engagement and contexts of meaning can be combined to form a meaningful engagement matrix (MEM), as shown in Figure 2.1. Most musical experiences can be located within one or more cells of this matrix. For example, public performance fits into the Cultural + Embodying cell of the MEM. Performance involves embodied engagement through gestural interaction with an instrument or voice, and when it is done in public, it can generate cultural meaning for the performer as a result of feedback from the audience.

This MEM focuses on the phenomenological experiences of students as they undertake musical tasks. At one level, there are similarities with Keith Swanwick's activity-focused

	Appreciating	Evaluating	Directing	Exploring	Embodying
Personal					
Social					
Cultural					

FIGURE 2.1 The meaningful engagement matrix (MEM).

CLASP taxonomy that suggests that students should be involved with Composing, Literature Study, Auditioning, Skills, and Performance.[25] The modes of creative engagement and the CLASP model share an intention to ensure that a music program is well balanced. The impact of digital technologies on music making, however, means that the distinctions between performer, composer, and listener inherent in the CLASP model have been blurred to such an extent that they are no longer clearly identifiable in contemporary musical practice. The ways of engaging with music articulated in the MEM overcome these limitations and are applicable to a wider set of cultural circumstances and musical styles.

The meaningful engagement matrix focuses on the roles that students undertake as they make music and seeks to focus attention on the creative capabilities that students will develop. For example, within a performance activity, the student may be engaged to varying degrees through playing (embodying), listening and being part of the ensemble (appreciating), and taking the lead (directing). In preparation for the performance, the student may help to select the repertoire (evaluating) and work on a unique interpretation of the score (exploring).

While activities may provide students with experiences that can be placed in more than one cell of the MEM, the diagram in Figure 2.2 shows how particular musical activities tend to be emphasized by one cell in particular.

The MEM makes explicit how experiences with music technologies can operate within each of the modes of creative engagement. The matrix also reveals how music technologies can be relevant in personal, social, and cultural contexts to help develop musicianship and a rich sense of identification. Teachers can use the MEM to map the range of experiences that an activity, or even a whole curriculum, might provide for students. Once several of the activities shaping a student's musical life have been mapped, areas of inactivity across the MEM may emerge, and complementary activities can be devised to address those gaps.

Different music technologies lend themselves to certain interactions that emphasize particular areas of the MEM. A range of music technologies (various software or devices) may be required to cover all of these contexts and modes of engagement. When considered as part of the overall music program, music technologies can fill particular niches that enable the student to be engaged in ways not available in other aspects of the music program.

	Appreciating	Evaluating	Directing	Exploring	Embodying
Personal	Listen, Read, Watch	Analyze, Select	Compose, Produce	Improvise, Experiment	Practice, Play
Social	Share files	Discuss, Share playlists	Conduct, Lead	Jam	Rehearse, Record
Cultural	Attend events, Patronage	Curate, Publish reviews	Promote, Manage	Publish research	Perform

FIGURE 2.2 The meaningful engagement matrix with exemplary musical activities in each cell.

Conclusion

When considering the role of music technologies in education, it is important to clarify some of the common assumptions and issues that often arise. This chapter addressed how technologies can be an important part of music education, regardless of whether they are a complementary resource to traditional instruction or the principle focus of study. In order to understand new technologies and their potential in music learning, we need to reassess educational and creative priorities. Technological change acts as a stimulus for the reexamination of many facets of music education and musical experience. Interestingly, the implications and indirect effects that technologies can have on music education may be as significant as their direct and visible effects.

Reflection Questions

1. What other issues, not covered in this chapter, might have an impact on the use of music technologies in education?
2. What are some examples of ways in which music technologies have been both a positive and negative amplification of your actions?
3. How might we apply the myth of the invisibility of technology to the piano as a technology for music making?
4. Do you think that the physical or the social context is more important to the successful use of music technologies?
5. If writing on manuscript paper is the analogy used by music publishing software, what kind of analogy is used by digital audio workstation (DAW) software?
6. What technological skills might be considered essential to contemporary musicianship?
7. What are some of the ways in which a tablet computer might be used to scaffold the learning of music composition?
8. While technologies might provide some intrinsic motivations for their use, what external motivating factors are also likely to be effective?
9. Between which modes of engagement would you expect to find the most overlap?
10. Which contexts of meaning would likely be present at a solo DJ gig?

Teaching Tips

1. Use recorded or sequenced backing tracks to scaffold junior student performances.
2. Encourage regular backup of data on digital devices, because a simple mistake can have disastrous results.
3. Consider how digital and traditional resources can complement one another in supporting musical activities.
4. Consider analogy as a powerful explanatory technique when introducing new concepts related to music technology.
5. Include the acquisition of digital literacy in musicianship lessons and tests.
6. Utilize mixed ensembles of electronic and acoustic instruments whenever possible.

7. Ask students to reflect on the influence of technology on their production and consumption of music.
8. Evaluate your music software to see how typical user experiences gravitate towards particular cells in the MEM.
9. Ensure that opportunities for personal, social, and cultural meaning are part of learning activities with technologies.
10. Share the MEM with students as a tool for self-reflection and evaluation of their musical activities.

Suggested Tasks for Educators

1. Select one piece of software you use, and analyze its design and effect with regard to the issues raised in this chapter.
2. Conduct a meaningful engagement audit of your music curriculum, in order to see how evenly the different modes and contexts are represented.
3. As follow-up, read some of the cited references to pursue areas of interest more thoroughly.
4. List the interface metaphors that are employed by the apps you use regularly.
5. There are many other philosophical issues important to music education that are not covered here. Think about how these might also apply to the use of digital technologies.

Chapter Summary

There are a range of issues, often unrecognized, that drive the development and use of technologies. In educational contexts these become especially pertinent when the lessons learned at an intuitive level can be as influential as the declared curriculum objectives. The issues covered in this chapter are the technological amplification of abilities, myths about the invisibility of technology, the significance of context in the effective utilization of music technologies, the important influence of analogy on the design of music technologies, the recognition of digital literacy as a musicianship skill, the ways that technologies can scaffold learning, the influence of technologies on the motivation for learning and making music, and the use of the meaningful engagement matrix as a framework for thinking about musical experiences with technology.

Notes

1. McLuhan, M. (1964). *Understanding media: The extensions of man*. London: Sphere Books.
2. Dewey, J. (1934). *Art as experience*. New York: G. P. Putman's Sons, p. 229.
3. Heidegger, M. (1977). *The question concerning technology and other essays* (W. Lovitt, Trans.). New York: Harper & Row, p. 34.
4. Postman, N. (1992). *Technopoly: The surrender of culture to technology*. New York: Vintage Books.
5. Norman, D. A. (1998). *The invisible computer: Why good products can fail, the personal computer is so complex, and information appliances are the solution*. Cambridge, MA: MIT Press.

6. Cycling '74. 1999-2014. Max. San Francisco: Cycling'74. www.cycling74.com.

7. Ibid., p. vii.

8. Thomas, D., & Brown, J. S. (2011). *A new culture of learning: Cultivating the imagination for a world of constant change.* CreateSpace Independent Publishing Platform.

9. Schaeffer, P. (1977). *Traité des objets musicaux* (2nd ed.). Paris: Éditions du Seuil.

10. Hofstadter, D., & Sander, E. (2013). *Surfaces and essences: Analogy as the fuel and fire of thinking.* New York: Basic Books.

11. Brown, A. R. (Ed.). (2012). *Sound musicianship: Understanding the crafts of music.* Newcastle upon Tyne, UK: Cambridge Scholars.

12. Piaget, J. (1970). *Structuralism.* New York: Harper & Row.

13. MakeMusic. (2005–2014). *SmartMusic.* Eden Prairie, MN: MakeMusic Inc. www.smartmusic.com/.

14. *jam2jam,* a research software application for collaborative control of generative music: http:// explodingart.com/jam2jam.

15. *GarageBand* for iOS, Apple's DAW and music performance app for iPad and iPhone: https:// itunes.apple.com/au/app/garageband/id408709785?mt = 8.

16. *iKaossilator,* an interactive music app for iOS with looping capabilities from Korg: https:// itunes.apple.com/au/app/korg-ikaossilator/id452559831?mt = 8.

17. Robinson, K., & Aronica, L. (2009). *The element: How finding your passion changes everything.* London: Allen Lane, Penguin Press, pp. 19–23.

18. Csikszentmihalyi, M. (1992). *Flow: The psychology of happiness.* London: Rider Books, p. 3.

19. Brown, A. R. (2003). *Music composition and the computer: An examination of the work practices of five experienced composers* (Doctoral thesis). University of Queensland, Brisbane, Australia.

20. Dillon, S. (2001). *The student as maker: An examination of the meaning of music to students in a school and the ways in which we give access to meaningful music education* (Doctoral thesis). La Trobe University, Melbourne, Australia.

21. Swanwick, K. (1979). *A basis for music education.* London: Routledge.

22. Elliot, D. (1995). *Music matters: A new philosophy of music education.* New York: Oxford, p. 53.

23. Small, C. (1998). *Musicking: The meanings of performing and listening.* Hanover, NH: Wesleyan University Press.

24. Dillon, S. (2007). *Music, meaning and transformation: Meaningful music making for life.* Cambridge: Cambridge Scholars Publishing.

25. Swanwick, K. (1979). *A basis for music education.* London: Routledge.

section II
Creation

three
Sound
Recording

Recording technologies have had the biggest impact on music making and learning in the last century. Since the emergence of digital recording in the middle of the twentieth century, digital technologies have become the dominant sound recording and distribution platforms. The range is vast: from voice recorder apps on smart phones to multi-track audio workstations and digital consoles in recording studios. Although different in scale, these devices make use of the same digital audio processes that allow seamless translation of audio data between devices and transmission over the Internet.

This chapter will introduce the basics of audio recording processes with a focus on digital audio capture and editing. It will also reflect on the opportunities for using audio recording technologies in educational contexts.

Elements of a Music Recording System

The sound recording process usually involves several pieces of equipment. Sometimes these are separate components, but especially in inexpensive setups they are integrated. It is important to become familiar with what each piece does, how it connects with the others, and how the sound signal flows through the system. A thorough understanding of signal flow will make problem solving much easier. There are several methods for learning about signal flow: practice in setting up and packing up a recording system, working with flow diagrams of various signal flow options, and talking-aloud the signal flow as it is traced from microphone to recording media and on to speakers for playback. Figure 3.1 shows a flow diagram that illustrates the main stages of the digital recording signal flow.

Most equipment and apps integrate these stages. Even so, it's important to understand the data (signal) flow—the journey of a sound signal through the recording process and back to the listener. It's difficult and frustrating trying to work out how a digital recording system operates or how to fix problems without understanding signal flow.

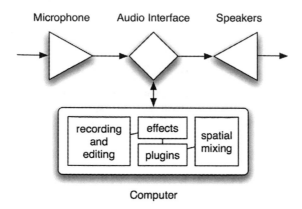

FIGURE 3.1 Digital audio signal flow in a simple digital recording system.

Sound is captured by a microphone (or perhaps comes as a signal from a guitar or other electronic instrument) and is converted to digital data by an audio interface. This data is stored in the device's memory for visualizing, editing, and playback. During playback the signal passes through various built-in plug-in effects that add equalization, reverberation, compression, and so on. When there are several tracks of audio, they are mixed with an appropriate volume balance and the tracks are positioned in space (panned), usually as a stereo image (two channel) or surround-sound plane (four or more channels). For playback, the audio interface also converts the data back to an electrical signal, which is then passed on to an amplifier and speakers (or headphones).

Operational difficulties with recording systems often come down to a kink in this signal pathway. The most productive method of solving these problems is to trace the signal as it makes its way along the (virtual) path until the problem is found.

Plugs and Connectors

There are a variety of analog and digital connections that can be used between hardware elements in a recording system. All-in-one devices, such as smartphones or tablet computers, include a built-in microphone and speaker and no hardware connections are required. However, the quality of these devices is often poor, and external microphone and speakers are often needed. External devices are connected either wirelessly or by cable. Common analog cable connectors, carrying very small electrical currents, are shown in Figure 3.2. One connector is the 3.5mm mini jack plug, used for output

XLR   jack   mini jack   RCA

FIGURE 3.2 Common audio connectors.

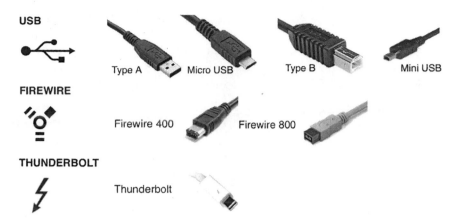

FIGURE 3.3 Common digital connectors for audio devices.

to headphone and audio input. Professional, external audio interfaces might use larger 1/4-inch jack plugs, like those used for connecting electric guitars; RCA plugs, often used for home hi-fi equipment; or XLR connectors, most often used on professional microphones.

Common digital connectors for audio are shown in Figure 3.3 and include USB, FireWire, and Thunderbolt. Often an external audio interface will connect to these, exposing analog connectors for audio equipment. Microphones with direct USB connection, usually referred to as 'USB microphones', are now readily available, and there are also wireless speakers with no physical connectors that transmit audio over Wi-Fi or Bluetooth. There is further discussion of these connection options in Chapter 7. Less common these days are optical cables that use a dedicated port or sometimes a 3.5mm mini jack for digital audio connection.

Playback

The final stage in the digital audio signal flow is playback via loudspeakers. At this stage there are many choices of equipment, depending on the listening context, individual preferences and, of course, varying budgets. Playback quality is a critical factor at the end of the signal chain just as microphone selection is at the start. Generally, the variation in quality within digital processing devices is minimal, but quality differences in the analog domain (microphones, audio interfaces, and speakers) can be dramatic.

The two major categories of playback devices are loudspeakers, for public or shared listening contexts, and headphones, for personal playback. Both are necessary at different times and in different environments. In classrooms, loudspeakers allow for group listening and for sharing of music. The minimum requirement in most cases would be a pair of stereo speakers of reasonable quality; the capability for streaming music to them wirelessly from any digital device in the space (computer, tablet, and so on) would be an added convenience. Headphones in classrooms are useful for private listening, and headphone distribution amplifiers are useful for dividing one signal into several, allowing small groups to listen together without disrupting others in the space.

Microphones

The microphone is a critical element of the audio recording process. Microphones come in a bewildering array of sizes, shapes, and costs. Because they have such a dramatic impact on the quality of a recording, it is worth spending the time to become familiar with their basic operation and use.

Two venerable microphones are shown in Figure 3.4. First is the *Shure SM58*, a dynamic mic with cardioid pickup pattern. It is very popular for live sound and for recording drum kits. Second is the *AKG C414*, a large diaphragm condenser with multiple pickup patterns. Historically, it has been one of the most used studio microphones, quite versatile but especially renowned for use with acoustic instruments and vocals.

Dynamic and Condenser Pickups

Microphones operate by converting sound pressure patterns in the air into electrical signals. There are several ways to achieve this. Most microphones use a delicate diaphragm that moves in response to sound waves. *Dynamic* microphones convert this movement into electricity using a magnetic coil. Dynamic microphones are robust and relatively inexpensive and therefore are often used in live performance situations. *Condenser* microphones measure the change in distance (electrical capacitance) between the diaphragm and a fixed plate. Condenser microphones can be quite delicate and capable

FIGURE 3.4 The *Shure SM58* and *AKG C414* microphones.

of high-fidelity recordings, and so they are frequently used in recording studio settings. Because they contain active electronic circuitry, condenser microphones need to be powered, either by a battery or by phantom power delivered via the microphone cable.

Phantom Power

Phantom power is a method of delivering a small amount of electrical power through microphone cables. The current is transmitted through two of the three wires within a balanced audio cable. Typically these cables use XLR connectors. Phantom power supplies are often built into mixing desks and computer audio interfaces. Typically, phantom power can be switched on or off as required; for example, phantom power is turned off when using a dynamic microphone. A condenser microphone, however, will not work without being powered, and so phantom power must be available and turned on to avoid an otherwise subtle error in the recording setup. For devices with built-in microphones, like field recorders or mobile computers, power requirements will be managed automatically.

Diaphragm Size

Microphones, especially condensers, are classified according to the size of their diaphragms: either small or large diaphragm microphones, and some in between. The classic large-diaphragm microphones are associated with recording studios and radio or TV presentations. They are usually vertically oriented in design, with a flat side as the front. They often have multiple pickup patterns (see below) and are versatile enough to record almost anything.

Small-diaphragm microphones are also widely used. They are pencil-shaped and designed with one end as the front. The smaller diaphragms can be very responsive and are used when it is important to capture the sparkle in the sound; for example, with acoustic guitar and percussion, or as drum overheads. Because these microphones are small and lightweight and can be unobtrusively positioned, they are frequently used for concert recordings.

Some microphones might have more than one diaphragm. There are a number of reasons for this. Stereo microphones have two diaphragms to capture sound from different directions at the same time. Some use secondary diaphragms to manage the directional response by combining the signals from each diaphragm in particular ways.

Directional Response

Microphones are typically design to point in a certain direction, meaning that they have a front and a back to best pick up sound from one or more directions. However, the directional response of microphones can vary. There are three main types of polar (or pickup) patterns—types of directional response—in common use: omnidirectional, unidirectional, and bidirectional. These are depicted in Figure 3.5.

Omnidirectional microphones pick up sound from any direction. This pattern is often used in lapel mikes, for public speaking, and for ambient field recording. Unidirectional

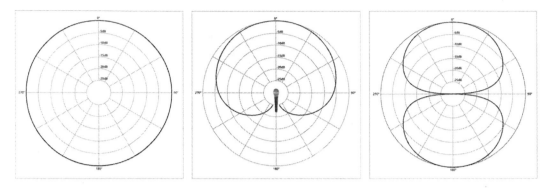

FIGURE 3.5 Polar patterns indicating common directional response of microphones.
(a) Omni (b) Cardioid (c) Figure-8

microphones pick up sound from in front and reject sound from the sides or from behind. They have a heart-shaped pattern (see Figure 3.5b), which is often referred to as cardioid. This is the most common pattern used for dynamic microphones and is particularly useful on stage where sound from surrounding instruments needs to be excluded. Bidirectional microphones pick up sound equally from the front and back and less effectively from the sides. Because of its characteristic polar shape, the bidirectional pattern is sometimes called a Figure-8 pattern. This pattern is useful for recording duets and interviews where one performer or participant stands on either side of one microphone.

There are many other types of microphones and details about how they operate. Finding out more requires only a simple search; a good place to start is Wikipedia.[1]

Microphone Techniques

This section outlines a number of basic tips and techniques for using microphones to record music. Before talking about using the technology, it's important to consider the recording environment. What are the characteristics of the space in which you will record? How quiet is it? What are its tone, color, and reverberation characteristics? These and other features of the environment can have a significant impact on any recording, so choose carefully.

Microphone selection and placement are critical to recording quality and there are a number of dimensions to consider. Choose microphones that suit the sounds you will record and the context in which they are being captured. For example, louder sounds in a noisy ensemble might require a dynamic microphone positioned close to the sound source, while a delicate solo vocalist will be better served by a closely positioned condenser microphone. Consider how sound projects from the instrument you are recording and place the microphone so that you have an even and desirable tone quality. Remember that the microphone is acting like your surrogate ear. For example, positioning a microphone close to and directly in line with the bell of a trumpet will produce a very brash sound, compared with placing the mic off-axis and a short distance away.

Remember that microphones at different distances from the source can change the timbre of what they record; lower frequencies are attenuated the further away the microphone is positioned. There might also be value in setting microphones at distance to picking up room ambience and blending this with signal from a close microphone.

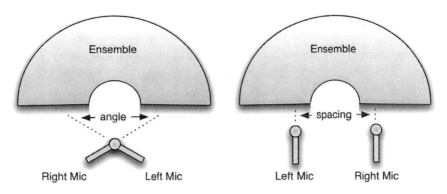

FIGURE 3.6 XY and AB stereo mixing methods for recording an ensemble.

Extraneous noises in the recording can be minimized in a few ways. Use close miking techniques and microphones with a cardioid pattern to minimize spill from other sounds in the recording environment. A microphone cradle can be used to keep the microphone isolated from the mic stand and any vibrations that are transferred through it. A wind shield or pop filter can be placed between a vocalist or wind player and the microphone, so as to minimize plosives and sibilance.

So far, the techniques have focused on solo instrumental/vocal recording. However, you might want to capture the overall sound of an ensemble for a stereo recording. A simple two-microphone setup can often be very effective, especially if recorded in an auditorium. There are two commonly used stereo miking strategies and each of them requires a matching pair of microphones, preferably small-diaphragm condenser microphones, which should be positioned 1 to 2 meters from the ensemble.

The coincident pair (or XY) method positions microphones together in the middle front of the ensemble. Two microphones with cardioid patterns are placed so that their diaphragms are very close together and at an angle of between 90 and 120 degrees from each other, as shown in Figure 3.6. This position enables the microphones to capture sounds from different sides of the ensemble and their close proximity maintains the time alignment of the two channels.

The spaced pair (or AB) method uses two omnidirectional microphones placed 1 to 3 meters apart and both directly facing the ensemble. Each microphone will pick up more loudly the instruments on its side of the ensemble than those on the other; instruments in the middle will be picked up equally. The use of omnidirectional microphones means that the ambience of the space will be clearly evident.

When the microphone capture is done, the recorder then converts the signal into digital audio data for storage, editing, and playback.

Digital Audio

Computers have been used for audio processing since at least the 1960s. The process of digital recording is called sampling. It involves measuring (sampling) the electronic sound signal from a microphone and storing the values as audio data.

There can be some confusion about the term *digital sample* because it is used to mean a few things. It can be both a verb and a noun. We can sample a piano, meaning we can take a digital recording of it (a verb). We can play a sample of the piano, meaning that we can listen to the recording we made (a noun). In this phrase the term sample refers to the whole recording of a piano sound. The term sample can also refer to a single element of recorded data; a single measurement of the signal is a sample. As this section unfolds these separate meanings will be explained as clearly as possible.

Digital sampling began in the 1950s and became popular in the 1980s at a time when the computer memory required to store the samples became affordable in small quantities. This led to new musical styles based on the reuse (looping and editing) of short sampled fragments.[2] One popular approach was to sample single notes from an instrument, for example, a drum kit, which could be combined to play back phrases of any length. Another technique was to sample a short musical phrase, say a drum beat, and loop that as the basis for a song. Computer memory is now much more affordable and so a musician can record hours of digital audio. However, the principles of digital sampling remain unchanged and the earlier techniques continue to be musically productive.

The process of digital recording (sampling) involves the rapid and regular measurement of the audio signal. Each measurement of the signal level is called a sample. This process is analogous to shooting a film, where every frame is a moment in time, but when played back in quick succession, together they simulate movement. In music, each sample is like a single frame.

Figure 3.7 shows how a continuous analog signal is described as a series of discrete digital samples. Samples values are quantized to the closest grid point, so the higher the rate and resolution, the more accurately the sample values represent the waveform.

The rate of audio sampling is the number of samples taken each second. For CD-quality audio, the signal is sampled at a *rate* of 44,100 samples per second. The sampling *resolution* is the precision of the sample measurement. Resolution affects the timbral accuracy and the dynamic range of a recorded waveform. CDs use 16-bit resolution. As a rule of thumb, higher rates and resolutions equate to better recording quality.

The numbers (digits) generated by the sampling process are stored as a list in the computer, and this list is saved as an audio file. A stereo recording will have two lists—one for

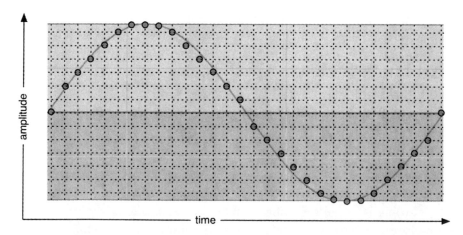

FIGURE 3.7 Low-resolution sampling of an audio signal. Sample points rounded to the closest grid values.

the left channel and one for the right—which are stored together in one file. For replay, the numbers are read back in order and passed at regular intervals for conversion to an electrical signal for amplification and playback.

Recording Level

The volume, or level, of the sound signal needs to be carefully managed throughout the audio signal path. If the sound is too loud or the digital values too extreme, the sound will distort. On the other hand, if the sound is too quiet or the signal too low, then unwanted background noise or processing glitches might be audible.

Recording equipment provides level meters that allow the visible monitor the signal level. There will be one or more input or volume gain controls to adjust the level. When using digital recording equipment, set the level by checking that the loudest sounds peak just below the meter's maximum and never exceed it. This is particularly critical at the recording stage, when capturing from a microphone. Adjusting the distance of the microphone from the sound source will also vary the input volume, so recheck levels whenever you change the sound source or the microphone position.

Editing Audio

Once a recording has been made, there are many ways in which it can be edited and changed. One of the features of digital audio processes is that they can be repeated and compounded almost indefinitely, because sound has become simply a list of numbers and audio processes—just mathematical functions.

There are a variety of software tools for recording and editing audio. The free *Audacity*[3] software, shown in Figure 3.8, is a popular choice in educational contexts. There are similar applications for tablet computers and smartphones, including *Hokusai Audio Editor*[4] for iOS devices.

Audio editors provide a waveform visualization allowing the user to select areas of the waveform for editing. They include tools for arranging segments and varying

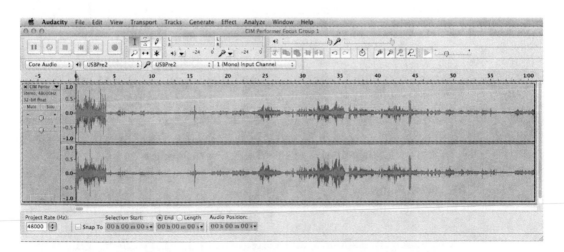

FIGURE 3.8 *Audacity* audio editing software.

timbre, tempo, amplitude and much more. Some of the more common editing techniques will be introduced in the remainder of this section.

Cutting and Pasting

A digital recording comprises a list of sample values. Sections of this list can be removed, reordered, or rearranged, using cut and paste. The technique can be used to edit out unwanted sections, to repeat segments, or reorder material. Segments can be as short as the attack portion of a note or as long as an entire chorus of a song. Cutting and pasting can be used compositionally to recreate *musique concrète* tape-splicing techniques or for rearranging (cutting up) drum patterns in electronic dance music styles.

Pitch Shifting

Varying the playback rate of a sample will change its pitch, not unlike changing the speed on a tape player. This process involves a technique called resampling. Shifting the pitch more than a few whole tones will introduce noticeable timbral variation to the sound. Simple resampling also changes the length of the recording. A quicker playback rate makes the sound faster and higher. The inverse is true when the rate is slowed down.

More sophisticated pitch shifting techniques can separately control the pitch and duration of a recording. Loop-based sequencing software such as *Ableton Live*[5] and *FL Studio*[6] use pitch-shifting and time-stretching to match tempos and keys between various sampled music clips. Synthesizers often use the pitch-bend wheel or lever to control pitch shifting as a smooth glissando, and when set to extreme ranges this can produce some very interesting effects. A range of manipulations, including pitch shifting, can be explored interactively with apps like *Sound Warp*[7] for iPad.

Filtering and Equalization

Filters change the timbre of a sound, for example, by increasing or decreasing the bass or treble. Audio filters can be compared with water filters: they let some signals pass through but extract unwanted elements on the way. Unlike water filters, however, audio filters can also accentuate elements of the sound.

Filters can affect different regions of the harmonic spectrum to create the desired result. The timbre of a sound is altered by changing its harmonic spectra. Filters are used to reduce or accentuate overtones at particular frequencies. Low-pass filters are used to reduce the brightness of a sound, and high-pass filters take out the lower frequencies. Filtering is used to help 'color' the sound as required. They can assist in providing clarity to multi-track mixes, to accentuate certain sounds, or to de-emphasize unwanted noise.

Audio editors apply various filters to sections of the recording. For example, in *Audacity*, equalization can be selected from the Effects menu and then a range of filtering options is available. On audio mixing desks and other audio equipment, equalization is called EQ for short. Channel strips on mixing consoles have EQ controls labeled Hi, Mid, and Low, which correspond with the frequency range they affect. A multiband EQ uses several band-pass filters, each covering a specific frequency range.

Fading In and Out

Audio editors can be used to fade the volume of a selection up (in) and down (out). Fading can be very effective over short durations to remove clicks or noise at the top and tail of a recording. Over longer durations, a fade out is a classic way to end a track. More generally, fading is used to vary the volume of sounds over time.

An important cue in identifying a familiar sound is how its volume changes over time. A piano sound, for example, has a quick attack and then decays slowly, while a tuba speaks more slowly and can sustain its volume for some time. Changing this characteristic volume shape, called a volume envelope, changes the sound—either subtly, to better suit the articulation of a phrase, or drastically, to create interesting new effects. A volume envelope of a sound is often simplified to four major stages; attack, decay, sustain, and release (ADSR), as shown in Figure 3.9.

Amplitude envelopes are also used in digital recording to crossfade between two sections of overlapping sound. On a larger time scale, they can vary the volume of a track in the mix. Amplitude envelopes are also used as mix automation curves in most audio editors and digital recorders. For example, *Audacity* has a dedicated Envelope Tool positioned right next to the standard Selection Tool that is used to cut and paste.

When changing the amplitude (volume) of the waveform, you should be aware that digital systems have a maximum amplitude that can be represented. If the signal is amplified beyond it, then all values above the maximum are limited to that maximum. This effect is called clipping. It produces a distorted sound and should usually be avoided when amplifying (or recording) a digital signal. In some styles of music, clipping and other glitches in the audio stream are used intentionally as a musical feature.

Reverb and Delay

Most recordings sound more convincing with the addition of some reverb. Unless you are fortunate enough to have a great concert hall in which to record, the original recording can often sound dry and lifeless. Acknowledging this, most digital audio systems include reverb and delay effects. A simple echo or delay is an easy process for

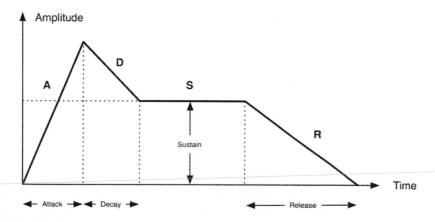

FIGURE 3.9 An ADSR amplitude envelope.

a computer. To achieve it, the sample wavetable can be read once for playing back the original sound, then again for each delay, usually decreasing the volume of subsequent delays. Reverberation is a more complex process, involving multiple overlapping delays of different durations, which simulate the many reflections a sound would undergo in a live space. It is common to say that reverb is like the ketchup of audio processes: you can put it on anything.

Plug-Ins and Digital Audio Routing

The audio effects mentioned above are likely to be built in to your digital audio editor, but alternative effects are often provided with additional software components called plug-ins. Plug-ins can be applied to an audio signal to provide additional processing or alternatives to the built-in effects. Some applications will include a range of plug-ins but they can also be purchased separately to extend the functionality of the digital audio system.

There are many protocols for plug-ins and for passing digital audio between applications. Because these protocols focus on moving sound between and within applications on one computing device, they are usually specific to particular operating systems, like Windows, Mac OS, Linux, iOS, or Android; a few are cross platform. It is important to make sure that any plug-ins you buy will operate with the plug-in architecture of your existing software.

The most common plug-in architectures for each platform are listed below:

- Mac OS—AudioUnits (AU), VST, TDM, RTAS, AAX
- Windows—DirectX, VST, TDM, RTAS, AAX
- Linux—LADSPA, DSSI, LV2
- iOS—Inter-App Audio
- Android—n/a

It can also be useful to route audio between apps, particularly from synthesizers to DAWs. The most common inter-application audio streaming protocols for each platform are listed below:

- Mac OS—JACK, Soundflower, ReWire
- Windows—ReWire, JACK
- Linux—JACK
- iOS—Inter-App Audio, Audiobus, JACK
- Android—Patchfield

Sound Recording in Music Education

There are many ways to use digital recording to assist music learning. Recording is a way to enhance listening. Following R. Murray Schafer's notions of 'ear cleaning',[8] recording sounds and listening to them carefully can be an effective way of hearing sounds around us in a fresh, new way, increasing our aural acuity and awareness. Audio recording, along with video recording, is extremely valuable for the documentation of our music activities, helping us to remember and reflect. Finally, and most importantly, sound recording opens up new horizons for musical creativity. This is clearly evident in the flourishing of its use by composers, producers, and performers over the past century. Contemporary digital technologies put the power of sound recording within easy reach of all music students and teachers in affluent countries, and allow us to share easily our creations and individual experiences.

Recorded Portfolios

One of the original motivations for the invention of audio recording was the opportunity of archiving speech as a record of events. In music education, record keeping and the monitoring of progress are enriched by the use of audio and video recordings. These can include routine recordings of performance progress, the capturing of presentations and performances, and assembling a recorded anthology of an ensemble or class.

Portfolios of recorded material are a useful way, especially for teachers, of recording and archiving individual student or class activities. Storage media are inexpensive and portable, and cloud-based storage sites with good wireless Internet access can be very efficient. Recordings are readily available to assist critical analysis, make assessment of progress, act as a reminder of work done, or to facilitate communication of standards and progress between teaching teams.[9]

Because audio recording for portfolios should be a regular activity in music education, the necessary equipment should always be available in the learning environment. This can be achieved with a portable device that teachers or students can carry with them. Alternatively, investing in a permanent recording setup with good microphones—on stands or hanging from the ceiling—provides the best quality audio.

Reflection

The most powerful use of recording for learning is to enable reflective feedback on music making. Recording for reflection enables self, peer, and teacher feedback. Students seem more willing to make, and take, criticism of a recording of their work because listening back provides a critical distance and emotional separation. The provision of recording devices for reflection can reduce the pressure on teachers in the classroom, as they can defer listening and comments to a later time. Students can peer review each other's recordings, which is both time efficient and educative.

A number of research studies have shown that reflection is more effective in discussion situations than through written processes.[10] Talking about music with the music present in the conversation can add value to the conversation. A recursive step would be to record these reflective discussions for later review. In this way the student(s) whose work is being discussed can have a record of comments which might otherwise pass by too quickly to be remembered.

Students can be encouraged to record lessons and then undertake reflective processes in their practice or home environments, allowing the positive feedback process to continue beyond the lesson rather than take up lesson time.

Assessment

Audio and video recordings are increasingly used for assessment purposes. Their practicality in managing geographic separation, scheduling, selective viewing, and reviewing as evidence is widely accepted. While there is general agreement that live viewings of music are preferable for assessment, the practicalities often outweigh these concerns.

Recordings need not be simply documentation or representation; they might be the original work itself. Music is often produced for a recorded medium: for music albums, film scores, and so on. They can be included in the same assessment and moderation process as performance recordings.

An increased reliance on recordings for assessment places a greater emphasis on teachers' and students' familiarity with recording processes. First, as producers they need to be able to make the best possible recording so that their work gets a fair hearing. Second, as critics they need to understand the medium sufficiently well to distinguish the quality of work being assessed from the quality of the recorded artifact. For example, is poor tone production due to inadequate microphone selection and placement or to flaws in the performers' technique?

Developing a consistent practice of recording audio opens new possibilities for comparison. For example, recordings from one year or semester can be heard alongside those of previous times. This might be useful in assessing progress, maintaining consistency of assessment standards, but might be unfair if other factors significantly change the learning opportunities over time. Recordings could be submitted for assessment as a portfolio, even if they were recorded at different stages in the learning process. As will be evident in many of the topics covered in this book, the issues raised about recording in assessment are often not so much about the technologies as they are about the ways in which they are used.

Conclusion

Sound recording has become such an influential part of music making that it is recognized as a fundamental skill for musicians. Making effective use of sound recording and editing need not involve complex and expensive equipment; it should, therefore, be available to all students. Digital recording involves converting sound into numbers by sampling. Sound sampling is used in synthesizers for instrument imitation, for creating musical collages from field recordings, for using musical fragments for loop-based music, and for capturing performances and compositions. Learning to capture and edit sounds can open up many creative and productive musical opportunities. Digital recording is the basis for larger scale multi-track recordings done in recording studios. Understanding the basics of sound recording provides a pathway to larger scale music production projects. The educational uses of digital recording range from everyday use in the documentation of activities for remembering and reflecting, to creative uses by composers, producers, and performers.

Reflection Questions

1. Which technology has reputably had the largest impact on the music industry in the last 100 years?
2. What is the difference between dynamic and condenser microphones?

3. What are three different uses of the term *sample*?
4. How does a digital device capture sound?
5. What do the rate and resolution of a digital recording refer to?
6. How many times can digital audio data be processed?
7. What effect might be used to enhance the timbre of a recording?
8. How can recordings assist the development of aural awareness?
9. Why are recordings useful tools for reflection?
10. How can recording technologies be used for portfolio assessment?

Teaching Tips

1. Have students investigate the history of sound recording technologies so they can better appreciate the value of the opportunities they have to record music so easily.
2. Students can use recording equipment to make a podcast (audio documentary) about a research topic.[11]
3. Obtain one of the many books on audio recording techniques as a resource for improving students' recording skills.
4. As a way of clarifying their understanding of recording terminology, have students work on definitions for a sound recording glossary.
5. Have students evaluate the recording techniques used in some of their favorite commercial songs.
6. Encourage students who have mobile digital devices to use them as pocket recorders.
7. Set up cloud-based audio portfolios, that can be shared by all stakeholders in a student's musical life.
8. Provide portable recorders for students to make field recordings to use in creating a soundscape composition.
9. Test students' understanding of signal flow by having them 'problem fix' a digital recording system that has been deliberately set up incorrectly.
10. Use the list of recording production techniques in this chapter as criteria for assessing student recordings.

Suggested Tasks for Educators

1. Record the same sound source with various microphones and their positioning to hear the difference that these make on audio quality and character.
2. Compare the reverberant qualities of different spaces around the school with the different presets on a digital reverb plug-in.
3. Explore audio recording techniques in a creative context by creating a composition in the style of *musique concrète*.
4. Make a recording of you speaking your name, then experiment with editing it in ways where the impact of the manipulations is both obvious and fun.
5. Draw a map of the signal flow diagram that corresponds to your recording system.

Chapter Summary

Recording technologies, collectively, have had an enormous impact on music making and learning. The integration of computing and recording in the form of digital audio sampling has the potential to turn any digital device into a digital recorder. This chapter provides a road-map of the principles of digital recording and editing. It explores how to capture audio with microphones and manipulate those recordings with audio software. The chapter provides some hints about how to assess and achieve good recording quality. Finally, there is discussion about the ways in which recording technology can be useful in music education.

Notes

1. Microphone: http://en.wikipedia.org/wiki/Microphone.
2. For a brief but creatively presented history of sampling in popular music, view the video *A Brief History of Sampling*, a video by Eclectic Method—http://youtu.be/crfyvWLLHbQ.
3. *Audacity*: http://audacity.sourceforge.net/.
4. *Hokusai Audio Editor*: https://itunes.apple.com/au/app/hokusai-audio-editor/id432079746? mt = 8.
5. *Ableton Live*: www.ableton.com/.
6. *FL Studio*: www.image-line.com/flstudio/.
7. *Sound Warp*: https://itunes.apple.com/us/app/sound-warp-free/id336052047.
8. Schafer, R.M. (1969). *Ear cleaning: Notes for an experimental music course*. Toronto: Berandol Music.
9. For more details about for the use of ePortfolios in the creative arts, see S. Dillon and A. R. Brown (2006), The art of ePortfolios: Insights from the creative arts experience. In A. Jafari & C. Kaufman (Eds.), *Handbook of research on ePortfolios: Concepts, technology and case studies* (pp. 418–431). Indianapolis: Idea Group.
10. For example, Price, S., Rogers, Y., Stanton, D., & Smith, H. (2003). A new conceptual framework for CSCL: Supporting diverse forms of reflection through multiple interactions. In *Designing for change in networked learning environments. Proceedings of the international conference on computer supported collaborative learning*, pp. 513–522.
11. Listen to Radiolab as an example of the excellent use of audio editing in documentary podcast. www.radiolab.org/.

four
Music
Production

The meaning of the term 'music producer' has changed over time. In the twentieth century, the term referred to a person who assisted musicians with the artistic and technical direction of a recording. George Martin, for example, was famous as the producer of The Beatles. In the twenty-first century, this meaning persists, but more often, 'producer' now refers to the artists themselves when they create and record their own music. This shift in emphasis from the producer as a professional with technical knowledge to one who has creative *and* technical control has emerged alongside a trend of increasing access to the technological means of production. Modern hardware and software have conflated the studio and the laptop, tablet, or phone. Digital technologies are now end-to-end in the process of musical experience, from capturing the original inspiration, through writing and performing, to recording and distributing. Mobile computing devices conveniently enable music production and listening anywhere and anytime. Building on the previous chapter's focus on sound recording, this chapter will explore the basics of music production, MIDI sequencing, editing and mixing, and discuss how these techniques can be used in music education.

Digital Audio Workstations

The desire to automate musical playback has a long history, stretching at least as far back as the player piano. Audio recording satisfied some of that desire, but its early inflexibility as an editable compositional format led to solutions like the sequencer. The sequencer is a product of the electronic music age that allowed a series (sequence) of evenly spaced steps to be programmed and looped. Typically these steps defined a series of notes by defining pitches and rests. Sequencers provided a way to automate music without the need to commit it to a static recorded format. The ability to automate music playback gave the musician an extra set of virtual hands, allowing the musician to play many parts at once.

Like recording, digital sequencers enhanced these capabilities greatly and allowed musical ideas to be crafted and saved for later review, assisting the musician's memory and the communication of his or her ideas. Software sequencers can capture and perform musical gestures (performances) as Musical Instrument Digital Interface (MIDI) data, rather than as sound. MIDI is a language for describing performance information, including controller movements and note attributes, such as pitch and dynamic. MIDI controllers—including piano keyboards, drum pad surfaces, and more—are used to perform; gesture data in the MIDI format is then sent to the sequencing software. Usually these controllers are connected to a computing device via a USB or MIDI lead, or connected wirelessly via Wi-Fi or Bluetooth.

The processes of audio recording and MIDI sequencing came together during the 1990s via software applications called digital audio workstations (DAWs). Examples of some of the more popular DAW software for Windows or Mac OS include *Cubase*,[1] *Sonar*,[2] *Logic*,[3] *Ableton Live*,[4] *Pro Tools*,[5] *FL Studio*,[6] and *GarageBand*.[7] DAWs for iPad include *Auria*,[8] *Cubasis*,[9] *BeatMaker 2*,[10] *NanoStudio*,[11] and *GarageBand*.[12] There are now audio recording and/or MIDI sequencing apps for many mobile computing devices. A simple example is the *Little MIDI Machine* sequencing app for the iPad,[13] shown in Figure 4.1, that emulates the function of a 16-step sequencer and outputs data via MIDI. As a result, music production technologies are now literally in the palm of a musician's hands.

For younger audiences, there are also a number of simple step sequencing applications, including *O-Generator*[14] and *Beatwave*[15] for the iPad and iPhone. These simple

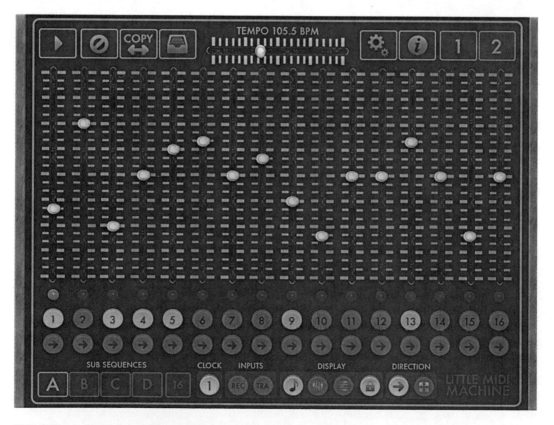

FIGURE 4.1 The *Little MIDI Machine* app for iPad.

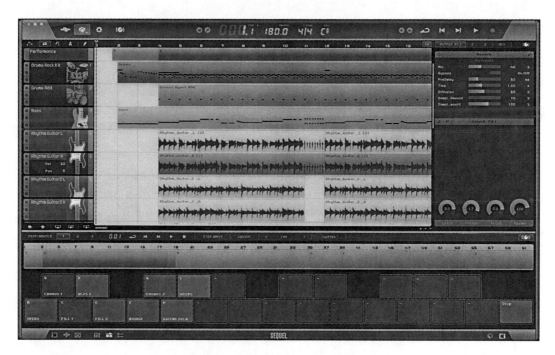

FIGURE 4.2 *Sequel* by Steinberg, a typical digital audio workstation interface.

sequencers can be a fun introduction to the concept of sequencing for junior classes, and clearly demonstrate the principles evident in advanced sequencing programs.

Music production software and apps (DAWs) follow a fairly familiar design pattern (see Figure 4.2). Based on tape recorder and musical score analogies, they feature a multi-track timeline, with parts on the vertical axis and time on the horizontal. Around this core there are user interface elements for record and playback, tempo, effect settings, and so forth.

Modern DAWs combine and extend both the tape recorder and musical score metaphors. Like a tape recorder, a DAW records and plays back music as 'tracks,' and utilizes a 'transport' control area to house the play, stop, fast forward, and rewind buttons. There are two types of tracks: audio and MIDI. Audio tracks contain recorded data often captured with a microphone or generated from electronic sources (see Chapter 3 for more on audio recording processes). MIDI tracks record data generated by performances on external devices, such as a synthesizer keyboard or drum pad control surface. A DAW's timeline can be divided into beats and bars, or minutes and seconds, with elements arranged by musical or clock time. All tracks follow a single tempo map that acts like a conductor to control tempo and keep all the parts together.

Within this multiple track structure, each track equates broadly to a part in a musical score. While audio tracks contain waveform data, MIDI tracks use musical notes as their basic unit of organization. Notes are grouped into patterns, regions, or sections that can be arranged on a timeline to form the structure of a piece. DAWs allow arbitrary segmentation of audio or MIDI tracks into regions, and provide functions for transformations such as duplicate, copy, remove, mute, solo, loop, transpose, pan, amplify, compress, and expand.

FIGURE 4.3 Track view.

Often DAWs will have different visual editors that display music at various levels of detail. Higher level groupings, such as phrase or section, are displayed as boxes in tracks on the timeline. Individual notes on MIDI tracks can usually be displayed as notation, as a piano roll matrix, or as a list. Audio track data can be viewed in an audio editor for detailed inspection. Learning when to use each visualization is a key component of becoming a fluent user. Below are the major visual displays found in DAW applications.

Track view—Each musical part has its own row that follows the timeline from beginning to end (see Figure 4.3).

Region editor—Groups of notes or sections of audio appear as blocks (see Figure 4.4). Multiple blocks can appear on each track; their position indicates their placement in time.

Piano roll editor—Each block represents one note; its vertical position indicates pitch and its length indicates duration (see Figure 4.5).

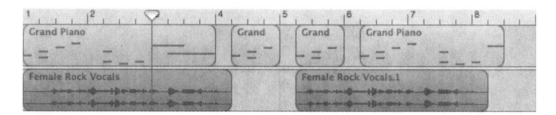

FIGURE 4.4 Region editor.

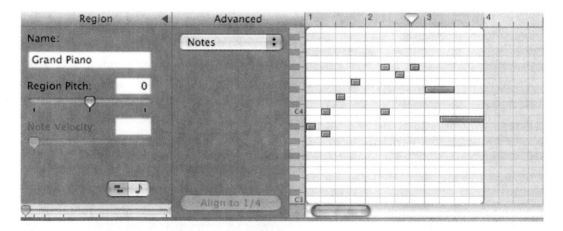

FIGURE 4.5 Piano roll editor.

FIGURE 4.6 Notated score editor.

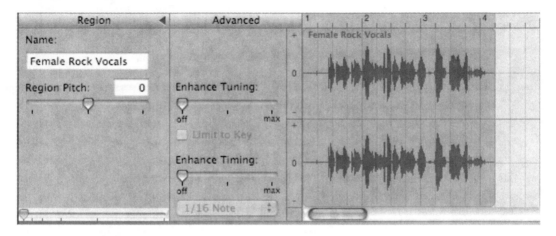

FIGURE 4.7 Waveform view.

Notation view—Some DAWs can display MIDI tracks as a notated score, (see Figure 4.6 from *GarageBand* for Mac).

Waveform view—The detailed visualization of an audio segment (see Figure 4.7).

Looping—DAWs allow regions to be repeated several time over (see Figure 4.8 for the repetitions of a one-measure loop).

Clip library—A library of musical fragments and sounds is usually preinstalled. Clip libraries are often arranged in hierarchical categories (see Figure 4.9).

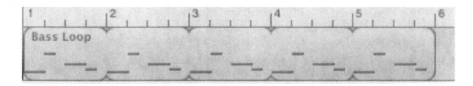

FIGURE 4.8 A looped MIDI region.

Loops ⇕	Instruments	All Drums	Name
All	Acoustic Bass	All Drums (280)	70s Ballad Drums 01
By Genres	Acoustic Guitar	Acoustic (176)	80s Pop Beat 07
By Instruments	All Drums	Arrhythmic (4)	80s Pop Beat 08
By Moods	Banjo	Beats (100)	80s Pop Beat 09
Favorites	Bass	Cheerful (39)	80s Pop Beat 10
	Beats	Clean (229)	Ambient Beat 01
			Classic Rock Beat 01

Scale: Any   176 items

FIGURE 4.9 Navigating a music clip library.

Digital audio workstation software has grown ever more sophisticated in its ability to help realize the musician's ideas from inception to completion. This evolution parallels the emergence of the contemporary music producer—a musician who is part composer, performer, and engineer, for whom the computer is the instrument of choice.

Some DAW software integrates video playback and synchronization as well. See Chapter 7 for more on video playback and synchronization.

Production Techniques

Digital audio workstation software and related music technologies are excellent tools for assisting with the creation of new music. They can be used for sketching or remembering ideas on one end, and the production of the final shareable version on the other end. Music projects that can be developed in this way include songs, movie soundtracks, podcasts, radio documentaries, advertisements, soundscapes, and more. This section will cover techniques that relate to each of the main stages of the music production process.

Understanding the production techniques, or production values, of the recording process is vital to making recordings, but it is also useful for those who simply listen to music. The ability to understand the intricacies of the production process can help an individual better understand differences in production style and fashion, which play a significant role in defining a musical genre.

The function of music technologies in music production is to allow musicians to externalize and refine their ideas. The musician focuses on translating an idea into sound and developing that idea as he or she reflects on and plays with sound. Becoming an expert at music production requires the musician to develop fluency with music technologies so that he or she can take full advantage of his or her imagination and critical listening skills.

Setting the Mood

It is important from the outset to create an environment that is conducive to creativity and good musical performances. While there are plenty of tips and tricks in operating equipment and making musical decisions, it is vital that during the production process, creative ideas are allowed to flow and musicians are able to do their best work. No amount of technical wizardry will compensate for a lack of creativity or musicality. Make sure the work environment is pleasant and the equipment is set up and operating correctly, and endeavor to set a collaborative and congenial relationship among those involved. When capturing ideas or performances, remember not to obsess about technical details. Prioritize expression over perfection.

Tracking

Tracking is the process of capturing ideas and recording performances. Often it is useful to start with a rhythmic part or a guide vocal playing along to a click track. This provides a foundation and context for the other tracks. In educational settings, tracking

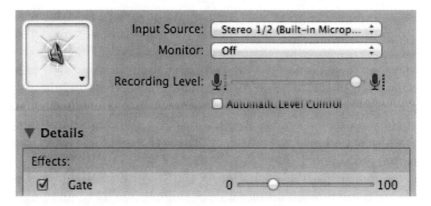

FIGURE 4.10 Setting the gate effect threshold in *GarageBand*.

may involve audio capture in noisy environments. The use of a noise gate can minimize the audibility of background noise. A noise gate operates by silencing the incoming signal, typically from a microphone, when the level is below a set threshold. The threshold needs to be set so that it is below the level of the desired sound, but above the level of the background noise. Figure 4.10 shows the gate threshold setting in Apple's *GarageBand* software. The result is that when the desired signal is present—say, of a singer's vocal performance—the gate is open and the voice is recorded, but in between phrases or in other gaps, the gate is closed and these periods are silent.

Your project may include virtual instrument, or MIDI, tracks as well. They utilize the rich palette of sound colors available in today's synthesizers and sample libraries; these need to be selected and combined with care. Try to choose sounds or music clips that complement one another—ones that are not too similar or too different. Remember that you can change the sound of the virtual instrument later, so sometimes it pays to record the part while the idea is fresh and finalize the sound selection later.

Whether you are tracking audio or MIDI performances, it often requires several takes to get a performance right. It is all right to record several takes—keep them all. With today's music technologies, tracks are plentiful and computer storage space is cheap. Having several takes allows you to decide later between them or combine sections from several into a final version.

Multi-tracking and Overdubbing

DAW software provides the luxury of either recording one track after another to build up a layered musical work—a process called overdubbing—or recording several tracks at the same time, a process called multi-tracking. For solo music projects, overdubbing tracks is the obvious choice; for a group, either approach can be taken. A technical limitation of multi-tracking is the number of inputs the recording device has. The Beatles recorded their early albums straight to stereo (two tracks), so this limitation need not be a barrier. However, they still required multiple microphones and a large mixing desk in the signal path, from which we can see that technical requirements cannot be completely ignored. Given the equipment limitations in most educational and 'bedroom' recording situations, overdubbing is an important skill.

The main considerations when overdubbing are how to hear back previous tracks while recording the next, and how to ensure the tracks are in time. DAW software will provide a cue system to enable the monitoring of tracks already laid down. Use of headphones for cueing is useful when recording audio to avoid spill from previous tracks into the microphone. When recording audio tracks, there may be a slight delay, called latency, between the heard and recorded tracks due to the time it takes for the signals to pass through the system. Applications and audio interfaces typically have some latency compensation or a zero latency feature to avoid these issues, but be aware of this potential problem.

When overdubbing, use the track muting and soloing functions so that only the desired parts are heard through the monitors or headphones. This can be especially useful if multiple takes of previous parts were recorded. Usually only one of each previous part will be required in the cue mix, and it is useful to set volumes in the mix so that parts with important timing or harmonic cues are clearly audible.

Editing

Editing techniques apply to altering captured data; they include deleting and correcting errors, making small variations and recombining sections from several takes. For more on audio editing techniques, see Chapter 3. This section will focus on editing MIDI tracks.

Large-scale edits, such as cutting and rearranging musical phrases, can be performed in the time line window. More detailed edits on one or a few notes, or even on parameters within a note, are performed in an edit window, as shown in Figures 4.5 or 4.6. Single notes or groups of notes can be selected and moved up and down to alter their pitch, or left and right to vary their beat position. Notes in piano roll displays and in some notation views can have their durations extended by dragging the right edge of the note block. Note dynamic can also be adjusted.

The volume, panning and other global features of a track, either audio or MIDI, can be adjusted by manipulating parameter automation curves. When examining projects from professional music producers, it is often surprising to see the extent and degree of detail of these parameter edits. When parameter automation is selected on a track, say, for volume, a horizontal line appears on the track indicating the default value. Clicking on this line and dragging it allows it to be segmented and varied over time. On playback, the level of the associated parameter will automatically follow the curve. This way, adjustments can be made to achieve crescendos and fade outs. Short-term dips and peaks can be drawn that compensate for unexpected levels in a performance. See Figure 4.11 for an example of the use of track automation curves for volume adjustments.

FIGURE 4.11 Track automation of the volume of a track.

Arranging

One of the strengths of digital audio workstations over previous technologies used for making music (such as tape machines or even paper manuscripts) is the malleability of digital data. Consequently, DAWs are ideal for arranging music. Tracks can be easily segmented or grouped into musically salient regions, and then moved or copied to create the desired musical form. Versions of an arrangement can be saved at any time, allowing the musician to maintain alternatives for later comparison or other purposes. This capacity is the basis for the popular practice of remixing.

When creating an arrangement, remember that a musical work needs to have some sense of drama—points of climax and repose—and enough repetition to aid familiarity, but not so much that it gets dull. Common techniques include building up layers of tracks so that the intensity of the work gradually increases, then, suddenly, parts are dropped out for dramatic effect, only to reenter again as the energy rebuilds.

If there are multiple takes of a particular section, these can be used to add subtle variety to repeated sections. Rather than simply copying the same performance and reusing it, use a different take for variety.

Mixing Music

The quality of a music track is influenced by practices at three stages: capture, editing, and mixing. Mixing involves more than volume balance between parts; it is adjusting timbre, ensuring the work follows the desired energy contour, and creating a sense of spatial organization and context. Mixing processes are done in the DAW software, and many of the elements of music production technologies discussed in this and previous chapters are employed at the mixing stage. To bring out the best in the production, their application must often be subtle and nuanced.

Because the mixing stage requires careful attention to sound, the way music is listened to during this process is a crucial consideration. While draft mixes can be done using headphones, it is best to complete the final mix using loudspeakers in a quiet environment. Because the musician has no control over how his or her recorded music will be listened to, it is prudent to check the mix on several loudspeakers and headphones to make sure it sounds acceptable on different systems. The characteristics of the mix will also vary with playback volume, so different level(s) should be considered. It is best to mix with loudspeakers set at a pronounced but comfortable volume level. The mix should be checked at varying volume levels to make sure important characteristics, like vocal track clarity, are maintained.

Read on for more factors to take into account when mixing.

Clarity

Recording quality is dictated to a large degree by the equipment and capturing processes discussed earlier. However, a goal of the mixing process is to ensure that parts can be heard adequately, and the use of the techniques below can ensure that each part of the music has its own sonic space. The clarity of the recording can also be improved by editing out extraneous noises such as page turns, coughing, foot tapping, and the like, which may be at the beginning and end of recorded sections if they were not removed at the editing stage.

Tone

The recording process will color each recorded sound. Once captured, the tone of each part can be adjusted using equalization (EQ). It is good production practice to pay attention to the timbre of each part and add or cut back the amount of treble, bass, or mid-frequencies to get the desired sound. Equalizing can also help clarify the sound by removing booming bass frequencies or emphasizing particular frequency ranges in each part to articulate them more clearly.

Balance

The volume mix between parts is very important. Use solo and mute buttons to isolate tracks and individual parts to make sure their contribution to the mix is appropriate. Some tracks need to be mixed so that they blend, while others need to be either more pronounced or restrained. The mix need not be static through the duration of a recording; adjustments at certain points, such as bringing up a soloist, may be necessary, and use of parameter automation can be helpful. Work through the piece section by section, noting points of adjustment. It may be useful to record the automation curves from live fader movements of the volume faders.

Spatialization

A spatial mix of the recording allows tracks to be positioned anywhere around the speaker array using the panning controls. Spreading the sounds across the spatial field creates a full sound and provides each part with its own location (or movement) in positional space. Sometimes the initial recording is done in stereo, for example, with two microphones, so those panning positions may need to be maintained. Usually the parts of most importance are panned to the center, such as vocal and bass in a pop song, while accompanying parts are evenly spread to the left and right. Spatialization can also be used to create an illusion of a stage setup, with instruments panned to appear left to right on the imaginary 'stage,' and volume and reverb used to provide depth perception from front to back. Mixes are most commonly done in stereo (two tracks) or in surround sound (six tracks for 5.1). However, it can be fun to mix for a custom speaker array.

Effects

Spatial attributes can be enhanced with various added effects such as reverb, delay, chorusing, compression, and so forth. The use of reverb is most common and can make the recording, or parts of it, sound like it is in a hall, a small room, a club, or any other space. If the room in which the recording took place has nice acoustics, then digital reverb may not be necessary. When it is added, apply it to the whole mix to provide a general sense of space, or to individual parts to bolster their sound. In complex productions, multiple reverbs may be used.

Effects can be added to each part, or to the main outputs where they are applied equally to all tracks. It is more efficient to apply common effects, such as an overall reverb or compression, to the master (main output) tracks. Specific effects can be applied to individual tracks as required, but be aware that computing power may limit the number of tracks and effects a device can support.

Delays are usually applied only to individual tracks to enhance them. Some delay on a lead vocal or instrument is the most common application. Chorusing provides the effect of doubling, with a second part slightly detuned. It is used to give a greater sense of an ensemble, for example, to string sounds. Compression reduces the dynamic range of a track, and is used most often to provide punch or emphasis to percussion or vocal recordings. It is used to reduce the dynamic range of a track to prevent, for example, the vocal part being subsumed by the rest of the mix in quiet moments. Reducing the dynamic range and increasing the overall volume ensures that such a part is always audible.

For more information on these and other production techniques, consult one of the many books and online videos on the subject. Take time to play with audio software to experience the range of sounds that can be created and to learn how to control its functions and effects. Listening closely to professionally produced recordings and analyzing how they are produced is another great way to learn more about music production techniques.

Learning through Music Production

This section outlines some of the many educational activities supported by music production technologies. These include many composition and recording projects. DAWs such as *Ableton Live* are well known for their application in electronic music performance, and mobile technologies such as music production apps are being increasingly integrated into the live music arena.

Creation

Digital audio workstation software systems have become the twenty-first-century equivalents of manuscript paper for the collection and development of musical ideas. Add to this that they have also replaced the tape recorder for audio documentation and production of recorded music, and their utility and centrality in modern music making is unsurprising.

In educational settings, a DAW can be central to individual or group composition tasks. The combination of audio capture and performance on virtual instruments (via MIDI keyboards and other controllers) enables DAWs to function as a musical sketch pad for ideas and as a central place for saving and sharing musical ideas as they develop. Students can compose their own music fragments and freely develop and arrange them on the time line and in various detailed edit views. An increasing number of DAWs include generative music processes, sometimes called 'smart' instruments, that the student can work with to guide a semi-automated compositional process.

An effective way to scaffold beginner composers is to have them work with the music clips supplied with many software packages. The assemblage and editing of these provides useful practice in arranging and mixing, even before the student is able to compose individual parts. In a similar way, the assemblage of soundscapes from the student's own audio recordings in a DAW represents an easy way to engage with concepts of structure, timbral integration, and dramatic development.

Presentation

Sound and video recording are the dominant music representation formats and the mediums through which most students will access musical ideas. Traditionally this access would have been through score reading, live performance, and written books. Therefore it is increasingly important that music education helps students to articulate and be fluent in digital recording media.

Audio production software can also support performance activities. This can be as simple as playing along to existing recordings or creating original backing tracks. There are many professional bands that have a lineup such as vocalist, guitarist, and laptop computer. Similarly, small student ensembles can use DAWs to augment their own performances. More interactive performances are possible when recording devices are used to delay, loop, or otherwise replay parts of the performance, which are in turn played against. Such techniques have their history in reel-to-reel tape loops, but they are more commonly found today in dedicated digital sample and delay devices.

A growing trend in live electronic music is to trigger music clips and sounds from control surfaces with a grid of button triggers. See Figure 4.12 for a typical grid control surface and an emulation of one on an iPad. These were originally popular as drum triggers, but are now used for playing pitched material and controlling (starting, stopping, and effecting) musical segments. As with any skill, with practice one can become quite virtuosic at interacting with these devices. Combine the live performance element

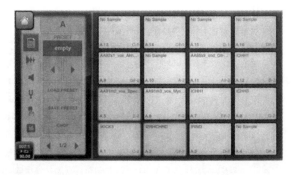

FIGURE 4.12 Examples of physical and virtual grid trigger controller surfaces.

with the compositional preparation of materials, and this becomes the basis for quite a complete music education.

The topic of electronic music performance is covered in more detail in Chapter 10. For now, the focus will remain on music production activities.

Analysis

Music production apps can be useful for music analysis, especially if multi-track versions of works can be sourced. Often MIDI files of pieces can be imported for this purpose. Analysis and investigation is facilitated by the software's ability to play back at various speeds, randomly access any part of the work for section comparisons, mute parts to isolate part relationships and interactions, and isolate solo tracks to hear the detailed inner workings of a part that might otherwise be obscured in the ensemble.

Investigation of a multi-track work can also be encouraged through remixing, that is, taking the existing work and rearranging it, even deleting parts and adding tracks. This encourages the remixer to understand each part and to imagine and develop his or her musical potential.

Conclusion

The digital audio workstation has remained a centerpiece of contemporary music technologies; it constantly reinvents itself to accommodate and influence the latest musical techniques and trends. At the heart of the DAW is the representation of music as audio and MIDI data. This data can be chunked into regions on a time line, or used as clips for triggering and looping. There is a variety of visual representations available, including track view, common practice notation view, piano roll editing, and audio waveform editing. These allow control at different time scales and in ways that accommodate most styles of music. This broad utility is also why DAW software is often the core software application used in music education. As music production systems evolve ever further and are increasingly available on mobile devices, their use is expanding from compositional activities to performance situations that involve improvisation with prepared materials. Consequently, there is sure to be a useful application of digital technologies for music production in every musician's life.

Reflection Questions

1. What musical parameters were controllable in the early analog sequencers?
2. What does the acronym DAW stand for?
3. What is meant by the term step-time in relation to sequencers?
4. What is the difference between a MIDI track and an audio track?
5. A linear timeline has been at the heart of DAW software for many decades. What other functionality do more recent music clip organizational features provide?
6. What is an audio plug-in?
7. Name three production techniques mentioned in the chapter.
8. What techniques are used to spatialize a track left-right and forward-back function?

9. What features of a DAW might scaffold beginner composers?
10. How is it suggested a student might use a DAW for music analysis?

Teaching Tips

1. Due to their wide variety of representational views, sequencing applications are useful in musicianship classes when discussing musical symbols and representations.
2. Teach both real-time and step-time data input so that students with and without some keyboard performance skills are accommodated.
3. It is common that, as with word processor applications, most people only use a small percentage of a modern sequencer's features. When selecting a sequencer for use in schools, be careful not to get one that is too advanced (and therefore complicated).
4. To underline the importance of structure in musical organization, import a MIDI file into a DAW and visually segment music into phrases and sections.
5. Use a DAW's looping feature to have students quickly create interesting polyrhythmic textures.
6. Have students explore the opportunities (or difficulties) of performative expression in music by playing with the note lengths, dynamics, and tempo on a provided MIDI sequence.
7. For an ideal environment for the student to create film scores, have him or her use a DAW to synchronize sound with a digital video file.
8. Clips from libraries that come with many DAWs can be used as a foundation for students to compose original parts.
9. Use an existing MIDI file as a starting point for a remixing project.
10. Consider using headphone distribution boxes to allow groups of students to collaborate in isolation on a project at one computer workstation.

Suggested Tasks for Educators

1. Record a MIDI track and compare the timing resolution of the piano roll and common practice notation displays of the same music. What are the differences?
2. Compare the features lists of the major DAW applications for your operating system. How do they differ and which might fit your situation best?
3. Try to circumvent the 'conductor' notion of track synchronization in a DAW by creating a version of Steve Reich's *Piano Phase* piece.
4. Use the copy, paste, and transpose functions of the DAW to quickly arrange a fugue.
5. Locate and download a number of free plug-ins that are supported by your DAW application and learn how to use them.

Chapter Summary

The automation of musical playback has a history stretching back at least as far as the player piano and the windup music box. Digital audio workstation (DAW) software has evolved significantly from these origins and enables the capturing, editing, and playback of music. The graphical interfaces of a DAW rely heavily on analogies from multi-track tape recorders and pattern looping sequencers. DAWs include audio and virtual instrument (MIDI) tracks and enable the visual representation and editing of recorded data in a variety of formats. Audio tracks allow sound recording and manipulation. Virtual instrument tracks accommodate musical performance data in the form of MIDI messages captured from piano keyboard, percussion, or other control surfaces. Representing music in this symbolic way allows for the deferral of choices about instrumentation and detailed editing of data at the note level. Like previous recording devices, DAWs enable the capturing of ideas for later review, thus assisting the musician with his or her memory and communication of his or her ideas. The multi-track aspect of DAWs provides the ability to overlay parts, enabling the musician to have several extra virtual hands to play many parts at once. DAWs are utilized for the whole music production process, from creating to editing and mixing. The educational applications of digital music production systems are vast; they can be used as composition and arranging tools, as performance partners, and as windows into the subtle nuances of musical construction. However, although digital systems provide significant support for music production, the process still demands both creative and technical skills. While the technical aspects of the process may at times seem daunting, ultimately music production is about making music. In the world of music technology, music comes first.

Notes

1. *Cubase*: www.steinberg.net/en/products/cubase/start.html.
2. *Sonar*: www.cakewalk.com/.
3. *Logic*: www.apple.com/au/logic-pro/.
4. *Ableton Live*: www.ableton.com/.
5. *Pro Tools*: www.avid.com/US/products/family/pro-tools.
6. *FL Studio*: www.image-line.com/flstudio/.
7. *GarageBand*: www.apple.com/au/mac/garageband/.
8. *Auria*: www.wavemachinelabs.com/Products/auria.
9. *Cubasis*: https://itunes.apple.com/au/app/cubasis-music-production-system/id583976519?mt=8.
10. *BeatMaker 2*: http://intua.net/products/beatmaker2/.
11. *NanoStudio*: www.blipinteractive.co.uk/.
12. *GarageBand for iOS*: https://www.apple.com/ios/garageband/.
13. *Little MIDI Machine*: http://syntheticbits.com/.
14. *O-Generator*, simple cyclic sequencer: www.o-music.tv/product.htm.
15. *Beatwave*, a simple step sequencer for iOS: https://itunes.apple.com/au/app/beatwave/id363718254?mt = 8.

five
Aural Awareness and Music Theory Training

Acquiring basic skills in music theory and aural awareness is a core aspect of music education. The term *ear training* is used here to mean developing an ability to perceive sonic features in music. George Pratt, in his book *Aural Awareness*,[1] outlined the importance and fundamentality of these features in music. Ear training includes the recognition of timbres, melodies, harmonies, rhythms, and other musical elements, although a contemporary approach to ear training includes aural perception of content outside purely 'musical' contexts as well.[2]

The basis of music theory is the organization of musical elements—in particular, the ways that pitch and rhythm work independently and in combination to form melody, harmony, texture, and so on. Music theory is often associated with music notation, but it is underpinned by audio acoustics, which give rise to timbre, frequency, pulse, and other building blocks of music.[3] Knowledge about musical elements and how they are structured can be represented in many visual ways including as graphic scores, sonograms, and listening maps.[4]

The aim of aural and theory studies is to develop students' skills and understandings and help them develop from novice into expert musicians. Students fluent in these areas will move from deliberate and conscious behaviors to a habitual and intuitive musicality. A significant part of this journey involves understanding the elements of music from the sonic perspective—much of what aural software focuses on. Music theory software focuses on the structural organization of music and how music is represented as notation as shown in Figure 5.1. This chapter explores the benefits and concerns to consider when using music technologies to support aural and theory skills development.

Training Software

Many software programs, particularly for ear training, use repetition to achieve graded skill acquisition. Typically, with this approach, students complete a series of short tasks or questions; success at these tasks leads to further tasks at the next level. Software

FIGURE 5.1 A melodic dictation window in *Auralia*.

using this approach include the *Auralia* and *Musition* applications from Rising Software,[5] which emphasize staged progression, regular monitoring and managed assessment. Another example is Alfred's *Interactive Musician*[6] series, which focuses on pitch training, rhythm, and sight singing, and features a colorful, notation-focused software environment.

These applications use progressive short-term tasks for cumulatively higher levels of achievement. This software style also uses gamification approaches of video games, which include high score features, staged levels, achievement badges, and peer competition. Some software developers view these features as trivial or distracting and consequently use more austere presentations. These task-oriented applications are most useful when an instructor has identified a specific skill needs to be worked on or when he/she requires close measurement of student progress or ability.

Mobile devices, including smart phones and tablet computers, are especially appropriate for training apps. Their mobility allows the student to use them frequently; they typically include headphones, which are handy for aural exercises and music listening; apps are generally inexpensive; and touch interfaces facilitate easy interaction. Ear training apps for mobile devices include *Right Note*[7] (Orange Cube), *Rhythm Sight Reading Trainer*[8] (Rolfs Apps), *Ear Trainer*[9] (Thoor Software), *Timing Trainer*[10] (AppicDesign), *Perfect Ear*[11] (EDuckApps), and *Interval Recognition*[12] (Marchantpeter).

Music theory training apps include *Theory Lessons*[13] (*MusicTheory.net*), *Music Theory Lessons*[14] (*NadsTech.com*), *Music Reading Essentials*[15] (Apricot Digital Publishing), *Music Theory for Beginners*[16] (Musicroom.com), and *Chords in Keys*[17] (Stuart Bahn).

These programs range from informational tours to drill-and-practice sessions. They integrate sound, image, and text in their presentations and use interaction and feedback. Aural and theory applications can also be web-based. Examples include *MusicTheory.net*[18] and *Online Ear Trainer 2.0*,[19] which provide comprehensive selections of exercises. The latter requires a Java plug-in, so it cannot be used on iOS devices, but there is an iOS app from the same developer called *Play By Ear*.[20] The site *EarTrainingMastery.com*[21] has a set of Flash-based interactive drilling web apps, while *Functional Ear Trainer*[22] is an Adobe Air application for ear training that runs on Mac and Windows. Another online resource is the "1–10" Ear Training Test,[23] which combines instructions and questions and provides downloadable MP3 files as audio examples. For even more downloadable MP3 resources, turn to *Ear Training Anywhere*,[24] a site that presents a series of downloadable ear training exercises in MP3 format. And the extremely geeky musician may wish to consider the command-line interface *GNU Solfege*.[25]

The software and sites mentioned thus far (and there are many more) are resources to augment a study program. However, there are complete, but often short, online courses in music theory and ear training in the form of massive open online courses (MOOCs); see Chapter 13 for more detail on them. MOOCs provide instruction, exercises, and assessment packages and can be especially useful for the self-paced learner, for remedial study, or to augment formal studies in school music programs. Examples of music theory MOOCs include *Developing Your Musicianship*,[26] a six-lesson music theory course offered by Berklee College of Music on Coursera that focuses on scales, chords, and musical form with an emphasis on popular music. Another example is the *Introduction to Music Theory*[27] course offered on ALISON, which includes basic music theory, notation, and aural skills in a five-module sequence. A third example is *Music Theory 101*;[28] offered on Peer2Peer University, it is a twelve-module course that covers elementary music theory and notation concepts. A more advanced ear training MOOC that focuses on contemporary musicianship is *Critical Listening for Studio Production*,[29] a seven-week course offered on FutureLearn by Chris Corrigan from Queen's University Belfast.

In addition to integrated sounds and images, music technology software can incorporate game-like elements that make them fun to use. These can enhance student motivation in an otherwise repetitive and tedious curriculum area. But even with these game-like motivating elements, long sessions on repetitive tasks can still be tedious; to avoid student burnout, assign ear training and music theory software judiciously. Even if a student achieves good test results, these results should not demand the student learns that music is no fun at all.

Musicians have long known that regular practice promotes physical and mental musical skills. With mobile devices so widely available, students can now use software apps to practice more regularly. However, the apps' costs and/or licensing restrictions remain barriers to student practice on these devices. Educators might consider free or low-cost web-based systems or software, and explore software with licenses that allow student home installation. A good place to start is the "1–10" Ear Training Test and

MusicTheory.net, which provide online ear training and music theory exercises, respectively, and are easily accessed over the Internet at school and at home.

Software Features

Strategies for teaching music skills exist on a continuum that ranges from imitation to application. A good software program, like a good curriculum, includes a range of activities along this continuum. Software programs should also reinforce the link between musical sounds and notation. Matching aural and theoretical concepts creates useful associations in the user's mind, and computer programs that explicitly represent these links are most likely to be useful. With these learning strategies in mind, below are some activities often found in aural awareness and music theory apps:

- *Identifying/naming*—Flash cards or similar activities help reinforce identification and labeling. Contextual examples can be used, in which the student has to name features of a musical excerpt, such as meter, instrumentation, style, and tempo.
- *Matching*—Reinforces associations between representations. For example, students are asked to locate notes on a staff, piano keyboard, or guitar fretboard.
- *Structuring*—Students demonstrate their understanding by appropriately using musical materials. This can include sorting notes into meter groupings, writing melodies to lyrics, or harmonizing solo lines.
- *Demonstration*—Students are asked to relate, describe, or demonstrate their understanding of musical terms and symbols. This can include tapping a rhythm, singing a pitch interval, or performing a diminuendo.

When selecting software for aural or music theory training, determine that its features intersect appropriately with learning objectives and offline learning activities. Consider also the software's level of interactivity, its ease of setup, notational representations, and the styles and genres of its example music—features that are discussed in depth below.

Interactivity

A number of music training apps ask the user to answer tasks by singing or clapping. The computer records the user's performance, analyzes it, and gives feedback. Most singing tutors and many ear training packages, such as *Practica Musica*[30] and *Auralia*, have this capability.

Many approaches to user interaction are possible. Although programs usually focus on one or two of these, more comprehensive applications may incorporate more. User interaction approaches can include:

- *Recognition/identification*—Intervals, scales, rhythms, or tones are played, and the user replies (usually with a multiple-choice answer).
- *Repetition/dictation*—Users imitate by singing, writing, playing, or drawing. These activities are often contextual and open-ended, and are preferable to simple identification activities.

- *Prediction*—The student suggests (or predicts) possible extensions to an example. Extensions may include the closing of a cadence or the rhythmic completion of an incomplete measure. These activities can allow for more than one correct answer, and clearly indicate a user's problem-solving ability in a restricted context.
- *Description*—This approach is similar to recognition, but requires the user to justify his/her answer.
- *Analysis*—This approach extends description to include critical judgments regarding a musical example. Users should be encouraged to reach this level, which allows them to comment on music in an articulate fashion, but few software programs extend to this level.

The quality of aural and music theory software depends largely on the appropriateness and regularity of the feedback users receive about their progress. Some programs provide simple true or false responses to answers and allow the user a limited number of attempts before displaying the solution. Some applications provide hints after incorrect answers, and a few suggest revision materials when users are not able to answer correctly.

The basis of all training programs is repetition, but how repetition is used and the requirements for developmental progress can vary widely. Music theory programs often use a repetitive quiz model with randomized question order, and some additionally allow the teacher to add quiz content. The best programs combine exploration (play) and achievement-based (test) incentives and progression. As always, the teacher's role in choosing software, setting tasks, and providing learning activities and clarifications is critical for students' successful use of musical software.

Access

Music technologies' utility for aural and theory skills acquisition depends on device and software availability. A straightforward solution for device access in schools is to use computer labs. While appropriate for rudimentary skill acquisition, labs are usually not appropriate for the majority of music education activities, in which group work and integration with other resources are necessary.

Group work can benefit students learning music theory, but it can sometimes conflict with individual skill development, so provide students with opportunities for both. For example, have students rotate through activities, including using a device running aural or music theory software, in the music classroom. Even more conveniently, assign students to work on skills development in their own time, at school and/or at home. Suggest students use mobile device apps, as seen in Figure 5.2, while traveling to and from school, or let students access devices in their school downtime. Set required achievement goals that students can work toward to motivate students in these less formal activities.

Music Representations

While aural programs deal with music as sound, music theory programs often rely on visual cues, including music notation and note position on instruments like the piano keyboard or guitar fretboard. For example, the *ClefTutor* app, seen in Figure 5.2, combines

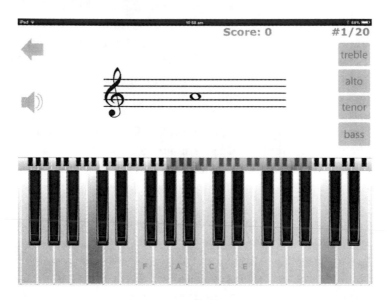

FIGURE 5.2 Music theory apps such as *ClefTutor*[31] can be used on a tablet computer.

piano keyboard and staff notation views, while the *Guitar Sight Reading Trainer*[32] from Rolfs Apps includes both guitar fretboard and staff notation views.

Theory programs mostly use staff notation or piano keyboard representations. Less conventional is music representation as graphic notations, typically as lines of melodic contour, pitch-color relationships, or cartoon-like height and length metaphors (such as a staircase). *TuneTrain*[33] by Jiyoung Lee, seen in Figure 5.3, uses this style of

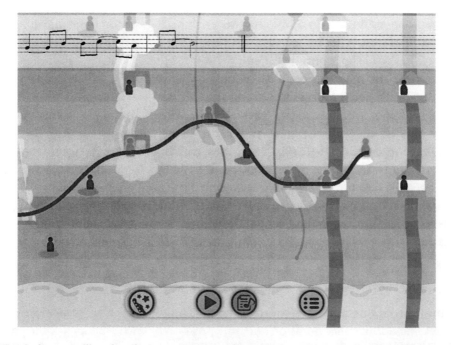

FIGURE 5.3 A game-like visual representation of a melody contour in the *TuneTrain* app.

representation. Many students may be more familiar with guitar tablature than staff notation, and they may benefit from apps that represent music as tablature.

While staff notation is pervasive in music education systems, teachers also use coding systems including tonic sol-fa, solfège, and French time signs. Some programs are available that support these representations. There are also occasional programs that use British, rather than American, duration terms (*crotchet* rather than *quarter note*, etc.). It is wise to remember that when choosing software, the software's musical representations—its language and symbol systems—should align with those relevant to the student's cultural context.

Genre and Styles

Ear training and music theory practice is significantly grounded in cultural conventions. Most software applications tend to revolve around diatonic Western music, lending themselves well to eighteenth- and nineteenth-century art music and contemporary rock and folk music. While practical, this approach is also limited. When choosing ear training software, make sure it covers the required curriculum areas. Some common musical topics that are less commonly found in apps include jazz chord terminology, atonal melodic material, polymeter rhythmic examples, spectral solfège,[34] and electronic and sampled acoustic timbres. It may be necessary or at least beneficial to get a program that focuses on some special aspect of your program; for example, *Absolute Pitch*[35] focuses on atonal pitch recognition.

While areas of pitch, harmony, and rhythm are well covered in most aural and theory programs, only a few deal with timbre and texture, and if they do, they often limit themselves to orchestral norms in these areas.[36] It is also uncommon to find programs that deal with tuning systems other than Western equal temperament. While some explore modal tonalities, non-Western harmonic systems are not widely supported. However, apps that engage with non-Western music include those focused on Indian classical music, such as the reference *Carnatic Raga*,[37] or quizzes like *Puzzle Me Raga*[38] and *RagaQuest*.[39] For increased focus on specific musical elements, some musicianship packages specialize in particular genres; the *Teoría*[40] music theory web site, for example, includes tutorials and ear training exercises that cover both Western classical and jazz harmony conventions.

Musical Examples

One of the most subjective areas in assessing ear training and music theory programs is the 'musicality' of their examples, even though it is arguably one of the most important considerations. Some programs use a database of prepared phrases for their examples, while others generate pitches, rhythms, or phrases algorithmically. Programs such as *MacGAMUT*,[41] for example, pay particular attention to the musicality of their generated melodic examples. Neither approach is inherently better than the other. A poor database selection can lead to predictable or already-known phrases, while overly simple algorithms such as random selection can result in counterintuitive musical examples. The aesthetic quality of the examples includes their compositional structure, their placement in a musical context, their sound quality, and their expressiveness. Thanks to devices' expanded memory capacities, the length and quality of recorded examples and sampled sounds is improving. Today there is little excuse for programs to employ poor-quality musical examples.

For full control of the musical examples used for ear training exercises, examples can be easily created using DAW or music publishing software packages. Alternatively, some software allows users or teachers to enter their own musical examples. For example, a user or teacher can add to the already rich and diverse selection in *MusicalEar*[42] by using *Sibelius* software or free *Finale Notepad* software.

Often in aural awareness training, examples isolate musical elements in order to focus the student's attention. While this approach is potentially useful in clarifying what students should attend to, isolating elements is generally undesirable. It can make it difficult for students to transfer what they learned in the exercises to real-world musical situations. The technical limitations of computer technology have historically reinforced this decontextualized approach. But as digital technology advances, richer musical examples can be expected. In particular, *MusicalEar* presents aural examples within their broader musical contexts.

Teaching Considerations

As with all resources for music education, there are logistical issues to consider when using aural and theory training software. One of the first considerations is deciding *who* will use the programs. If the students are of a broad range of skills and ages, then the breadth and depth of software content is important. In addition, consider the software's example customization options and the instructor's capacity to specify sets of tasks for different groups of students. If instructing many students, consider how students will access the devices and the costs of appropriate software licenses. When selecting specific ear training or music theory apps, consider how their stylistic emphases and the types and complexity of the skills they cover relate to your curriculum.

One of the often-cited advantages of computer programs in aural and theory training is the instructor's ability to monitor student progress. But educators wishing to use these features need to consider a number of factors. First, what is the program monitoring? Some programs keep records of all student activity—both practice and assessment exercises—while others keep records of high score achievement only. Second, can the software individualize a program of study for students or groups of students in an appropriate way? A number of software applications have provisions to track the activities and achievements of users. Some also allow the instructor to set activity pathways along which students can progress. Third, is customizing worth the effort? While a few aural programs allow sophisticated individualization, the question remains: Who is going to take the trouble to use such features and keep track of student progress at this detailed a level? Larger online educational sites, such as Khan Academy, commonly claim that data tracking and customization can bring significant benefits to student learning. However, there seems to be a gap between the infrastructure available to these large online services and teachers' manual setting options in desktop software applications.

There are a couple of solutions between these extremes. Students can be instructed to set their own task pathways, thus freeing the teacher from setting them, or frequent assessment feedback can be used to consistently reset short-term goals rather than attempting to plot (and then re-plot) long-term learning trajectories. But can you trust software assessment? And what part will computer-based results play in the student's grade? Many educators prefer to use aural and music theory programs to support their curriculum, but to personally gauge the student's progress and achievements through individual examinations and tests. As the data management processes improve, especially in online services, it is likely that results from automated testing will become quite reliable. This should allow educators to focus on the impact such training has on more holistic activities, such as student performance and production projects.

For aural or theory training to be effective, its use cannot be ad hoc. Time needs to be regularly allocated for work on these tasks for them to be effective. Many short work sessions are more productive than a few extended sessions. Students' mobile devices allow for convenient engagement with these activities. Regular progress monitoring is required to keep students on task and to make sure that training time is well spent.

Conclusion

Helping students perceive and understand the elements of music and how they operate is fundamental to music education. An important part of acquiring these skills is listening, identifying elements, and performing exercises that reinforce the basic principles of music. Such repetitive tasks are well suited to music technologies, and it is not surprising that there are a wide range of software applications that support aural and music theory training. The challenge for music educators is how to use these wisely. Practice can be engaging and fun, but a tireless computer can exhaust the easily bored student. Music educators also face another challenge: how to continually relate the (at times) abstract exercises and tasks to real-world musical situations and activities. Yet, used prudently, music technologies can be a powerful ally in ear training and music theory instruction.

Reflection Questions

1. Ear training software tests sonic features including which musical elements?
2. What additional skills and knowledge are beneficial for contemporary musicianship?
3. What are some apps for mobile devices related to ear training?
4. Which video game characteristics are often used in ear training software?
5. What visualizations do theory and ear training apps use to represent music?
6. Name some of the activities used in aural awareness and music theory apps.
7. Name some MOOCs that focus on musical ear training or music theory.
8. How do aural and theory applications incorporate style and genre diversity?
9. What does 'musicality' mean regarding music samples in training software?
10. What questions does the chapter raise about training software as a monitor of student progress?

Teaching Tips

1. Choose software that allows for self-assessment at any time (especially prior to formal assessment gateways).
2. Focus on measurable competency outcomes. Allow students to regulate their independent practice as required to achieve those outcomes.
3. Provide supplements to music theory and ear training studies through composing, arranging, and performing exercises in which students apply their knowledge.
4. Ensure that students have off-hours access to aural or theory training software.
5. Use software that provide different types of interaction so students can develop a variety of abilities and stay interested.
6. Have students work in pairs at times, so they share problem-solving skills and develop a healthy competitive spirit.
7. To familiarize students with the features of ear and theory training software, ask students to search for and evaluate apps.
8. Keep a mobile device with appropriate apps in the music room for students to use in 'down time' between activities.
9. Make sure that software employ visual representations (staff, tablature, etc.) that are relevant to students.
10. Provide a range of software to accommodate differences in student learning styles, and allow students to pick the software they are most comfortable with.

Suggested Tasks for Educators

1. Test your own aural abilities using a ear training software package.
2. Choose an example curriculum and match up its aural and music theory requirements with software systems that meet those needs.
3. Explore the content of ear training or music theory MOOCs, and reflect on how these resources might be useful in your own teaching.
4. Take time to investigate some of the more exploratory software packages, such as *MusicalEar*, rather than settling for easy-choice didactic systems.
5. Choose a musical practice and find out the aural and theory skills it requires. How might a study program develop these skills?

Chapter Summary

Skills development in music theory and aural perception continues to be a core part of music education. These skills include the recognition of timbres, intervals, melodies, harmonies, and rhythms, and understanding harmonic and rhythmic musical structures and how to represent them symbolically. An extensive assortment of software exists to support ear training and the study of music theory. These apps come with a broad range of features and capabilities. It is critical to match an app's capabilities with the student's educational requirements. When relying on a computer-based training regime for skill training, the question of access to devices and software needs to be addressed. Mobile music technologies—including smartphones, MP3 players, and tablet computers—are proving to be particularly useful in this area, as students can use them regularly, at times convenient for them. There is, however, a risk that abstract training exercises will bore students, and there is no guarantee that skills gained through these exercises will be transferred to real-world music-making activities. Despite these cautions, when appropriately incorporated into a music program rich with holistic music-making activities, music technologies can be very effective for ear training and developing an understanding of music theory.

Notes

1. Pratt, G. (1990). *Aural awareness: Principles and practice.* Buckingham: Open University Press.
2. Tsabary, E. (2012). Electroacoustic Ear Training. In A.R. Brown (Ed.), *Sound musicianship: Understanding the crafts of music* (pp. 313–323). Newcastle upon Tyne: Cambridge Scholars.
3. Wolfe, J. (2012). Musical Sounds and Musical Signals. In A.R. Brown (Ed.), *Sound musicianship: Understanding the crafts of music* (pp. 14–27). Newcastle upon Tyne: Cambridge Scholars.
4. Listening Maps are described in more detail at Arts Education Ideas: www.aeideas.com/text/articles/listeningmaps.cfm.
5. Rising software, developers of *Auralia* and *Musition* software: www.risingsoftware.com/home.php.
6. *Interactive Musician*, pitch, rhythm and sight singing software drills: www.alfred.com/sub_software/aim/aim.htm.
7. *Right Note–Ear Trainer*: https://itunes.apple.com/us/app/right-note-ear-trainer/id427276222?mt=8.
8. *Rhythm Sight Reading Trainer* for iOS: https://sites.google.com/site/sightreadrhythm/home.
9. *Ear Trainer* for iOS: https://itunes.apple.com/us/app/ear-trainer/id358733250?mt = 8.
10. *Timing Trainer* for iOS: https://itunes.apple.com/us/app/timing-trainer/id500704297?mt = 8.
11. *Perfect Ear* for Android: https://play.google.com/store/apps/details?id=ru.exaybachay.pearfree&hl=en.
12. *Interval Recognition* for Android: www.marchantpeter.co.uk/android-interval-recognition.php.
13. *Theory Lessons* for iOS: www.musictheory.net/products/lessons.
14. *Music Theory Lessons* for Android: https://play.google.com/store/apps/details?id=nadsoft.musictheorylessonsfree&hl=en
15. *Music Reading Essentials* for iOS: https://itunes.apple.com/us/app/music-reading-essentials/id501483486?mt = 8.
16. *Music Theory for Beginners* for iOS: https://itunes.apple.com/gb/app/music-theory-for-beginners/id435161137?mt = 8.
17. *Chords in Keys*, theory app for Android: https://play.google.com/store/apps/details?id=appinventor.ai_kissmyaxe.MusicTheoryChordsInKeys&hl=en.
18. *MusicTheory.net*, online aural and notation skill exercises: www.musictheory.net/.
19. *Online Ear Trainer 2.0*, web-based exercises using Java: www.iwasdoingallright.com/tools/ear_training/main/.
20. *Play By Ear*, ear training app for iOS: www.iwasdoingallright.com/playbyear/iphone/.
21. *EarTrainingMastery.com*, web-based interval exercises: www.eartrainingmastery.com/en/ear-training-exercises.
22. *Functional Ear Trainer*, software for Mac and Windows using the Adobe Air plug-in: www.miles.be/software/34-functional-ear-trainer-v2.
23. The "1–10" Ear Training Test web site: www.hearchords.com/ear-training-test/.

24. *Ear Training Anywhere*, MP3 audio files of aural exercises: www.eartrainanywhere.com/.
25. *GNU Solfege*, ear training software written in Python: http://savannah.gnu.org/projects/solfege.
26. *Developing Your Musicianship*, a MOOC by Berklee College of Music: www.coursera.org/course/musicianship.
27. *Introduction to Music Theory*, a five-module MOOC: http://alison.com/courses/Introduction-to-Music-Theory/content.
28. *Music Theory 101*, music MOOC on P2PU: https://p2pu.org/en/groups/music-theory-101/tasks/.
29. *Critical Listening for Studio Production*, ear training MOOC: www.futurelearn.com/courses/critical-listening-for-studio-production.
30. *Practica Musica* by Ars Nova software: www.ars-nova.com/practica6.html.
31. *ClefTutor*, music theory tutorials and exercise app: www.cleftutor.com/.
32. *Guitar Sight Reading Trainer* from Rolfs Apps for iOS: https://sites.google.com/site/guitaratsight/home.
33. *TuneTrain* music game: www.etc.cmu.edu/projects/bravura/.
34. *Sound Chef Pro* and *Train Your Ears* software can be used for spectral solfège training: www.soundchefpro.com/ and www.trainyourears.com/.
35. *Absolute Pitch*, ear training software that includes atonal examples. From Silvawood software for Windows OS: www.silvawood.co.uk/pitch-intro.htm.
36. Davidson, R. (2012). Notating music and sound. In A.R. Brown (Ed.), *Sound musicianship: Understanding the crafts of music* (pp. 277–288). Newcastle upon Tyne: Cambridge Scholars.
37. *Carnatic Raga*, an app reference for Indian ragas: http://carnaticraga.com/.
38. *Puzzle Me Raga*, an app quiz about Indian and South Asian classical music: https://itunes.apple.com/us/app/puzzle-me-raga/id661453233?mt = 8.
39. *RagaQuest*, app by Sriram Emani for aural identification of Indian ragas: https://itunes.apple.com/in/app/ragaquest/id659252437?mt = 8.
40. *Teoría*, a comprehensive web-based music theory and ear training site created by José Rodríguez Alvira: www.teoria.com/.
41. *MacGAMUT*, ear training software for Mac and Windows: www.macgamut.com/.
42. *MusicalEar*, software focused on developing ear training and music theory skills developed in the context of complete musical examples: www.musicalear.com/.

six
Music
Publishing

One of the most popular applications of computing in music education is the publication of notated musical scores. Although music notation packages are popular with users, their development remains a veritable minefield for software developers as they attempt to accommodate hundreds of years of notational conventions and stylistic interpretations. Conventions of notation that are commonly encountered and understood by musicians can cause significant problems for computers attempting to interpret these incoming musical gestures. Even so, the major music publishing packages do a great job of navigating this minefield. Once published, screen displays are increasingly used for reading notation during performance and for study. The wide adoption of tablet computers since 2010 has accelerated the acceptance of screens in this way. In this chapter we will explore some of the major features of music notation software and their use in educational contexts.

Notation as a Representation

Fundamentally, all music notation is a visual representation of music: an abstract representation of the ideas and sounds we embed in musical expression. As with all abstractions, music notation brings particular elements of music to our attention while deferring others to cultural context and performer/reader interpretation. Digital systems can struggle with issues of context and interpretation and so rely heavily on assumptions of their designer and choices of their users to operate effectively. In this way music publishing systems are a clear case of music technologies acting as a tool, designed to operate with clear human direction—a topic explored in some detail in Chapter 1. Of course, screen-based notation is a clear analogy to paper-based notational displays and thus digital notation also acts as a medium. As a medium it imitates features of the older print medium and adds new features of digital systems including ease of editing or manipulation (e.g., transposition) and hands-free page turning.

FIGURE 6.1 Music publishing systems can handle many common notational conventions.

Fortunately, the demands of music publishing in educational situations is often rudimentary and focused in areas that software applications handle well. The score in Figure 6.1 provides an example of conventional uses of stave notation including for percussion, guitar tablature, and chord symbols. This chapter will begin by addressing the uses of music notation apps in education to make clear the features most often required in music publishing systems. Following this is a discussion of the strengths and weaknesses to keep in mind when selecting music technologies for music publishing.

Learning with Digital Music Notation

Traditionally the use of music manuscript is widespread in music education. Most educational uses of manuscript paper transfer easily to digital music notation systems. Because of the strong metaphorical links between notation on paper and on screen, most educators will be able to easily think of additional applications to those outlined here.

Arrangements

The ease of editing and printing legible scores makes the preparation of arrangements the single most common use of music publishing apps in schools. Capabilities such as being able to quickly prepare neat scores, easily copy and paste sections, automatically extract parts from a full score, and effortlessly transpose keys makes the digital arrangement of scores and parts an efficient task. This is particularly useful for teachers who regularly manage ensembles with unusual or varying instrumentation. Saved scores can be the basis for quickly creating new or substitute parts on demand. The digital playback of the score provides a convenient audition while arranging. Audio renderings of completed scores and of individual parts are useful for learning parts and rehearsing. Recordings of scores can be rendered at different tempi, with or without some parts omitted, for additional flexibility and learning support.

Worksheets

Educators often need to prepare printed material as handouts. For music classes these often incorporate notated examples. Interoperability between word processors and music publishing progress can be as easy as copying and pasting, but this process is not always as straightforward as it should be. Surprisingly, some of the lesser-known software programs implement this feature best. However, all major music publishing applications allow some way to capture score selections for transfer into another application. At the very least a screen shot can be captured and cropped using image editing software.

Making score segments look correct for use in handouts can require some special editing because layout conventions for printed scores may not always be appropriate. The handout shown in Figure 6.2 includes examples of some unconventional layout requirements.

Typical layout challenges include needing to prepare several self-contained examples in one notation file, or the use of nonstandard or absent stave or bar line layout. For example, it is likely that clef changes between examples will result in courtesy clefs at the end of preceding lines which may not be desired but cannot be deleted. Also, it may be difficult to turn off automatic features such as bar numbering or staff justification.

These edge cases aside, once handouts have been created in a word processor with musical examples pasted in, these can be easily printed or sent electronically to students.

Composition

Music publishing systems are widely used for composition for the same reasons of neatness and efficiencies that assist arranging tasks. However, because the compositional task not only requires efficiency but also malleability, many composers find their compositional process interrupted or restrained by the limitations and/or implementation of a program's editing capabilities. With improvements in score navigation, note entry and playback features more composers find programs such as *Sibelius*[1] and *Finale*[2] useful compositional environments, but for many tasks, simpler and less expensive applications such as *Musescore*,[3] *Noteflight*,[4] *Reflow*,[5] or *Finale Notepad*[6] may be quite adequate. The direct manipulation possible with touch screen interfaces have also reduced barriers to entry for many composers. Apps such as *NotateMe*[7] for iPad and Android, shown in Figure 6.3, are leading the way.

Many digital audio workstation software packages, described in Chapter 4, have support for music notation. Often this is quite adequate for educational examples and simple scores. The ability to also edit music in non-notational views can be an advantage in some cases; however, these apps will not be as fully featured for music publishing as dedicated ones.

Instrumental Exercises
for Trumpet/Cornet

Introducing **6/8** Time

6/8 time has six eighth note (quaver) beats to a bar, split into two sets of three:

These make up two dotted quarter notes (dotted crotchets):

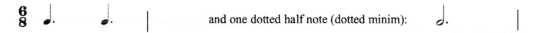

and one dotted half note (dotted minim):

Other combinations of rhythm can be created which include:

EXERCISE 1

Clap the rhythms above individually and in sequence, to get used to the timing.

EXERCISE 2

Now try playing this exercise, which uses these rhythms and is based on the scale of C major (below). Some fingerings have been added to help you along the way.

C Major scale

EXERCISE 3

Now try playing this melody from a well-known traditional song, but watch out for the accidentals!

FIGURE 6.2 An example of a music handout prepared in the *Sibelius* software.

FIGURE 6.3 Handwriting recognition of notation with *NotateMe* on the iPad.

Animated Playback

As most music notation software has the ability to play back the score, this can be very useful for music theory exercises, either as teacher-operated demonstrations or for self-directed student exercises. The addition of aural feedback and visual scrolling that follows the playback location can greatly improve student engagement and understanding. For extensive or specialized aural training activities there are specialized applications that are more appropriate; these are discussed in Chapter 13.

Analysis

Another educational usage of these programs is for analysis. This has much potential but is not well supported by features in existing packages which focus on publishing. Notation software can be utilized for analysis by part-muting to isolate elements, comparison of score segments displayed in different tiled windows, and allowing the playback of discrete sections at any tempo and with variations of orchestration. Some applications also have features that highlight pitch range boundaries within the score, which could be tweaked for purposes of analysis. Many provide annotation tools to draw on the score. These could be used to mark up features as part of an analysis process. A small number of applications can be scripted; that is, short software algorithms can be written, to automate, or search. These could be adapted by a keen user for locating repeated themes or counting the occurrences of particular features.

Score Reading

Music publishing systems can be deployed in performance too, if required. The most obvious use is to have the program, or output from it, displayed on a tablet computer, the screen of which is positioned on a music stand. There are some specialist applications, such as the *ForScore*[8] app, that are dedicated to this task. Readers are available for major music publishing formats, including the *Scorch*[9] app for *Sibelius* files, and the *SongBook*[10] app for *Finale* files. Often a music publishing package used to create the score will be sufficient, or even a PDF or image reader such as Acrobat can display score pages saved in an appropriate format. The advantages of screen reading include carrying many scores in a lightweight package, reading visibility in low-light conditions, hands-free page turning, and erasable annotation.

Scanning and Transcription

Because it is often easier to store and manipulate scores in electronic form than in paper form, some music publishing software allows for the scanning of printed scores into a digital format. Scores may be scanned as graphic images or, in other cases, into an editable notation file via optical character recognition (OCR) processes. The accuracy of the OCR transcription process varies significantly depending upon the print quality and complexity of the original score. When OCR works well it can save considerable time in note entry, but when transcription is inaccurate the task of correcting errors in the score can be tedious.

Another method of quickly entering note data is to read in a MIDI file of the score. Most applications do a very good job of interpreting the MIDI file into a notated score, even if the MIDI file was created from a human performance of the work. Music publishing systems can usually save scores and MIDI files also if required. This facilitates data transfer to other music applications.

Sharing and Collaborating

The sharing of electronic scores can go much further than passing around files. Online music libraries and collaboration services are increasingly available for scores in various formats. Examples include the *Scorch* software for *Sibelius* files and the *SongBook* app for *Finale* files. These apps allow the sharing of prepared score files for practice, homework, or assignment submission.

Some music publishing systems like *Noteflight* are entirely online, allowing score entry, playback, and sharing in a web browser. These can become truly collaborative, allowing files to be shared between users and even collaboratively edited. The advantage of having everything online is that only a web browser is required to run and access the account, which does not restrict the software to a particular computer or device. While online editors like *Noteflight* are not as fully featured as the larger applications, they are surprisingly feature rich and often more than adequate for most educational uses. In addition, being online they can also provide basic learning management facilities, such as file distribution, tracking user access and usage, and online assignment submission.

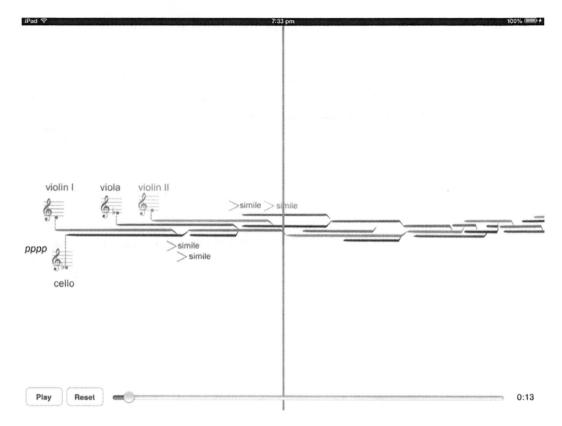

FIGURE 6.4 *ScorePlayer* app scrolling through *Simile* by Lindsay Vickery.

Animated Scores

In a digital age, there is no need for scores to be static objects. Scrolling through the music as its plays is a simple example of score animation, but this is only the tip of the iceberg. A notable example is the *Decibel ScorePlayer*[11] app, shown in Figure 6.4, that allows the creation and playback of animated, especially graphic, scores. It also supports synchronization of score playback between devices. For more information on this topic consult the blog of animated music notation maintained by Páll Ivan.[12]

Selecting Music Notation Software

Music publishing packages are complex software systems and people's requirements are diverse. However, there are some common technical features to be aware of when assessing music notation systems. In educational situations the appropriateness of a system will depend on who is using it (staff or students), their experience and expertise, and the styles of music being notated.

Complexity

As with all technologies, it is critical with music publishing software to choose the right tool for the job. Given that the demands of professional music typesetters and student composers are vastly different, it is not surprising that different tools best suit each instance. Less expensive apps often limit the maximum number of staves in a score or the range of symbols or features. Elements such as adding lyrics or chord symbols may not be present, and it may not be possible to import or export MIDI or audio files. Software for mobile devices is likely to be more limited in capabilities than desktop computer software, but this may be an advantage in not confusing students with unnecessary options.

Print Quality

It can be most important to look first at the score output when evaluating music publishing systems. The way the score looks on screen and when printed depends significantly on the notational font being used and on the quality of the screen display. Look for clarity, openness, and readability at a variety of font sizes. Things to notice include the note head size and shape, beam thickness and slant angles, and the spacing between notes and accidentals (particularly in dense chromatic clusters). The range of notation size(s) may be an issue, particularly if preparing music for a young (or much older) audience is a priority, where larger notes are required. The ability to view a score on screen in high resolution can help to accentuate the spacing and positioning of symbols and reduce the need for excessive draft printouts or file transfers. Many systems offer a choice of fonts that allow for an authentic appearance in genres such as jazz and early music.

For those that take their music engraving seriously there are specialized programs for this too. Notable among these applications is *LilyPond*,[13] written by Han-Wen Niehuys and Jan Nieuwenhuizen; and *Belle, Bonne, Sage*[14] by William Andrew Burnson, which produce excellent and sometimes astounding output. However, their operation can be very complex.

Input Methods

Entering notes and other symbols can be easy or frustrating. This primarily depends on matching the input method with the character of music. For example, with rhythmically simple phrases, real-time performance on a MIDI keyboard is quick, whereas for rhythmically complex scores, note-by-note input using a QWERTY keyboard will usually be less frustrating in the long run. Note-by-note methods include mouse-dragging from a pallet or menu, clicking on an on-screen keyboard, use of the QWERTY keyboard, and handwriting recognition.

Methods of scanning and transcribing printed scores were canvassed earlier. An example of specialized music scanning software is *SharpEye*[15] for Windows computers. This can be useful for clean and straightforward scores but, except for very large score entry tasks, is often not worth the effort. Applications like *ForScore* treat the score as simple image files, which works fine for score reading but not for editing or arranging.

Rhythmic Transcription and Rendering

While pitches are highly constrained in Western music and generally cause few problems in notation systems, rhythmic accuracy can be quite problematic. First, some programs simply cannot display certain complex rhythmic groupings (such as those found in contemporary music or non-Western music). Difficult rhythms include those with arbitrary tuplets, embedded tuplets (one inside another), groupings across staves or bars, or unusual beam groupings within a bar. Second, the ability to appropriately transcribe real-time input from performances can vary greatly. Interpreting the differences between triplets and dotted note patterns can cause problems for software, as can rubato and swing articulation. If these are important in the music you write, then it is wise to test examples containing these features with various applications to see which deals best with them.

Staves, Clefs, and Articulations

Note symbols are central to music notation, as are staves, clefs, slurs, ties, accents, and other articulations. Most music publishing software will provide a full range of the most common of these symbols. Beyond that, however, features may vary. For example, lack of access to percussion staves of fewer than five lines can be a source of frustration. For guitar music a tablature (TAB) stave is useful. At times the changing of clefs can be problematic, particularly if midway through a bar, and courtesy clefs are often dealt with in different ways. Staves should be able to be grouped as required.

Another variable is the number of articulations that can be associated with a single note and how elegantly they are positioned in relation to one another. Articulations such as accents, staccato marks, pauses, slurs, and so on are generally well catered for in simple cases. Both the print quality and positioning of slurs, and the ease of positioning and editing articulation locations can vary widely between applications. It can be wise to examine some published scores in the style(s) of music you write to make sure that all necessary bracketing, beaming, trills, barline extensions, repeat time bars, D.C. and D.S. signs, and so forth are available.

Editing and Transformation

Composers often use repetition, sequences, and variations in their scores; therefore, having software functions for moving and transforming groups of notes can save a lot of input time. Basic copying and pasting functions are to be expected, while the extension of these might include functions to create multiple repeats and the use of aliases (duplicates that reflect any changes made to the original).

Depending on your composition or arrangement needs, the use of note transformations can be either helpful or vital. Manipulation can include transposition, duration extension or reduction, and the retrograde or inversion of a phrase. More complex functions may be available such as modification by similarity, automatic harmonization, note range limiting based on instrument ranges, and spelling correction of accidentals. Programs can vary widely in the types of transformations available and can even vary the terms used to describe them.

Text and Drawing

Although scores are focused on music notations they often include text and simple graphical elements. Text is used for titles, stave names, lyrics, chord symbols, and interpretive indications such as 'allegro'. More direct methods of input (clicking any-where and typing) are quicker and more intuitive for small amounts of text, while the dedicated text-area approach is more productive for complex scores and large blocks of text, such as lyrics.

It is surprising how often simple shapes and lines can be useful in a score. Drawing tools are useful for simple lines, boxes, and ovals that can be used to border rehearsal markings, highlight form repeat indicators, and indicate extended notational conventions. An extensive set of tools for drawing is required only for those doing more professional score output, or dealing with graphical conventions often encountered in contemporary works.

Playback and Audio Rendering

It is often useful to have an audio playback of your score to assist in hearing the composition or arrangement. It is also useful to be able to make a recording (an audio rendering) of the score or parts of it. As discussed above, recordings can assist in learning and rehearsing the parts or as a demonstration of how the final performance might sound. The ability for music publishing software to perform expressively and with high quality sounds has increased significantly over the decades. Most music publishing applications include a software synthesizer or sample library—or the option to add one as an additional plug-in. These plug-ins allow the user to select the types and quality of sounds used for playback. The variety of instruments available can impact the diversity of musical genres that can be adequately supported.

The expressiveness of music playback can vary between software applications on two counts. There can be a general performance interpretation applied to the playback that takes into account emphasis on downbeats and subtle variations in note loudness and duration. Secondly, playback can respond to articulation markings such as dynamics, slurs, accents, diminuendos, rallentandos, and so on.

Display and Page Turning

As screen reading has become more frequent, the ability of software packages to support animated playback or page turning has improved. One consideration is controlling the page layout so that page breaks are in appropriate locations. Typically software includes the facility to adjust the number of measures (bars) in a system, or the number of systems on a page. At times there is computational assistance in page layout, such as with *Finale*'s *Smart Page Turns* plug-in or the *Suggest Page Turns* plug-in for *Sibelius*. A second consideration for page turns is activating them when reading from the screen. Touch screen devices allow a tap or swipe which is usually no harder than a paper page turn. This can work even if using a general purpose document reader like the *Kindle* app or PDF reader. Hardware devices, such as the *Air Turn*,[16] which support hands-free page turning are quite popular. These foot pedal devices connect wirelessly via Bluetooth and operate with a wide variety of apps on most platforms.

Priorities for Music Publishing Hardware

A complete music publishing system will consist of a computing device, software, and optionally a printer, a MIDI keyboard, and audio playback equipment. Having previously discussed software features in detail, this section examines the requirements for individual hardware elements.

Computing Device

In many situations the choice of computing platform will be made for reasons well beyond the considerations of music publishing. But assuming the choice is driven by the needs of music publishing there are some features to take into account. Most important is software availability for your platform. Simply pick a device that runs your preferred music publishing application and supports your preferred input method: touchscreen, mouse, MIDI controller, and so forth. If this still leaves some choice, then ensure that connection to other hardware is well supported; for example, connection to a MIDI keyboard, audio interface, secondary screen, and printer. Following these considerations are general computing considerations of size and mobility, speed and memory capacity, Internet connectivity, and the like.

Screen Size and Resolution

Where there is a choice, the size and resolution of the device (or external) screen should be as large and clear as possible for score display. Having to continually scroll around a page becomes annoying. Being able to see at least one manuscript page at full resolution is desirable. There can be a tradeoff between resolution and image size. There is little point in having a very high resolution if it means the notation size is too small to read clearly. Keep in mind that desktop or laptop computers will allow the screen resolution to be varied, but tablet computers may not. Even so, for tasks in music education even a relatively limited display size can be quite effective. For example, Figure 6.5 shows that even a quite limited screen size can support basic music publishing. Music notation apps can allow zooming in and out of the score, and so take time to juggle zoom, resolution, and size to achieve a desirable balance.

Input Devices

There can be a variety of methods to enter score data. Step input is achieved with the computer or MIDI keyboard, computer mouse, stylus, or drawing tablet. For most users, the input method can make a significant difference to work efficiency and ergonomics. So, it is worth taking time to explore the range of devices available and choose carefully. Real-time input through live performance capture can be useful for competent players and for experimenting with musical ideas before committing them to the score. In this case considerations for the instrument include interface (piano, wind, percussion), pitch range, dynamic responsiveness, and portability. Audio input (transcription) is possible on some systems but works best with monophonic lines and can produce inconsistent results. As discussed previously, scores can be digitally scanned and there

FIGURE 6.5 *Noteflight* software running in an iPad web browser.

is OCR software that transcribes these images to editable score data. A general-purpose optical scanner should suffice for music scanning.

Playback Quality

Most applications include a sound library for audio playback. In these cases hardware playback options include headphones and loudspeakers, as for other music technology tasks. If the software supports MIDI output then it is possible to use an external synthesizer or sound module for playback. It is common for a school or college to have a digital piano and this may provide better quality playback than the built-in software.

Local and/or Cloud Storage

Provision of file storage and backup needs to be considered, but may vary somewhat depending upon the devices in use and the way they manage storage. Music notation files need not be large compared to audio or video files, but keeping them organized and backed up still requires some attention. File organization is particularly important when students are sharing a notation system, sharing files, or using personal devices where files need to be synchronized with institutional storage. A way of collecting and maintaining files for devices with traditional file systems, like PCs, is to use an external storage device such as a flash drive or hard drive where files for individual or groups of students are maintained. These can be moved from device to device as required. Often a school or college will have central computer server space on which data can be backed up or stored. Online, or cloud, storage can be a convenient and flexible alternative to physical external storage where Internet access is readily available. There are a number of cloud storage providers, including Google, Amazon, Microsoft, and Dropbox. However, operating systems vary in their support for these services, especially with regard to allowing group collaboration and file sharing.

Printing

When hard copy score publishing is the goal, printers become a most important element of the system. For student exercises or handouts output quality may be less critical. Modern computer printers are of quite reasonable quality, but paper handling size can be a consideration for score printing. Printer quality should, of course, be as high as is affordable, which typically means laser printers with a resolution of at least 600 dots per inch. The speed of printing a page can vary, and if high volume printing is expected this can be a consideration. The common paper handling size for printers is A4 or US Letter. Many musical score formats are larger, including the convention of B5 for orchestral parts, and even larger for some conductor scores. Therefore an A3 printer can be a considerable asset. An alternative is to print at a smaller size but at a very high resolution and then enlarge on a photocopier to the required dimension. Color printing is of little concern for traditional scores but it may be important for color-coded graphic scores and for printing attractive class handouts.

Equipment Location

Music publishing systems can take many forms, from an app on a personal mobile device to a dedicated notation workstation setup with a printer, keyboard, and loudspeakers. Remember that laptop computing systems need not be any less powerful than desktop systems and can be conveniently used in a variety of locations. Output from fixed or mobile devices can be sent to fixed printing devices over a wireless network or directly connected via cables as required. Internet-based notation solutions can be conveniently accessed from any networked device with a modern web browser. Tablet computers with a touch interface make good sense for notation input and can even be used in classrooms, concert halls, or at home. While smaller mobile devices are attractive, remember that fully featured music publishing packages will always be restricted to, and certainly operate most effectively on, the most powerful computing devices. This may mean that a variety of systems that suit different notational tasks is the best solution.

Conclusion

Music notation plays an important part in music making and therefore in music education. It is a primary means of storing musical knowledge and a major means of communicating that knowledge. The computer as a symbolic processing machine is well suited to the tasks of handling music notation, and music publishing applications generally do a good job of this. Digital music technologies can assist in creating clear musical scores by imitating paper and printing processes. They can transform performance gestures into notation and so speed up the writing process, and they can provide convenient and powerful notation transformation functions to assist the arranger and composer.

As with all music technologies, access to the benefits of digital music publishing brings with it challenges such as the provision of devices and software, the reassessment of what notational systems are relevant to contemporary music contexts, how symbolic representation of music assists learning, and how screen-based scores integrate into established musical practices and create new ones. The extensive uptake of digital music publishing indicates that the many benefits of neatness, efficiency, audible feedback, and file sharing make engagement worthwhile.

Reflection Questions

1. What are the ways in which digital music publishing software is similar to or differs from paper-based publishing?
2. How can the audio rendering of a digital score be useful?
3. How can a music publishing application be integrated with other software for educational purposes?
4. What are some of the potential issues in the preparation of score examples for printed handouts?
5. How can music publishing software files be shared?
6. Why might some composers still prefer to use paper and pencil over a digital scoring system?
7. How might digital music scores be used in performance?
8. Why might the ability to scan an existing printed score be useful?
9. What features of a computing device are important for use in music publishing?
10. What drawing capabilities would be most useful for creating graphic scores?

Teaching Tips

1. Use computer-based notation tasks as a way to introduce students to music theory concepts and music representation conventions.
2. Have students explore the editing possibilities of the software by correcting a score file that includes deliberate errors or incomplete sections.
3. Use the entry of nonstandard notation symbols used by some twentieth-century composers as a way to discuss their performed interpretation.
4. Use music publishing software for styles of music usually represented as scores and avoid using it for those styles that are not.
5. Use the editing and playback features of music notation systems to support sight-reading and transcription tasks by having students check their interpretation against the computer playback.

6. Provide a range of notation input options so that students can find the method that works best for them.
7. Have students arrange pieces for different voices or instruments but aim to preserve or enhance the expressive effect of the music.
8. Introduce percussion notation and guitar tablature by having students enter short musical passages into appropriate notation software.
9. Use the table of supported articulations that can be found in the music publishing software's manual as a stimulus for students to investigate what they all stand for.
10. Utilize the lyric function of notation software to support songwriting activities.

Suggested Tasks for Educators

1. Check the difference in efficiency between paper and computer scoring by timing how long it takes to do the same notation task each way.
2. Use a music publishing package to create a music-minus-one audio recording of an arrangement for use in rehearsal.
3. Explore the capabilities of music publishing software by entering the first eight bars of a complex work such as Stravinsky's *Rite of Spring*.
4. Use a word processor to create a handout using musical examples prepared with a music publishing application.
5. Experiment with screen-based score reading apps and wireless page-turning hardware.

Chapter Summary

Music publishing is one of the more popular applications of digital music technology, particularly in educational circles. Although music notation packages are popular with users, their development remains a veritable minefield for software developers as they attempt to accommodate hundreds of years of varied notational conventions and stylistic interpretations. Despite these difficulties, a number of highly advanced software programs are available for writing and arranging music as common practice notation. Using these, a wide variety of computing devices can become efficient tools for composing and arranging music, for the creation and display of scores used in performance, and for the generation of notational examples for music lessons.

Notes

1. *Sibelius*, music publishing software: www.sibelius.com/cgi-bin/home/home.pl.
2. *Finale*, music publishing software: www.finalemusic.com/.
3. *Musescore*, free and open source music publishing software: http://musescore.org/.
4. *Noteflight*, online music publishing environment: www.noteflight.com/.
5. *Reflow*, music publishing software: www.reflowapp.com/en.
6. *Finale Notepad*, free music publishing software: www.finalemusic.com/products/finale-notepad/.
7. *NotateMe*, handwriting-based notation entry: www.neuratron.com/notateme.html.
8. *ForScore*, music reader app for iPad: http://forscore.co/.

9. *Scorch*, software for viewing *Sibelius* score files over the Internet and on tablet computers: www.sibelius.com/products/scorch.
10. *SongBook* app for reading Finale files: www.finalemusic.com/products/finale-songbook/.
11. *Decibel ScorePlayer*, an iOS app for playing back animated graphical scores: https://itunes.apple.com/us/app/decibel-scoreplayer/id622591851?mt=8.
12. Animated Notation web site: http://animatednotation.blogspot.com.au/.
13. *LilyPond*, music publishing software: http://lilypond.org/.
14. *Belle, Bonne, Sage*. Music notation library in C++: http://bellebonnesage.sourccforge.net/.
15. *SharpEye*, music scanning software: www.visiv.co.uk/.
16. *Air Turn*, Bluetooth foot pedal for hands-free page turning: http://airturn.com/.

seven
Music and
Other Art Forms

There is a strong tradition of collaboration between music and other art forms. Creating music for visual or performing art contexts can be a popular music learning activity. It can be an authentic project echoing those undertaken by professional musicians, and often involving music technologies in its creation and delivery. Inter-arts collaboration results in forms such as opera, ballet, musical theatre, film, TV, music videos, and more.

Digital technologies can be useful in inter-arts projects because of their ability to synchronize with and map data between different media (e.g., sound and image). There are also many apps that support production processes in the creative arts. It has become commonplace for composers to produce entire music sound tracks on computer, and the ability of digital devices routinely to handle both image and video has made interdisciplinary work even more viable. This chapter will focus on some of the issues, techniques, and processes for using music technologies to create, synchronize, and deliver music and sound for productions involving collaborations with other art forms.

A common theme in creative arts productions is the linear narrative, broadly characterized as storytelling. The creator of a film, a dance, or even an art exhibition plans how to guide the viewer through the work. The role of music is to enhance that story, often adding an emotional layer. The overall impact of these productions relies heavily on sound design. This involves several tasks: dialogue recording and editing, sound effects, music selection, atmospheric sounds, audio mixing and, at times, computer programming. Music and sound design contribute to an experience of immersion for inter-arts works, filling the venue with sound that envelops the audience.

Many inter-arts projects are created by teams, and require interpersonal skills beyond those normally associated with a solitary artist. These ensemble skills can be, and often are, quite well developed in musicians through group music activities. It is increasingly evident that media artists, particularly in smaller projects, will be required to work across graphics, video, sound, and programming. For larger productions the specialized jobs of sound designers and musicians will continue to be necessary, but these opportunities might become increasingly rare.

When music has a collaborative role, accompanying a visual narrative, its responsibility is to carry the storyline or convey a mood. This is a different role from that of a purely musical work. This type of music has reduced density and complexity so as not to overwhelm the visual aspects of the work. As Earle Hagen writes in his book *Scoring for Films*, "The natural tendency for a composer starting out in film is to overwrite. Too much music, and not enough time to say it."[1] This is not just good advice for the student film composer but also hints at why music for visual narrative can be educationally effective; it might not involve a high degree of musical complexity nor the associated skills. This is not to say that inter-media collaboration is easy. However, minimal but appropriate compositions can produce effective results and are within the capacity of less experienced musicians.

Inter-arts projects often have an externally defined artistic vision. This can also be an educational positive because it is usually much easier to have some defined boundaries within which to work creatively. Having a written brief to focus students' creative attention on desired elements of the task can emphasize these constraints.

Music for film, dance, theatre, or any other collaborative project usually provides another constraint: time. Deadlines and the lack of time both influence the rhythm of production, and it is common that the creative process under these circumstances will "march to the beat of a different drum." Because these projects tend to come together only at the last minute, it is important for musicians to develop the skill of imagining the context within which their music will eventually operate. Tight time lines also emphasize the need for technical fluency in the use of music technologies to maximize the efficiency gains they provide.

In inter-arts projects there can be various media that help provide musical inspiration. Having visual materials in front of them as they work helps students to contextualize their compositions. Useful support materials include draft edits of films or scripts, rehearsal videos, storyboards, and so on. The digitization of these media allows the integration of such materials into the computer music workspace.

Technologies and Inter-arts Collaboration

The use of digital technologies in inter-arts work provides three major advantages:

- interoperability of media
- flexibility of editing
- conflation of the writing and recording process into one production process.

Digital systems allow tight synchronization between media. Videos can be aligned to music tracks; choreographic software sequences can be tied to music applications; and stage plans, scripts, and set designs can be stored together with other project files and made available with cue points and hyperlinks marked in them. All this can happen within the one virtual working environment that musicians can carry with them.

Creative processes are fluid at the best of times, and collaborative ones can be especially volatile. Flexibility in digital production processes and tools, therefore, is vital. Commitments made earlier in the process can be amended, edited, or undone in a nondestructive way. It is empowering to hold a production meeting around the computer and explore the implications of changes to the structure of a work as part of the decision-making process. Maximizing the advantages of such flexible working methods requires appropriate design choices by software developers and sensible practices by users; for example, regular work backup and the use of muting or hiding rather than deleting.

Digital tools have streamlined or conflated the processes of inter-arts projects. Media productions in the twentieth century resembled assembly-line processes where elements of a production passed from task to task. For example, film scoring started with a script and cue sheet, then a composer wrote a sketch score, an arranger orchestrated the score, a conductor and orchestra played the score, Foley artists created sound effects, actors provided dialogue, a recording engineer mixed the score, and effects and dialogue and post production houses integrated the score into the film. In the twenty-first century, many of these processes are done, in parallel, in an integrated digital context. While large studios may still have specialists, smaller filmmakers handle the whole process with one or two people.

This conflation of processes into music production systems has blurred boundaries between composer, arranger, performer, and sound engineer, and created a new class of audio, image, and video software. Accessible versions of tools like Apple's *GarageBand* and *iMovie*, which combine audio and video editing, are easily accessible to students. Figure 7.1 shows the integration of movie, dialog, music, and sound effects in *Garage-Band*. The integration of these processes means that students can be trans-disciplinary in their abilities and understandings. As a result, educational practices must also reflect this blurring of disciplinary boundaries and skills.

FIGURE 7.1 Applications such as Apple's *GarageBand* can be used to synchronize music and video.

There are general tendencies in inter-arts projects, as we have seen, but there are also particular features inherent in collaborations with different art forms. In the next few sections collaborations between music and number of other arts forms are explored in detail.

Film, TV, and Video

There is a century-long tradition of music for motion pictures. Live solo performances accompanying silent films in the early 1900s evolved into elaborate scores written for live orchestral performances. Movies with recorded sound—'talkies'—replaced live performance in the 1920s and '30s but not without some agitation from musicians at the time. The addition of the spoken word as a sound source changed the role of the score and of sound design quite significantly. The advent of television in the mid-1900s expanded the opportunities for musicians with the need for theme music, under-scores for TV dramas, and advertising jingles. At the start of the twenty-first century, streaming video on the Internet became widely available, and with the establishment of *YouTube* in the middle of the first decade, audiovisual media on the Internet became increasingly common. In this chapter the term *film* will be used as a shorthand for all time-based movie image forms, including TV, video, and animation.

Despite the changes in the technologies of production and distribution, there are processes and principles that are important in the use of music technologies for film composing—for example, structural organization and synchronization.

Structure

A major structural element in film is the use of character themes and variations on those themes. Once written, these themes become the basis for musical sections within the work that align with the plot. Themes reinforce character identity and the overall narrative. Once established they can be used to refer to characters that are alluded to in the script but are not present in the scene. Because thematic material can be copied, pasted and edited, it can easily be varied and repeatedly reused.

The constraints on the duration and placement of music and sound effects in a film (the macro structure) are determined by visual cues and the way the scenes are edited. The composer, sound designer, and director collaborate in deciding where the music and sound effects will go and what role they should have in each scene. This process is called spotting the film. The spotting process results in a list of cues—moments in the film where music should start and stop. Using this cue list, the composer is aware of the number and type of musical materials that need to be produced.

Many music production apps allow for markers or cue points to be added to the timeline. These provide a visual reference as the musician works on the score. Usually there will be editing functions to enable the moving, tempo mapping, or time stretching of material to match the cue points. Before the use of computers for music production, there were many tedious manual calculations necessary to ensure that the duration and timing of musical passages would correctly align with the pictures. Modern applications usually support zooming of the visual display so that the musician can set the level of detail to allow precise alignment of music cues and video frames.

Synchronization

When music, sound, and visual elements are created separately it is important to be able to synchronize their playback when assembled. Traditionally this involved the complicated interconnection of different machines, using click tracks, time code, and other connecting standards. Fortunately, the digital process has made synchronization much easier to the point where it is an almost transparent process in computer-based editing. However, careful placement of audio elements against the video track and even more careful setting of tempo to align beats and video cues are still required for an accurate result. There are differences between musical beat timeline subdivisions, video frame subdivisions, and clock time. Editing software usually allows the setting of timeline preferences to show the preferred time base.

Given that the timing of cues in film needs to be very accurate, musical decisions have to be made about how to shorten or lengthen a phrase to fit the allotted time. As a first rule of thumb, most composers advise changing the phrase structure by rewriting to add or remove notes. Then, if the musical style allows, they would modulate the phrase length with some rubato or a slight tempo change. If required, audio elements can be time stretched to fit. Working through these alternatives and hearing the difference between them can help students to understand better the subtle musical effects that tempo, melodic shape, and rubato have on the aesthetic qualities of music.

Theatre

There are many occasions in schools and colleges when plays and theatrical productions require music. These provide the opportunity to connect composition, performance, and sound design activities in the music program. This section will focus on how music for theatre productions can be enhanced using music technologies.

Sound Design

Even more than film, theatre productions have sonic requirements that are heavily focused on sound design and less on music production—except perhaps if it is a musical theatre production. Sound design includes the creation of Foley effects, including gun shots or automobile engine sounds; the assemblage of atmospheric soundscapes, such as thunderstorms or party chatter; and the selection of small musical clips for use as transitions between scenes. In these situations the focus is on the tasteful application of music and sound and the live performance of those sounds during the show.

These materials can be prepared using sound recording and editing software and techniques discussed in Chapter 3. The playback of the sounds is often triggered by a sound operator, who uses a sampler and control surface with percussive triggers. Touch screen tablet computers provide a compact and inexpensive solution, using sample triggering apps such as *Noisepad*,[2] as shown in Figure 7.2.

Another solution is to assemble the sound in a DAW with each sound spaced out on one track, and with markers set to the start of each sound cue. Jumping from cue to cue and playing or pausing can be done using the QWERTY keyboard.

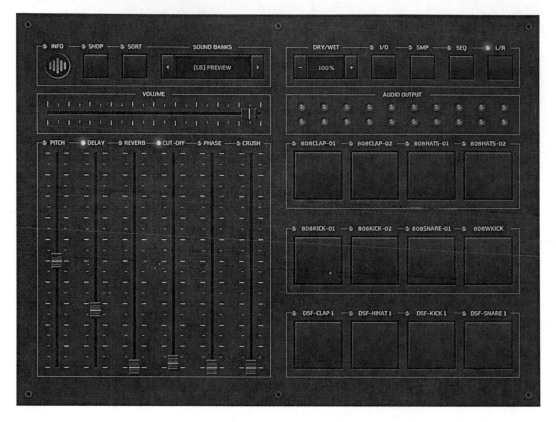

FIGURE 7.2 Sound effects can be triggered by an operator from a touch screen app.

Audio Spatialization

An important consideration in live theatre is the placement and movement of sounds in space, or audio spatialization. Good sound spatialization can greatly enhance a theatre production. It requires a multi-speaker array to be installed in the theatre and an appropriate multichannel mixing console, or software equivalent, to be available. The uses of audio spatialization are many and varied, including the positioning of Foley effects to match their physical (or offstage) location, the panning of ambient sounds such as weather or traffic noise around the audience, and the playback of music tracks in 5.1 or other surround formats.

The heart of a digital multi-track playback capability is a computer with a multi-channel sound card or interface. Each output can be sent to different speakers located around the theatre; most major audio applications will allow multichannel mixing of each track to position the track as required. The preparation and delivery of spatialized audio require careful listening to the real-world environment that is being imitated or the creative imagination of a virtual space, as required by the theatre production. Undertaking projects that involve sound spatialization can greatly enhance the aural awareness of students and affordable multichannel audio systems make this achievable in educational environments.

Atmospheric Music

Selecting or writing music for a theatre production provides many of the challenges that have been discussed in relation to film music, including contextual appropriateness to the topic of the play. Some works are period pieces that require research into the musical styles and conventions of that period or culture. Older plays, such as Shakespeare's, are often put into contemporary settings; then the focus is on identifying the emotional or narrative intent of the original and how that can translate into a contemporary context. This approach allows students to use music of their own time and to reevaluate its meaning in terms of how meaning can transcend time and place.

Like any other compositional task, the creation of atmospheric music can be achieved with the help of digital production software. It can be quite exciting to have students perform these ambient musical tracks live during the theatre production. An electronic music ensemble is appropriate here because of the sounds that can be produced and because control over volume can be important. Live performance of the music allows for subtle changes in timing and expression that respond to variations in actors' delivery from performance to performance. Many of the considerations for live theatre apply equally to music for dance productions.

Dance

Choreographed dance productions almost always have a strong musical element. Therefore, dance collaborations provide the musician with an inter-arts context where the music has quite a high profile and where artistic license can be quite liberal. Dance productions are often contemporary and experimental which makes them ideal for using electronic music and exploratory techniques. It is here that digital music technologies come into their own.

The history of music and dance goes back further than we know, with examples in indigenous cultures stretching back tens of thousands of years. Even in Western fine arts history, ballet has a long tradition. In the second half of the twentieth century, choreographers were quick to collaborate with the emerging electronic and experimental music scenes; for example, the notable partnership between composer John Cage and choreographer and dancer Merce Cunningham. Connections between rock music and dance are inherited from African American traditions and have produced genres such as jive, disco, punk, soul, and techno—each with its own distinctive dance style.

The music producer and dance choreographer can forge strong collaborations because both art forms have a degree of abstractness that provides flexibility. Contemporary dance projects can often enable the musician to escape tight cue points and even strict tempo or rhythmic constraints. However, as noted above, freedom from constraints can also make the production of appropriate music somewhat confronting. Often a number of draft ideas are required before a composer and choreographer agree on a suitable direction. Example music, selected by either party, can often serve as a way to explore possible directions quickly. However, avoiding the attachment to the draft or example, sometimes called 'demo love', can be tricky.

Once a creative direction is established, a digital music system can be a useful tool for trialing a variety of arrangements, given the ease with which sections can be moved about and tempo maps redrawn. Working with a flexible tool can speed up the collaborative process enormously compared with having to wait for redrafts and re-recordings when using less dynamic media.

Another connection between dance and music, and possibly the reason they are so strongly related historically, is that they are both about gesture. A key to connecting music and dance is to work at the level of gestural correspondence—not necessarily in a direct or imitative way but rather at the level of overall energy or intensity. When writing with a focus on gesture, it is worth exploring ways in which drawn curves can be used to make these connections. Curves are routinely used in music software for parameter control; for example, volume, dynamic range, pitch bend, amount of reverb or delay, spatial positioning, and so on. Simply using the mouse to draw curves with an appropriate gestural style and then mapping these to elements in the music is a way to use music technologies to connect gesture and sound. A more direct way is to track and map the dancer's movements during a performance.

Often, choreographed music is tightly scripted and so is usually best presented as a recording, given that there will be little variation between performances. However, in more loosely choreographed works, where there are elements of improvisation, it makes sense for the music to be performed live, in a semi-improvised sense. See, for example, the work *Dancing With Laptops,* which was a collaboration between the Concordia Laptop Orchestra (CLOrk) and the dance company Collab'Art de Stéph B in Canada in 2014.[3] The kinds of sample triggering and lopping methods described for theatre productions can also be employed for dance performances. A mixture of prepared recorded material, improvised electronics, and acoustic sounds can provide a rich palette of timbres and structures and, in educational contexts, interested students can form small ensembles to work on such projects. The combination of prepared material and semi-structured improvisation provides enough continuity for the choreography but still allows for a responsive performance that takes into account the physical context, the mood of the audience, and the variations in delivery that inevitably occur.

Many schools hold rock music dance contests, which usually feature well-known popular songs. These can be arranged or remixed by music students to suit choreographic requirements. Dance events can often tie in well with music technology performance practices such as DJing and live electronic dance music. These are discussed further in Chapter 10. A plethora of music technologies support these practices, from dedicated hardware such as the AKAI MPC series[4] to tablet computing apps including *djay*[5] and *Traktor DJ*.[6]

There are many instances in contemporary dance performances where dance gestures directly control musical events. Technologies that support this include MIDI dance suites, pressure pads, light sensors, video tracking, and other motion tracking technologies. Simple trackers can work quite effectively in an abstract or simple triggering situation, but where tight synchronization is required more sophisticated motion tracking systems are needed. Gesture capture can be used to trigger single sounds, to start or end musical processes, to control parameters of compositional processes or sound synthesis, and to act as cues for the music system. It is also quite common, as part of dance performances, for motion tracking systems to control visual effects and real-time computer graphic data projections. An impressive example of combining video tracking with interactive music and projection mapping is the work *Seventh Sense* created by a collaboration between Anarchy Dance Theatre and UltraCombos in 2011.[7]

Visual Arts

While visual art exhibitions have traditionally been silent affairs, the increase in electronic and digital art works has been accompanied by an increase in audio as part of works and exhibitions. Audiovisual art works might have visuals and sound created by the one artist, particularly in digital arts that reflect the convergence of art forms and digital space. An example of a solo audiovisual artists is Ryoji Ikeda. His *Test Pattern* series includes generative computer-based works where large data projected images and multi-speaker sounds fill the gallery space, as shown in Figure 7.3, creating an immersive and quite physical experience.

Audiovisual works may involve collaboration between visual and sound artists. Many collaborative projects have been inspired by Modest Mussorgsky's *Pictures at an Exhibition*, where musicians compose music inspired by visual art works. The exhibition of collaborative audiovisual works can follow several conventions. Each visual artwork can be hung in the gallery with its own sound system, using either loudspeakers or headphones. The image in Figure 7.4 is from the *Affecting Interference* exhibition by Daniel Mafe and Andrew R. Brown where speakers are hung over paintings, becoming

FIGURE 7.3 Participants experiencing Ryoji Ikeda's *Test Pattern [No.5]*.

FIGURE 7.4 Paintings with integrated sound from Mafe and Brown's *Affecting Interference.*

part of the art work. The sound for each painting is played from its own portable MP3 device and the soundscape composed so that all sound tracks blend together in the gallery with the mix varying as the viewer moves about the space.

An exhibition can include multiple visual art works with a single sound system filling the gallery space or several works, each with its own music and sound system. The sound system for a gallery might use mobile devices loaded with location-specific music tracks played through headphones. In the latter case, tracks can be triggered by the user or via place-based tags or location tracking.

Working through the aesthetic and practical considerations for presenting music in galleries can be a useful exercise for music students who would rarely otherwise be challenged to question the concert-stage or recording-headphone modes of music consumption.

Sonification of Digital Images

Music and visual art can be combined by creating sound directly from images. Sonic rendering, or sonification, of visual images can be automated using computing technologies. Data from a digital image can be mapped as audio data. For example, pixel location might represent pitch and time as in the work *Sounds of the Americans* by Andrew Emond.[8]

More complex mappings are also possible, such as a type of steganography that uses a digital image as a spectrograph, which is transferred to sound using an inverse Fourier transform. This means that the image is scanned from left to right over time and each column of pixels, when scanned, determines the frequency spectra, thus the timbre. Techno musician Aphex Twin (Richard James) used this technique in a section of his track *Windowlicker*.[9] The *MetaSynth*[10] software uses a similar approach to 'paint' sound with a palette of colors that map to particular timbres. The *VOSIS*[11] app for iPad provides interactive image signification using a process of scanning synthesis to generate continuous sound. This app is very playable and could be used for sonification performances. The *SonicPhoto*[12] app for Windows makes a similar conversion but with a less interactive interface.

A similar process of 'drawing' note-based music can be achieved using the piano roll view in a DAW. Images like those in Figure 7.5 are easy and fun to create and listen to, even if their sound might be unconventional. To explore further the turning of images into music via MIDI files, try the *RBG MusicLab* software.[13]

As a reversing of the sonification process, images can also be created from sound. This process of audio visualization can be used for scientific or artistic purposes. In the artistic space, this practice is often referred to as *visual music* and can include generative graphics, like the iTunes *Visualizer*, that respond to beats and frequencies in music. A more interactive example is Yamaha's *Visual Performer* for the iPad.[14] Further details about scientific uses of audio visualization are discussed in Chapter 8.

Relationships Between Music and Visuals

Starting with a visual artwork as inspiration, musicians will often try to reflect the mood or ambience of the work, and the challenge can be to understand the structure and range of interpretations that the work presents. Different ideas inspired by the work can become the stimulus for musical sections or layers within the musical texture.

Unlike any of the previous art forms discussed, visual art works are often fixed in time, not temporal like the performing arts. This raises questions about the music that

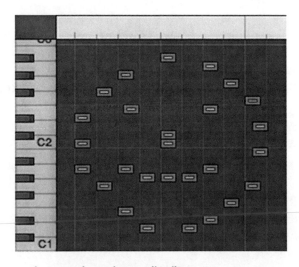

FIGURE 7.5 Drawing music notes in a piano roll editor.

is to accompany an image or a sculpture. How long should the music be? What tempo? Should it be looped? Should it play all the time or be triggered by the exhibition visitor?

In one sense, the reading of a fixed visual art work is always temporal as the eye scans it, so hints about how to approach timing in the musical work can come from the musician's own experience of viewing the work—a kind of human sonification. Parallels between music and visuals may be drawn between levels of activity and intensity in the colors and shapes of the artwork that can translate to musical activity and pace. The lack of an obvious temporal frame may be liberating for musicians, who can then please themselves about what music will complement the visual work.

Conclusion

There are contexts in which music supports a visual experience for the audience, including film, theatre, dance, and the visual arts. Digital music production and sound design methods can be applied to inter-arts projects either for solo artists or for collaborations. Digital tools are particularly useful because of the interoperability of data between digital media: images, text, gesture tracking, and sound. Working with computing devices in these contexts makes apparent the abstractness of the digital representations. Given that the computer can represent not only music and sound but also text, image, and moving picture, the structural relations between these modes of expression are highlighted and the possibilities for future creative expression are stimulated.

Producing music and sound for use with other art forms requires reflection on the uniqueness of aural senses and how they interact with other modes of experience. This reflection, in turn, strengthens a musician's music-only practices through better understanding of the expressive power of music and sound. In creating music for projects where storytelling is clearly articulated, as it is in film and theatre in particular, musicians come to understand that music can have a narrative too. From an educational perspective, the fact that students find inter-art projects engaging makes them doubly valuable.

Reflection Questions

1. What art forms provide a narrative visual experience for which music could be produced?
2. What kinds of tasks does a sound designer perform in a film or theatre production?
3. How does the role of music in cross art collaborations differ from its role in concert hall presentations?
4. What was Earle Hagen's advice to student film composers quoted in this chapter?
5. How might the constraints imposed by collaboration be constructive for the creative process?
6. Why is the flexibility of digital production tools useful for collaborative projects?
7. In film scoring, what is the process of spotting?
8. Merce Cunningham was famous in which creative arts discipline?
9. What is sonification?
10. What are some of the ways in which music can be presented in visual arts exhibitions?

Teaching Tips

1. Use movie trailers as short film scoring exercises for students.
2. Have students use a piano roll editor to draw a picture in notes or write their names, then play it back to hear how it sounds.
3. Use students' own artworks, or those of their peers, as inspiration for compositional activities.
4. Collaborate with creative arts classes that are scheduled at the same time as your music classes.
5. Encourage small ensembles to select and rehearse pieces for performance with silent films as a backdrop.
6. Using sound editing software, have students create sound effects for a theatre production.
7. Locate videos of contemporary dance productions and lead students in an analysis of how music and dance are integrated.
8. Use signification software to explore the sonic possibilities of images.
9. Create a 'pictures at an exhibition' web page with contributions from each member of a class.
10. Utilize students' mobile devices as media recorders and editors.

Suggested Tasks for Educators

1. Watch the film *Blade Runner* by Ridley Scott to be inspired by Vangelis's effective use of electronic music technologies.
2. Download a movie trailer, import it into a music software package, and record a simple sequence.
3. Sequence a short melody, then use software tools to create versions that are exactly one second shorter and one second longer than the original.
4. Create a sound collage, as if for a theatre production, that sounds like an open-plan office.
5. Locate an app for your computing device that can load and trigger music clips and sound effects.

Chapter Summary

Musical outcomes need not only be for the concert hall or recorded media. There are many opportunities to create music for visual experiences such as film and video, theatre, dance, or the visual arts. When combined with other art forms, the narrative and emotive nature of music is emphasized and simple musical expressions are often adequate counterparts to visual stimuli. These attributes make the integration of music with other art forms a productive educational experience. When producing music for visual narratives, considerations include working within the constraints imposed by the collaboration; coordinating and synchronizing music with other media and events; understanding that musical intelligence is required for tasks such as music selection and sound design; meeting the challenges of presentation in different performance or exhibition environments; appreciating the similarity of structures across art forms and media; and understanding how media come together in digital form. Computational tools that integrate multiple media in one digital platform can support musical collaborations with other art forms. These provide a flexible production environment for media creation and presentation.

Notes

1. Hagen, E. (1971). *Scoring for films: A complete text.* Miami, FL: E D J Music, p. 74.
2. *Noisepad*, sample player for iPad: www.noise-pad.com/.
3. *Dancing With Laptops.* Concordia Laptop Orchestra (CLOrk) and Collab'Art de Stéph B. http://youtu.be/lOIzk6Rr14k.
4. AKAI MPC (music production controller) instruments: www.akaipro.com/category/mpc-series.
5. *djay*, iOS and Mac DJ software from algoriddim: www.algoriddim.com/djay-ipad.
6. *Traktor DJ*, iOS DJ software from Native Instruments: www.native-instruments.com/en/products/traktor/traktor-for-ios/traktor-dj/.
7. A video excerpt of *Seventh Sense* by Anarchy Dance Theatre and UltraCombos: http://youtu.be/iQlDEPLHPyQ.
8. *Sounds of the Americans*, videos of this audio sonification work are online: www.soundsoftheamericans.com/index.html.
9. Aphex Twin (Richard James). *Windowlicker.* Sire Records, 1999.
10. *MetaSynth*, OS X software for sonification and sound painting: www.uisoftware.com/MetaSynth/.
11. *VOSIS*, interactive sonification app for the iPad and OS X: www.imagesonification.com/. There is a published paper on its operations: McGee, R. (2013). VOSIS: A multi-touch image sonification interface. In *Proceedings of the New Interfaces for Musical Expression Conference.* Duejeon, Korea: Korea Advanced Institute of Science and Technology. Retrieved from www.lifeorange.com/writing/McGee_NIME_2013.pdf.
12. *SonicPhoto*, a Windows application that converts images to sounds: www.skytopia.com/software/sonicphoto/.
13. *RGB MusicLab*, software for Windows and Mac that maps image pixels to music that can be saved as a MIDI file: www.kenjikojima.com/rgbmusiclab/.
14. *Visual Performer*, an interactive music and visual effects app for iPad from Yamaha: http://usa.yamaha.com/products/apps/visual_performer/.

section III
Presentation

eight
Presentation Platforms

The documentation and communication of knowledge are core elements of education. The ways of expressing knowledge, especially in the arts, can take many forms; in more formal terms, expression is multimodal. The presentation of information as part of music education needs to take account of these multiple channels of communication wherever possible. Both teachers and students are engaged in presenting information and demonstrating knowledge and understanding. This chapter will explore methods of presentation using digital technologies and discuss how they can be applied to learning and teaching music.

As discussed in Chapter 1, digital technologies can be a medium for storage and transmission of text, image, sound, and music. Digital media allow the integration of these media forms and, in many cases, for interaction, navigation, and dynamic variation. Digital convergence is the term given to the conflation of a variety of media, including still images, moving pictures, sound, and text into numerical representation—that is, digital data. In digital form these media become interoperable and practices previously considered hybrid or multi are integrated. Emerging from this trend is the capability of incorporating many media types into one document or format as depicted in Figure 8.1. Forms that integrate media include PDF documents, web sites, and mobile apps.

Communication and Education

Rich media presentations include a variety of media types and, as a result, they serve a number of educative purposes. They assist in information sharing. They are used as 'media to think with' and can help make sense of information and experiences. They provide a vehicle for capturing and expressing knowledge and understanding. They become artifacts of creative expression.

The choice of presentation medium has important pedagogical implications because it privileges content that is easily presentable in the elected medium. This might, in turn,

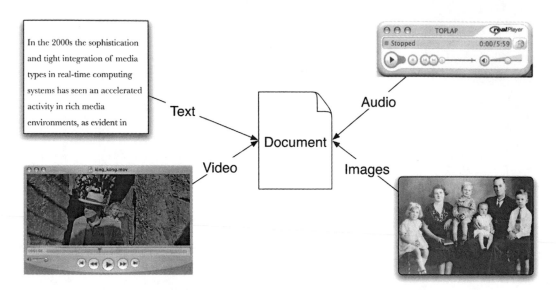

In the 2000s the sophistication and tight integration of media types in real-time computing systems has seen an accelerated activity in rich media environments, as evident in

Text

Audio

Document

Video

Images

FIGURE 8.1 Rich media documents incorporate multiple types of media on one page.

lead to a distortion of perceptual priorities. The medium of paper privileges static content and best suits persistent data like historical information and musical scores. The strength of digital media is in their dynamic and interactive nature. This flexibility of digital media has an impact on the exploratory tendencies of the thinking that is done while using them. Digital data can also represent a variety of traditionally separate media—including text, image, animation, photography, film, and sound.

Building on the work of psychologist Jean Piaget and anthropologist Claude Lévi-Strauss, the computer scientist and educator Seymour Papert emphasized that children are concrete thinkers, and that therefore the relationship between knowledge and its medium of presentation is critical to understanding. He was a strong proponent of constructivist pedagogy where students developed understanding through exploration and experience. "[T]raditional epistemology," he wrote, "… is closely linked to the medium of text—written and especially printed. Bricolage and concrete thinking always existed but were marginalized in scholarly contexts by the privileged position of text."[1] Any writing about music is, in Papert's terms, a "proposition" about music; an abstraction. Because digital media representations of musical information can include audiovisual material and interaction, they rely less heavily on the abstractness of text or graphical representations. Also, the malleability and interoperability of digital data afford exploration and integration that are not possible with analog media.

To utilize digital media effectively, music students need to acquire skills and abilities that include the development of techniques in sound design and music visualization; an awareness of the structural connections between sound, image, and textual expressions; and intuitions about the importance of the experiential nature of interaction design. Students' musical skills combine with those they have acquired from media studies, computing, visual arts, graphic design, filmmaking, and communication design. Far from being overwhelming, this list of competencies gives the musician license to draw on a wide range of knowledge, skills, and activities when creating rich media presentations.

As the use of interactive media for capturing and evaluating student work continues to expand, rich media presentations have an important role to play in assessment. Students should be encouraged to demonstrate their understanding through rich media assignments and the documentation of their musical practices. For example, it is common to moderate performance examinations using videos of school-based performances, and students can present assignments as web pages rather than as printed pages—creating opportunities for integrated sound and video examples. Audio and video documentaries and in-class presentations can include material in verbal, visual, textual, and performance formats, enabling students to express themselves more fully.

The expectation to create rich media place similar demands on staff and students' skill development in media authorship and critical evaluation of media forms, and on providing adequate infrastructure for production and use. Questions for educators implementing such curricula include:

- Do students and teachers working in media formats have flexible and sufficient computational resources to create and assess such work?
- Are timelines varied to reflect changes in development and production from text or performance equivalents?
- Are the curriculum objectives able to be met by, or redefined to account for, such changes in media?
- How best are the artificial barriers between instrumental and classroom music education dissolved to enable a focus on integrated music education that embraces music production outcomes?

It is commonly understood that the best way to learn something is to teach it, and so students should be encouraged to use digital media for organizing and communicating their understanding. In fact, the use of digital media by students can be more educationally efficient than its use by teachers. However, for teachers, rich media documents are effective for organizing their own thinking about curriculum design.

Digital Documents for Curricula

An obvious implication of the widespread availability of rich media formats is that the music curriculum itself, which is traditionally a text document, needs to be developed as a rich media form. Writer Steve Dillon was quick to recognize this. He noted, in discussing music education and multiple logics, that "Print and its linear processes no longer dominate thought and communication and we now combine the word with images and sound in multi media communication which represents actual or imaginary experiences."[2]

Chapter 1 emphasized how changing technologies directly influence students' understanding; the same is true for educators. Musicians know that different media and their associated properties, conventions, and metaphors determine what can be expressed with them, and so the curriculum document needs to expand its communicative power by becoming a rich media document. Communicating artistic curriculum intent through text alone involves unnecessary abstraction and disembodiment, as William Barrett noted in the late 1970s:

> Statements may be the instruments of enlightenment, but not the only ones. As soon as we are freed from the notion of the single proposition as the ultimate locus of truth, which [sic] each proposition carrying its truth on its back like a rider on a saddle, we are also freed toward understanding other modes through which truth may be realized. In particular, we might begin at last to ask seriously in what way truth may be embodied in works of art.[3]

Evidence of a rich media expression of music curricula is seen where video and audio exemplar materials are prepared as support for music syllabuses. The future of rich media expressions of music curricula might be difficult to predict; for example, when will a national curriculum be delivered as an app for mobile devices complete with interactive audiovisual exemplars? We can be confident, though, that when it arrives, its expression in rich media is more likely to be sympathetic with communicating musical intent than a text document could ever be.

Graphical Representations

Music has long been represented graphically, most obviously as common practice notation—as discussed in detail in Chapter 6. Graphical scores provide an abstract visual representation of music and may be in the form of static diagrams or animations. Some computer music systems provide graphical interfaces for creating, rather than simply depicting, music. A historically important example is the collection of curves and arcs that describe sound parameter trajectories in the *UPIC* computer music system, designed by Iannis Xenakis.[4]

Visual notations of music can be saved in digital form as graphic files, videos, or programmed animations. Most music publishing software systems enable scores—whole or in parts—to be saved as image files. In cases where the program does not support output of a graphic file for inclusion in presentations, then a screenshot can usually be taken and edited as required. Graphic scores can be created using a range of painting and drawing software tools, or can be drawn on paper or other analog media and photographed for inclusion in digital media presentations.

Structural representations can be as visually interesting as they are informational. The field of data visualization has a number of examples of music as a stimulus for artistic visualizations; one that is both structurally informative and quite beautiful is Martin Wattenberg's *The Shape of Song* process.[5] A simple example based on Wattenberg's technique is shown in Figure 8.2. The potential for cross-curriculum projects between music, visual arts, and computer science around music visualizations is rich indeed.

FIGURE 8.2 The structure of repetitions in this music is visually highlighted by the arcs.

Audio Visualizations

Most audio editing software packages, including the freely available *Audacity*[6] software, can display audio in a variety of ways. Sound is usually depicted on screen as a waveform that reveals its change in loudness over time. A sound's waveform might also be shown as a more transitory oscilloscope view. Another popular visualization is the timbral perspective, where the presence of various frequency components is displayed—either instantaneously as a spectrum analyzer or over time as a spectrogram. These graphs can be either two- or three-dimensional.

Oscilloscope

An oscilloscope is a device for visualizing differences in electrical potential. It is primarily used by electrical engineers to test equipment, but electronic musicians also use oscilloscopes to display the waveform generated by their sounds. An oscilloscope displays the signal over a small time frame, redrawing the wave across the screen at a fast rate, as shown in Figure 8.3. Digital oscilloscopes display the audio signal being captured (or generated) in real time, through an iterative process of buffering and displaying a short sample of the wave.

Oscilloscopes and other real-time displays are excellent tools for helping students understand the relationship between sounds and their visual appearance. They can see that noisy timbres have a more jagged shape, that louder sounds are larger on the vertical axis, and that higher pitched sounds have more tightly packed (shorter) cycle lengths. Because these features are immediately visible, a student can experiment with different sounds in front of an oscilloscope and quickly get a feel for the relationship between heard and seen representations of sound, and a clearer insight into sonic elements. Images from, or video of, oscilloscope displays can be captured for inclusion in rich media presentations.

Waveform Display

Like an oscilloscope, a waveform display shows the sound signal as an amplitude-time graph, like that shown in Figure 8.4. However, the waveform shows the sound's history,

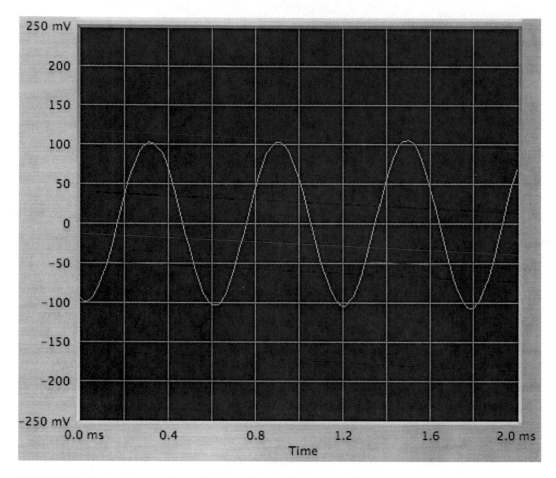

FIGURE 8.3 A simple waveform displayed in a software oscilloscope.

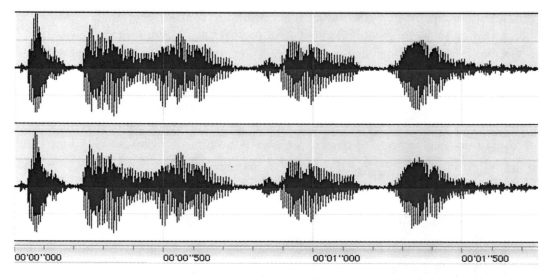

FIGURE 8.4 A stereo waveform; left and right channels have their own tracks.

rather than a glimpse of its current state, as depicted by an oscilloscope. The waveform view is particularly useful for displaying a recorded sound. Because it is a static display, it can be understood as a very detailed 'score' of the audio. The waveform display has the same advantages as a notated score, being useful for reflection, analysis, editing, and arranging, and is therefore the most common visualization of music in digital music systems.

The digital waveform display is a graph that looks like a continuous line but is, in fact, a line that connects the dots between individual samples. Because the time between samples (dots) is very small, this granularity can only be seen when the display is magnified to show this detail.

Spectrum Analyzer

The spectrum analyzer shows the instantaneous frequency distribution of a sound. Unlike the oscilloscope and waveform displays, which work in the time domain, graphing amplitude over time, the spectrum analyzer operates in the frequency domain, graphing amplitude over frequency. Figure 8.5 shows a spectrum analyzer and its amplitude (decibel) and frequency axes. Spectrum analyzers operate in real time, so the points on the display bounce around as the sound input varies.

The frequency spectrum has similarities to pitch distribution on the piano keyboard—a range from low to high pitches or frequencies from left to right. Just as the piano divides the pitch range into 88 *pitches*, a spectrum analyzer divides the frequency spectrum into a number of *bands*, typically between about 10 and 30.

The vertical axis indicates the loudness or intensity of each frequency band. Because audio recordings capture sound in the time domain, the signal must be processed to obtain data about the frequency spectra. This process involves a fast Fourier transform (FFT), which breaks the sound down into its constituent harmonics. The spectrum analyzer operates by repeatedly capturing a small segment of recorded sound (a window or buffer), performing an FFT on that data, and displaying the results. This occurs so quickly as to appear instantaneous—this is why it is referred to as a real-time process.

Spectrum analyzers operate in real time and the height of each frequency band dances around as the sound signal varies. Like oscilloscopes, spectrum analyzers are

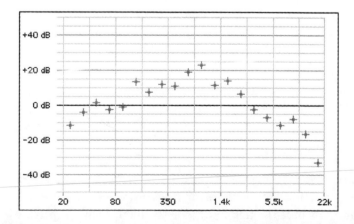

FIGURE 8.5 A 20-band spectrum analyzer; each cross represents one frequency band.

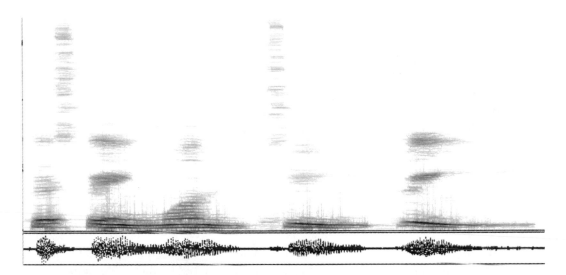

FIGURE 8.6 A spectrogram with the corresponding waveform view below.

useful for immediate feedback of timbral features, and have a similar educational value in developing aural perception of timbre through experimentation. They are useful for checking the frequency (timbral) balance within a recording and are used in live sound reinforcement as a way of determining the frequency of microphone feedback.

Spectrogram

A spectrogram, also called a sonogram, shows the frequency spectrum over the duration of a sound; see Figure 8.6. The spectrogram is to a spectrum analyzer what the waveform is to an oscilloscope; it uses the same process but shows the accumulated results over time. Spectrograms can operate on an audio file or from real-time input. The spectrogram reveals the changes in frequency distribution of audio input over time. For example, a spectrogram will clearly show a crash cymbal starting with a wide frequency range that then narrows over time.

The spectrogram in Figure 8.6 differs from the spectrum analyzer in Figure 8.5 in that the vertical axis is the frequency—lowest at the bottom, highest at the top. The horizontal axis is time; each horizontal line in the spectrogram corresponds to a frequency band and the line's intensity indicates its amplitude. Spectral analysis of recorded music is often used as an analytical technique in the same way that a textural analysis of a notated instrumental arrangement is—that is, to reveal the timbral variety or density and to reveal structure over time.

Presentation Platforms

The representation of information affects its interpretation and meaning; therefore the careful presentation of information is a mainstay of education. Modes of educational presentation include the telling of stories, the drawing of pictures and diagrams, the writing of texts, the production of videos and software, and the demonstration of practice. The presence and potency of the performer, or presenter, in this communication cannot be underestimated. In this section, however, we will pay particular attention to various digital media presentation platforms and their roles in communicating musical knowledge.

Multimedia Documents

Many digital document formats allow for embedded media. These include word processors, note-taking programs, PDF editors, and so on. These simple tools can provide a quick method of preparing a rich media document but usually provide limited means of interaction and embedded audio or video.

Word Processor

The humble (or not so humble) word processor usually displays much more than text. It can include images, sections of notated scores, scanned drawings and diagrams, and inserted audio or video annotations. Word processed documents can be distributed electronically to students and projected from the computer for in-class presentation. It is important to make sure that word processor file formats are readable across all the devices that students will use. There is a growing number of cloud-based word processors such as *Google Docs*, Apple's *Pages*, and Microsoft's *Office Online*, and these can be useful for collaborative document development and make distribution straightforward wherever there is reliable Internet access. While word processors might not enable highly sophisticated direct presentations, in terms of visual appeal they are certainly functional and widely available.

PDF

Adobe's Portable Document Format (PDF) is a format that is widely used and provides vector-based graphical descriptions of text and images that be compressed into a small file size. PDFs can be rescaled for printing or presentation making them useful for distributing musical scores and text documents. PDF documents can be read with freely available viewer programs and, with advanced editors, can contain media elements and hypertext links.

Digital Slide Show

Dedicated software applications such as Microsoft's *PowerPoint*, Apple's *Keynote*, or *Prezi*[7] are purpose built for integrating different media into slide show presentations. Information is organized as a series of pages, or slides, each of which can contain any digitized media. When projecting presentations it is important to ensure that text and image sizes are large enough to be seen clearly from the back of a room, that appropriate stereo amplification is available to play back embedded audio and video, and that presentations contain material that augments rather than duplicates what is spoken or offered in a printed handout. A slideshow application is as simple to use as a word processor but is better suited to information that does not rely heavily on text. It delivers a more polished on-screen presentation than print-oriented documents. Because it includes (ideally) all media within the file format, it is a reliable option when Internet access cannot be assured.

A slideshow can also be created using a clip book or magazine app to collect links to online materials and display them in a sequence. The *Flipboard*[8] app, for example, is a virtual magazine that curates content from the Internet on a given topic. It allows users to create their own magazine and to add web content to it, while browsing it on the app or via the *Flip It* extension for desktop web browsers. Articles, videos, and other online materials are curated into the custom magazine, which can be shared with other *Flipboard* users (e.g., students or peers). The app displays and sequences the materials as the user flips through the pages.

Web Pages and Blogs

The most pervasive rich media environment is the World Wide Web, the dominant Internet transfer protocol. It started as a text-oriented platform but now makes extensive use of rich media elements. Web pages are widely accessible and read in web browsers, like *Internet Explorer*, *Firefox*, *Chrome*, and *Safari*, which come as standard issue on Internet-capable digital devices. Web pages are constructed using the HyperText Markup Language (HTML) and other technologies including Cascading Style Sheets (CSS) and JavaScript. However, there are many tools for creating web sites without having to interact directly with these languages, and they are also as easy to use as a word processor. Alternatively, many document editors allow exporting to a web format. Web site creation tools are integrated into web hosting and blogging services, such as *WordPress*,[9] *Tumblr*,[10] *Google Sites*,[11] *Wix*,[12] and *Blogger*.[13] These provide fairly straightforward creation and administration interfaces, as shown in Figure 8.7, and are accessible through any modern web browser.

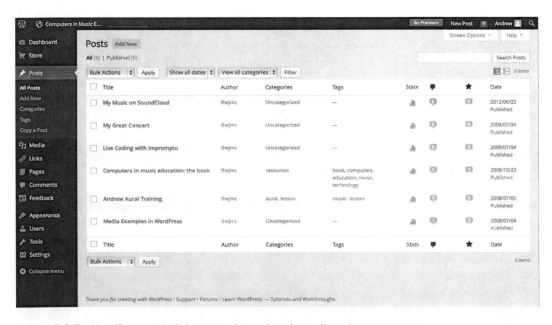

FIGURE 8 7 *WordPress* administrator view, showing a list of recent posts.

Podcasts and Videos

Audio and video material can be stored as files for downloading to a portable player or device, such as Apple's iPod—hence the term *podcasting*. Podcasts can involve subscription services, automatic downloads, and even manual downloading of material. There are many potential uses. For example, radio programs often provide shows as podcasts on their web sites, and museums might offer exhibition audio guides that can be downloaded prior to a visit. Apple's iTunes and other aggregators have catalogs of podcasts; iTunes includes a special section for educational materials called *iTunes U* (university). Podcasts, or audio tutorials more generically, offer a viable option for lesson materials or archives of classes or lectures. Students can download the files and listen at any convenient time. Audio files can easily be uploaded to services such as *SoundCloud*[14] for public distribution. For students, podcast production is a useful vehicle for developing audio recording and editing skills, a good option for an assessment item and a way of sharing information among peers.

Video authoring has become mainstream, with *YouTube* being the dominant hosting and distribution platform for video materials. Videos on services such as *YouTube* or *Vimeo* can be embedded into other rich media documents, especially web pages. Videos published on these host platforms can be public or private, so educators and students need to be careful of copyright and privacy considerations. Creating and editing video material are inherently more time- and computer-intensive tasks than producing audio alone, but provide a rich experience suited to the documentation of musical performance. Videos can be embedded within presentations and accessed at school or at home. Tools like *MASHER*[15] or *Animoto*,[16] which automate the video creation process and provide libraries of stock footage, can assist productivity in some cases. Most digital devices include video cameras, and so there is unlimited opportunity for capturing footage. Video production is particularly suited to musical demonstrations and documentary assignments.

Lecture-Recitals

This chapter focuses on digital media documents but it is important to remember that digital media resources can also be used to augment in-person presentations. In music education, the integration of performance exemplars into the educational process is especially valuable. The combination of live performance and presentation with rich media examples can be useful in diverse situations, from an instrumental lesson to a university graduate seminar. Slide presentations, prepared video examples, charts, and diagrams support verbal delivery and musical performance to produce an enhanced music presentation. This format takes advantage of face-to-face interaction and presence, and combines it with digital media materials that can be prepared in advance.

Via Internet communications, these presentations can be transmitted over video conferencing systems and might include participants at multiple sites. The uniqueness of the lecture-recital format is its quality of being live and responsive to interaction with the audience.

Interaction and Automation

The presentation formats considered in the previous section can be located along a spectrum of interactivity, from static documents for reading, through navigable materials typical of web sites, to in-person dialog and conversation. Interactive media systems allow the user to move about the content or become active in exploring it. Interactivity moves control away from the system or author and toward the user. In music, this is similar to moving control of the orchestra away from the conductor and to the audience.

The challenge of interactivity in nonlinear structures, like most web sites, is that the order in which the information is accessed might not be predictable. However, nonlinearity can provide opportunities as well. Users can visit sections of a multimedia document in the order that interests them and repeatedly revisit some pages, as necessary.

Interactive connections (i.e., links) between information in a rich media document reveal relationships between ideas and activities. For instructional purposes this format makes those relationships explicit to the learner. When students build interactive documents, the way in which they link content within them will reveal their understanding of the network of relationships. Students can demonstrate their understanding of connections relating to a topic or activity by creating multiple pages and linking between them and to relevant external sites. This kind of activity is a rich media extension of footnoting or referencing in text publications and reinforces similar educative values.

The construction and revealing of knowledge through media interactions and presentations underpinned the educational use of microworlds in the latter decades of the twentieth century. Microworlds were digital environments that enabled users to play with materials in a scaffolded and delimited space. Activities could be automated (programmed) in microworlds as a way of articulating ideas and simulating them for reflection; this allowed students to explore ideas and activities in an accessible way, with some useful building blocks to get them started and in a context protected from the full complexity of the world. In music, it began with the musical microworlds of Jeanne Bamberger, such as the *TuneBlocks* compositional world,[17] and lives on in general purpose systems, like the *Scratch*[18] environment shown in Figure 8.8, that include sound and other media properties.

The enthusiastic embrace of virtual worlds for learning peaked in the late 1990s with sites like *Second Life*[19] based on 3-D worlds featuring avatars that inhabited shared virtual rooms and spaces. The computational space was the virtual world and real voice communications (Voice-over-Internet Protocol, or VOIP) between people was the preferred mode of communication. This trend dissipated in the early years of the twenty-first century as mobile devices flipped the model on its head. The site for exploration shifted to the real world and messaging with mobile devices became the means of communication with others. Presentational media, especially video, came to dominate virtual 3-D environments and asynchronous interactivity with others around these media became the dominant form of communication. Examples of these new educational arrangements include *Kahn Academy*[20] and various massive open online courses (MOOCs), about which there will be more discussion in Chapter 13.

Interactive media presentation is considered by some to be a form of creative practice—particularly where it includes live performance with technologies, interactive installations, or mobile apps.

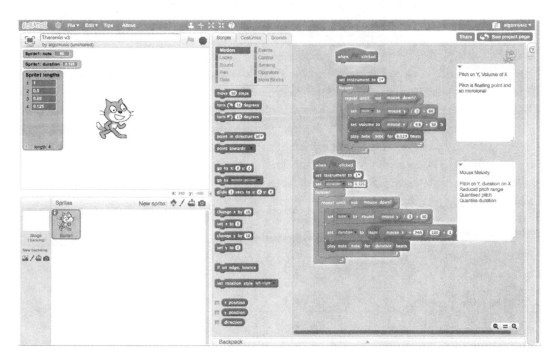

FIGURE 8.8 An example student-built interactive application built in the *Scratch* environment.

App Building

More and more information is being accessed via apps for mobile devices. They allow students to access information whenever and wherever they wish and, unlike web sites and blogs, in many cases do not necessarily need Internet access to view content. There are many tools to help teachers and students create their own apps, but even so, making an app is certainly more complex than putting together a slide show.

Apple's *iBooks Author* can be used to create an eBook—not actually an app—for iOS and Mac OS devices. The tool runs on a Mac and operates like a desktop publishing program, where text, image, video, and other elements are arranged into pages. eBooks can be submitted to the iBooks store and made available free or for purchase. For a great example of how this can be applied to music education see the video by music education lecturer James Humberstone from the Sydney Conservatorium of Music.[21]

Another pseudo app maker is *Nearpod*.[22] It is an interactive mobile presentation platform. Content is created on a computer and made available to students via the Nearpod app for iOS and Android platforms. Students can interact with the content and provide feedback via the app. Content is available free or for purchase via the Nearpod online store.

Real apps can be built using a variety of app development toolkits. Three accessible examples are the *MIT App Inventor*,[23] *Windows App Studio*,[24] and *PhoneGap*.[25] These environments require some programming but scaffold the process effectively. Other more commercial solutions for supported app development continue to become available, and include *iBuildApp*[26] and *iGenapps*.[27]

Conclusion

There are many ways to use digital media in educational presentations, to incorporate music and sound in an integrated, and in some cases interactive, way with other media. Both students and teachers can benefit from working with rich media documents. Teachers can effectively express ideas to students through rich media communications and also reshape their pedagogy to encourage the use of rich media documents. Students can both consume and create rich media presentations. They can use digital media environments to express themselves using sound, diagrams, video, text, and animations in ways that suit their abilities and help develop their communication skills. The digital convergence of previously separate mediums onto a computational platform provides the opportunity to make explicit connections between different knowledge representations; this can assist both the development and the expression of musical interpretation and understanding.

Reflection Questions

1. Why does the medium of presentation matter educationally?
2. What is meant by the term *rich media document*?
3. In the quote by Seymour Papert, what is meant by the term *bricolage*?
4. Why might rich media documents be useful for music education?
5. In what ways are oscilloscope and waveform displays similar?
6. Name some of the digital media presentation platforms discussed in the chapter.
7. What are the distribution channels for podcasts and videos mentioned in the chapter?
8. How might rich media documents be useful for assessment?
9. What does interaction add to the learning potential of a presentation format?
10. Name some of the development tools available to create mobile apps for education.

Teaching Tips

1. Transfer printed handouts to a web site to make them more widely available to students.
2. Provide access to a digital camera and digital video camera for students to document their music activities.
3. Use a whiteboard to map out the connections between all media that have been collected on a project before making a rich media environment from the material.
4. Have students create a digital media profile of their own music making, complete with examples of their music and photos of them producing music.
5. There can be technical hurdles in using digital media presentation software, so make sure students have a few practice tasks before they complete one for assessment.
6. Require that in-class student presentations include audio, image, and video elements.
7. Have students bring all manner of noisy objects from home for a session with real-time visualization tools including an oscilloscope and spectrum analyzer.

8. Work with music teaching colleagues to identify activities in which they can make greater use of digital media teaching resources.
9. Teaching is a good way of learning, so have students design a web site that is a tutorial for younger students on a topic you want them to learn about.
10. Work with the Information and Communications Technology (ICT) teacher to explore how best to enable media-rich documents to be created on the school's computers.

Suggested Tasks for Educators

1. Visit the web sites of some musical artists to see how they present themselves in a 'rich media' way.
2. Gain insight into a familiar piece of music by listening to it while watching its effect on a spectrum analyzer.
3. Look over a music curriculum document and identify how it could be enhanced by the addition of musical examples and images.
4. Examine how advertisers, as professional communicators, use multiple media to communicate; plan to employ those techniques in your own teaching materials.
5. Revise some of your frequently used lesson plans to see how you might make them more media rich.

Chapter Summary

The bringing together of a variety of media, including still images, moving pictures, sound, and text, into rich media environments or documents presents opportunities for teachers and students to communicate their musical understanding. Musical knowledge can be represented in many of these media forms, which augment text—the traditional medium for knowledge representation in education. Understanding how digital media operate together through various software presentation tools will help teachers and learners better exploit the opportunities for rich media communication of ideas and understanding. The tools and techniques for presenting material in digital media allow educators to create resources and assessment items, and encourage students to enhance their expression and reflection. The skills required to make effective rich media presentations include an understanding of digital audiovisual technologies, methods of representing music as images and diagrams, and the use of hyperlinks to indicate the nonlinear organization of ideas and content.

Notes

1. Papert, S. (1993). *The children's machine: Rethinking school in the age of the computer.* New York: Basic Books, p. 156.
2. Dillon, S. (1995). *The student as maker: An examination of making in music education and the implications for contemporary curriculum development.* Master of education thesis, La Trobe University, Melbourne, Australia. p. 21.
3. Barrett, W. (1978). *The illusion of technique: A search for meaning in a technological civilization.* New York: Anchor Press, p. 143.

4. Lohner, H. (1986). The UPIC system: A user's report. *Computer Music Journal, 10*(4): 42–49.
5. Wattenberg, M. (2005). *The shape of song.* Retrieved October 2005 from www.turbulence.org/Works/song/.
6. *Audacity*, audio recording and editing that includes a number of visualizations: http://audacity.sourceforge.net/.
7. *Prezi*, dynamic presentation maker: https://prezi.com.
8. *Flipboard*, a magazine app for mobile devices: https://flipboard.com.
9. *WordPress*, blog hosting and creation: http://wordpress.com.
10. *Tumblr*, blog hosting and creation: http://tumblr.com.
11. *Google Sites*, web site hosting and creation: https://sites.google.com/.
12. *Wix*, web site builder: www.wix.com.
13. *Blogger*, blog hosting and creation: www.blogger.com/.
14. *SoundCloud*, audio hosting online: https://soundcloud.com.
15. *MASHER*, online video maker from images and sounds: www.masher.com.
16. *Animoto*, online video remixing from images and music: http://animoto.com.
17. *TuneBlocks*, interactive music composition software: www.tuneblocks.com/.
18. *Scratch*, a media programming and sharing: http://scratch.mit.edu.
19. *Second Life*, a virtual world often used as a virtual classroom: http://secondlife.com.
20. *Kahn Academy*, online tutorial and learning site: www.khanacademy.org/.
21. Humberstone, J. (2013). Tips on using iBooks Author for creating music education resources. www.youtube.com/playlist?list=PLntCjmpNLUUfxo5-bk0A4oeubR1R6JDWm.
22. *Nearpod*, app-based presentation system for mobile devices: www.nearpod.com.
23. *MIT App Inventor*, app development environment for Android: http://appinventor.mit.edu/.
24. *Windows App Studio* phone: http://appstudio.windowsphone.com.
25. *PhoneGap*, multi-platform app development environment: http://phonegap.com.
26. *iBuildApp*, commercial app development environment: http://ibuildapp.com.
27. *iGenapps*, commercial app development environment: www.igenapps.com.

nine
Sound
Reinforcement

Electronic and digital music technologies rely heavily on loudspeaker and headphone playback, without which most of the music and sound created would not come to life. Loudspeaker systems are used, quite literally, to amplify sound making. Their invention enabled new music genres, like those featuring subtle vocal techniques; think crooners like Frank Sinatra in the 1940s. Amplified sound has also allowed more experimental music—for example, John Cage's pieces for amplified cactus in the mid-1970s, or the glitch music that arose around the turn of the century that utilized and embraced the sounds of malfunctions and misuses of electronic or digital systems as musical materials.

More customarily, amplified sound allows small ensembles or bands to be heard in large venues or stadiums, and it enables the arbitrary volume balancing of instruments in an amplified setting. This kind of use is what is traditionally called sound reinforcement and is associated with sound systems for live performance. In private and classroom settings, the management of sound amplification of music technologies has become commonplace. This chapter will survey the technologies of sound amplification, paying particular attention to their application in educational settings, where public, group, and private monitoring of music need to be accommodated.

Uses for Sound Reinforcement

Music technologies that make sound require amplification. What form the amplification takes depends largely on the context in which the technology is used. In educational settings, these contexts include amplification for public, group, and personal use. In public settings, loudspeakers are employed to provide a shared musical experience. Loudspeakers may be used from music playback in the classroom or music studio to presentations in halls and theaters. Often music needs to be shared among a small group for collaboration or rehearsal. In classroom situations, there may be several groups working in one space. In these situations, it is typical to have either a small loudspeaker system or a distributed headphone mix. Playback for personal use follows similar trends, with headphone use recommended when isolation from external sound sources is required or to minimize disruption from the surrounding environment. Loudspeaker playback is generally preferable when isolation is not required. While this chapter will give some consideration to small-scale loudspeaker and headphone playback, accommodating these circumstances is reasonably straightforward; therefore, this chapter will focus on sound systems for public performance.

Signal Flow and Connections

Understanding signal flow is central to setting up and managing a sound system, as previously discussed in Chapter 3, including one for sound reinforcement. See Figure 9.1 for the basic flow of a signal through a live sound system. Sound sources—including microphones, computers, and electronic instruments—are fed into a mixing desk, where signals are combined. The output of the mixed signal is amplified and played back through loudspeakers.

There are many possible elaborations and simplifications of this basic setup. For example, commonly the amplifier is incorporated into the computer, mixer, or speakers, as shown in Figure 9.2. It is much simpler and more convenient to use powered speakers, because they reduce complications when interfacing devices and allow for direct connection to a computer's headphone output.

Increasing the simplicity is the fact that the mixing functions are handled in software, typically by a digital audio workstation application, rather than externally by a mixing desk. In this case, it is likely that an audio interface is connected to the computing device to allow input and output with external sources that can be mixed with recorded or synthesized sound from within the computer. See Figure 9.3 for this setup.

Chapter 3 outlined the types of cables and connectors likely to be used between components of a sound system. To summarize, the most common leads will be XLR microphone cables and 3.5-mm or 3/4-inch jack leads between other audio components. Computer connections to the audio interface will likely be via USB, FireWire, Thunderbolt, or a proprietary plug such as Apple's Lightning connector.

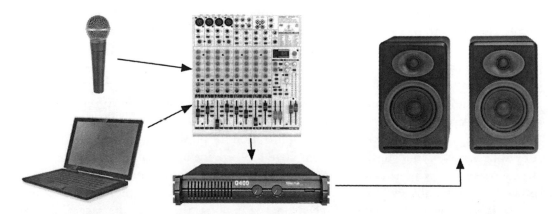

FIGURE 9.1 Signal flow through a basic sound system.

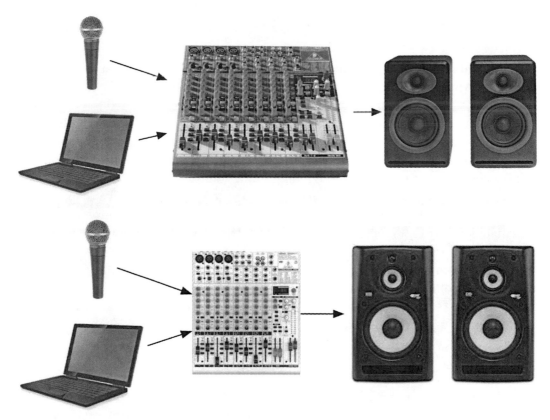

FIGURE 9.2 Integration of an amplifier into (i) a powered mixer and (ii) powered speakers.

FIGURE 9.3 A sound system using an audio interface, software mixing, and powered speakers.

It is increasingly common that audio connections occur over wireless connections. This saves on running cables and can allow for quick reconfiguration, but the process of setting up and finding errors may become more opaque. A later section of this chapter will cover the details of wireless audio connection.

Those are some of the basic sound system configurations. Read on to learn about a more involved system—one typically used for live concert sound reinforcement.

The Elements of a Live Sound System

A sound system for concert performance includes the basic components outlined above, but adds additional components as shown in Figure 9.4. For a live performance, the mixing console is typically positioned in the audience, so that the sound operator can hear what the audience hears and make adjustments accordingly. Because of the distance between stage and mixer, microphones are plugged into a stage box; a multicore collects all the mic cables and connects them to the mixing desk. Electronic instruments, such as synthesizers and computers, use a direct input (DI) box to facilitate connection to the stage box. The mixing console does its customary job, and, so that the performers can hear themselves on stage, a separate monitor mix is sent back to the stage through foldback speakers or in-ear monitors. Effects, such as compression and delay, are added to channels as desired. The main mix passes through equalizer (EQ) and effects for added treatment before being amplified and projected through the front-of-house speaker system.

It is increasingly common that a computer or digital mixing console will combine the functions of mixer, graphic EQ, and effects, somewhat simplifying the setup shown in Figure 9.4. The following sections provide further detail about the operation of each component in a live sound system.

Stage Boxes, Microphones, and DIs

In order to achieve a unified sound through the amplification system, all instruments and vocalists on stage should be amplified. To avoid spill when mixing vocals or acoustic instruments, microphones with a cardioid pattern should be used. For vocals, dynamic microphones will be less prone to popping and moisture damage from the singer's breath. See Chapter 3 for more details about different types of microphones. For even a modestly sized ensemble, quite a few microphones may be required—possibly one per instrument—but the number is restricted by the available channels on the mixer.

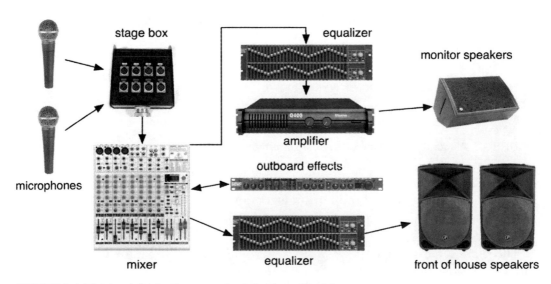

FIGURE 9.4 The layout of a live sound reinforcement system.

Microphones should be placed on stands close to instruments and vocalists. Keep them in fixed locations to maintain a consistent signal level and avoid potential feedback from the mic being moved around on stage. For guitars with amplifiers, position a dynamic cardioid microphone on a stand a few inches in front of the guitar amp's speaker. For a drum kit, place a dynamic mic near the kick (bass) drum, one near the snare and hi-hat, and two or more overhead to cover the rest of the kit. If there are enough microphones and channels, each tom-tom can be miked individually. The leads from the microphones can then be connected to the inputs on the stage box. Take care to keep track of which microphones are in which inputs and channels.

Electronic instruments will typically have a mono or stereo jack output, which is at line level (high impedance[1]). In order to convert these to a balanced mic level (low impedance) for input into the stage box, use a direct input (DI) box. DI boxes may be passive (unpowered) or active (powered). They contain jack inputs and XLR outputs, and may be stereo (two-channel) or mono. Connect the electronic instruments to the DI box and run a mic cable from the DI box to the stage box.

The multicore from the stage box runs leads back to the mixer, where the leads are connected to the channel inputs. Leads should be numbered so that the stage box inputs match the channels.

The Mixing Console

The main job of the mixer is to combine all the inputs and provide a well-balanced output to the main speakers and a foldback mix to the stage. Mixers can be analog, digital, or hybrid, but their tasks and operations are similar. Often the layout of an analog desk is more straightforward than that of a digital desk, which may have more functions and use pages of interface controls to manage them. Mixers have a number of channels, usually a multiple of four, and each channel has a strip of controls, including input level, EQ, sends, pan, and volume.

Input level

In the setup shown in Figure 9.4, all the sends from the stage box are at microphone level and DIs convert electronic instruments to mic level. The outputs from the stage box are connected to the microphone inputs (usually XLR connectors) on the mixer, and these need to be set to mic level input to match. There may be a gain (trim) control for each input that allows more nuanced attenuation (increase or decrease) of each input's level.

Inserts

On larger desks, each channel will have an insert jack for sending and receiving the signal to and from an external device, typically to be used for an effect such as compression. When cables are connected to these inserts, the signal is diverted to the inserted device before continuing its way through the remainder of the channel strip.

Channel EQ

This section of the channel strip affects the tone of the sound. By varying the high (treble), mid, and low (bass) frequencies, the EQ section enables an appropriate tone color to be achieved. This is useful when, for example, compensating for coloration from the microphone and adjusting the tone to add sound clarity.

Sends

A *send* involves a routing of the audio signal from the channel to another location. There are two types of sends: effect sends (auxiliary) and group sends (buses). Depending on its complexity, a mixer may have one or both of these. In either case, a send's function is to route the output of the channel to one or more outputs. Auxiliary sends typically allow a specific amount of signal from the channel to be sent to that output, while buses more commonly act as switches that send (or don't) the signal to a subgroup. For the purposes of the scenario in Figure 9.4, in which the secondary output is a monitor mix on stage, an auxiliary send can be used to allow a different mix on stage than the main mix. In the simplest case, the monitor mix is in mono and one auxiliary send is used. Different monitor and main mixes can be achieved by independently setting the auxiliary send level and the channel fader volume.[2]

Panning

Most live sound systems will be in stereo and will have their main output going to speakers on either side of the stage. The panning control enables one to position each channel's sound from left to right across this stereo spectrum.

Volume

The volume fader controls the level of the channel. This is a mixer's critical function. Of all controls, the fader is the one most frequently adjusted during live performances to compensate for variations in the performance, to feature a particular instrument for a time, or to adapt to different performers using the same microphone. Mixing desks have mute and/or solo buttons that allow each channel to be silenced or individually isolated. These are used for troubleshooting during sound check and for silencing channels when not in use.

Digital Control Surfaces

In a digital audio system, there may be no need for a separate mixing console. Instead, a multichannel audio interface may accept the inputs from the stage box, allowing the mixing process to be done in software on an attached computer. In order to provide a degree of physicality to the mixing process, a control surface—such as the 8-fader Avid *Artist Mix*[3]—may be attached to the computer. A multi-touch screen may display an on-screen mixing layout for use as a control surface. For example, the *Wireless Mixer*[4] app for Android provides virtual faders that communicate via MIDI to the mixing software. In these systems the sound does not pass through the control surface; rather, the app acts as a remote control for the digital signal processing done in the computing device.

FIGURE 9.5 A mixing console with multi-touch interface on an Apple iPad.

A related approach is to combine a mixing desk with a touch screen control surface. This method simplifies the hardware component, reduces cost, and provides the flexibility of various screen appearances. Software updates can add future functionality. The Mackie *DL1608*, shown in Figure 9.5, is an example of such a hybrid mixer and control surface that uses an iPad as a built-in control surface.

Effects

Effects can be added to a particular channel using the insert jacks on the mixing console. A common use for insert effects is compression, especially for vocal channels. A compressor reduces the dynamic range of the signal, helping to keep the volume consistent. Note that when an effect is inserted on a channel, it only affects that channel; thus, adding effects via inserts to many channels requires many external effect units or plug-ins. When using a digital mixer or computer software, virtual effects can be added as plug-ins on channels or on the main mix.

Some mixing desks include on-board effects, but all include auxiliary sends designed to work with external effect units such as a delay or reverb. As discussed earlier, auxiliary sends can be used for creating a monitor mix. Assuming there is more than one auxiliary send, a send can be used for the monitor send and another (or more) as an effect send. As shown in Figure 9.4, a signal is sent to and received from external effects devices via auxiliary sends. The most commonly added effect is reverb, which is especially useful in a dry performance space, but should not be added in an already reverberant gymnasium or concert hall.

The auxiliary output from the mixer is connected to the inputs on the effects unit, and the effects unit's output returns the signal to the mixer's auxiliary return. A number of levels will need to be adjusted: the auxiliary send for each channel will be used to control the degree of reverb for each instrument or voice, the effects unit's input level will be set to match the signal from the desk, and the auxiliary return on the mixer will be used to control the overall amount of effect that is added to the main output.

It is usual for the main mix and the monitor mix to pass through their own graphic equalizers just before reaching the amplifier and speaker. This allows the system to be tuned to the room, a process discussed in more detail in the section on sound system setup below. A graphic equalizer has a series of sliders (usually between 8 and 30), each corresponding to a particular frequency band. Adjustments can be made that increase or decrease frequency regions to achieve a flat frequency response that compensates for resonate peaks and dips in the environment. In a digital mixing system, a graphic EQ plug-in can be applied to the main and auxiliary outputs to achieve a similar result.

Amplifiers

Power amplifiers are fairly simple to operate. They have inputs for each channel (usually two) from the mixer and outputs to the speakers. Front panel controls are limited to an on/off switch, gain controls for each channel, and LED level indicators. The power of an amplifier is measured in watts. Desktop sound systems require only around 20–50 watts, but amplifiers for large public address systems will measure in the hundreds of watts. It is important to match the power and impedance of amplifiers and speaker combinations.

Separate amplifiers of this kind are less common these days; more often an amplifier is built into either the speaker or the mixer. Powered monitors are particularly practical, as they avoid the need to match components, are easy to set up, and can receive input from a variety of sources. Almost all computer speakers designed to connect to a device's headphone output are powered.

Speakers and Headphones

Loudspeakers are at the end of the chain of technologies in the audio signal path. They turn electrical current into vibrations in the air that we can hear. Speakers come in many shapes and sizes, but they all operate by using the electrical impulses from the amplifier to drive wire coils in a magnetic field that, in turn, move the speaker cone and thus the air around it. Speakers of different sizes are suited to reproducing particular ranges of frequencies. Generally, large speakers have more accurate bass response, and smaller speakers have more accurate high frequency response. As a result, quality speaker systems utilize several speakers of different sizes. The speaker cabinet's design and construction is also relevant to a speaker's frequency response. So, too, is speaker placement—both the speaker's height and its distance relative to the listener. Because our perception of direction is largely derived from our perceptions of high frequencies, it is best to have speakers that reproduce those frequencies at head height, facing the listener. According to what is known as the inverse square law, the volume of loudspeakers dissipates with distance. As a result, speaker cabinet designs differ; those intended for close monitoring are different from those designed to project sound. In particular, those designed for use in public address systems use a flared cabinet shape to focus (or *throw*) the sound forward.

Taking these factors into account, speakers suitable for a modest live sound reinforcement system are often two-way (two speakers/drivers) powered monitors that have a 10- to 15-inch woofer (low frequencies) and a flared horn for the tweeter (high frequencies). For the best audio quality, these should be paired with a matching subwoofer for very low frequency response. The speakers should be mounted on stands and positioned at, or slightly above, audience head height. As shown in Figure 9.6, the Behringer *EuroLive B112D* is typical of this kind of speaker and can be augmented with an active (powered) subwoofer.

Monitor, or foldback, speakers will have similar properties, only their cabinet design needs to allow them to sit on the floor at the front of the stage, facing up toward the performers. Other monitoring options include the use of small near-field speakers for each musician, or in-ear headphones. These options allow the onstage volume to be kept lower, but setup is more complex.

Headphones are also speaker systems; they utilize a single very small speaker per ear. They rely on proximity to the ear and an enclosure design to achieve a full-range sound from such a compact space. Earbuds fit into the ears, provide the most compact listening experience, and are designed to physically block external sounds from the ear. Larger over-the-ear headphones are more traditional and still quite popular. Closed-back designs prevent sound leakage, which is good for use in public spaces, recording sessions, and cueing during DJ performance. Open-back designs are considered to be more comfortable for long periods of listening. Headphone quality varies considerably both for earbud and over-the-ear styles.

FIGURE 9.6 A powered, two-way speaker for live sound reinforcement.

Wireless Audio

Connecting audio technologies with cables often results in a spaghetti-like mess of connected components, a scene that has become almost synonymous with electronic music. Indeed, the forest of patch leads connecting analog synthesizer modules has been romanticized in some DIY communities and is emulated in a number of virtual synthesizer applications, such as the Arturia *Modular V*.[5] However, the advent of wireless audio connections is a step toward a neater future for music technology—thankfully, many would say.

Wireless microphones have been available for some time. They use an FM radio transmitter (located in the microphone body) and receiver to communicate an audio signal. The receiver device is then connected to the sound system in the normal way. Additionally, lapel microphones can connect to belt-mounted transmitters and are useful for hands-free amplified presentations.

Digital wireless audio is a newer technology. These protocols enable digital audio data to be streamed between computing devices and to suitably equipped speakers and headphones. Combined with protocols for wireless MIDI and video streaming, a future with more seamless interfacing of digital technologies is now imaginable. The advantages of this for the music classroom are many, not least of which is the flexibility students now enjoy to stream their work on the fly to peers' or teachers' devices for presentation, comment, and review. The ability to quickly reconfigure technology in the classroom audio configuration to complete different tasks and projects is another significant advantage.

There are wireless audio protocols for Wi-Fi (wireless Internet) and Bluetooth. However, as always in the early days of such innovations, there are incompatibilities and competing standards to sort through. The Wi-Fi protocols include Apple's *AirPlay* and Android's *Wireless Direct*, which is an emerging Wi-Fi standard. There are also a few proprietary systems such as the one from Sonos. These Wi-Fi systems offer good audio quality and the ability to stream to multiple locations simultaneously. The range of a Wi-Fi signal is around 20 meters (65 feet), which should be ample for most environments. Each of these protocols supports the communication of metadata along with the audio—for example, song lyrics, analysis annotations, images, and so forth. The complexity of the Wi-Fi protocols means that compatible devices are more expensive than those using Bluetooth.

Bluetooth audio streaming gained prominence with the rise of wireless headsets for mobile phones and in-car Bluetooth-compatible stereo systems. The same technologies allow streaming of audio data between devices and Bluetooth-equipped speakers. Devices are paired before communicating, which currently means that Bluetooth audio streaming is limited to one-to-one device communication. The audio data is compressed; consequently, much like an MP3 file, the audio quality is not optimal, although in many cases it is acceptable. The range of a Bluetooth signal is about half that of a Wi-Fi signal—still quite sufficient for devices in the same room. An advantage for Bluetooth is that the Advanced Audio Distribution Profile (A2DP) standard is universal and should work in cross-platform device ecologies. Be aware that some incompatibilities may arise because there are two Bluetooth codecs in common use across A2DP—the default sub-band coding (SBC) and the newer aptX, the latter featuring higher audio quality.

When looking for loudspeaker playback options for mobile computers, tablets, and smart phones in the music classroom, it is wise to consider a wireless speaker solution. This would keep mobile devices untethered while enabling higher quality and more audible sound playback than the devices' built-in speakers allow. When selecting wireless audio devices, make sure the devices are compatible with your current equipment. Know that there are a growing number of wireless audio receivers and speakers that conform to more than one protocol, providing added flexibility.

Surround Sound

This chapter has so far assumed a stereo (two-channel) audio system, the most common configuration. Systems with larger numbers of speakers are also possible—in theory, any number—and for film music in particular, surround sound systems using 5.1 and 7.2 configurations are quite common. Electronic and electroacoustic music performances often use quadraphonic (four-speaker) and octaphonic (eight-speaker) arrays. During the mixing process sound sources can be positioned in, or moved through, the sound field created by the speaker configuration.

A stereo field allows for the panning of sound from left to right in one dimension. It is possible to use timbral and reverb treatments to impart a sense of depth perception in the stereo field. See Figure 9.7 for a diagram example of this.

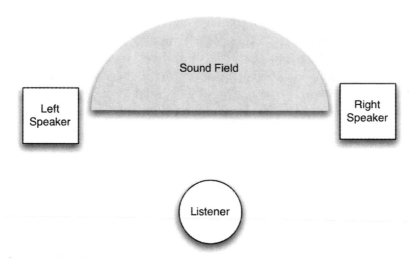

FIGURE 9.7 The stereo sound field extends between the speakers and back in an arc.

Using more than two speakers allows one to position the speakers in a two-dimensional plane around the listener. Different numbers of speakers and various positioning arrangements provide particular advantages. An even number of speakers—say four or eight—allows for even distribution around the listener without prioritizing any particular orientation as the front. Odd-numbered systems—say five or seven—have a speaker in the center-front position, which for film is often used to ensure that spoken dialogue appears to come from the screen. The '1' in 5.1 or '2' in 7.2 surround formats refers to subwoofer (low frequency effects, or LFE) channels that ensure that the sound-effect rumble is felt in the space. The location of the subwoofer is not considered very critical, but it should not be in a corner or a confined area.

Setting up a surround speaker array for your digital audio sound system means having a desk or audio interface with sufficient outputs—six outputs for 5.1, for example—and an appropriate number of powered monitors. The positioning of speakers for correct 5.1 or 7.2 conditions is quite specific, so refer to a guide as required.[6] Surround sound panning of channels generally requires a digital desk or software with an appropriate interface, such as the one shown in Figure 9.8 for a 5.1 surround sound setup. The panning control shows a plan of the speaker layout, and a dot indicates the position of the channel in the sound field. A surround panner can be activated per channel or track, to position (and move) as many sound sources as required.

Sound System Setup and Operation

Setting up a live sound system, as seen in Figure 9.4, can take some time. It is best to work methodically and systematically. Begin by setting up the basics of a mixer, amp, and speakers, and check that they are working with a microphone or music player. Then add the additional components, testing with each step. If possible, have plenty of spare leads in case of breakages. Make sure there are sufficient power extension leads and power boards.

When setting up, tune the main system and monitor speakers separately with their own graphic EQs. Figure 9.9 shows a 31-band graphic EQ in which each fader increases

FIGURE 9.8 The 5.1 surround panner in *Logic Pro*.

FIGURE 9.9 A typical 31-band graphic EQ.

or decreases the frequencies within a narrow range. Virtual graphic EQs will have a similar on-screen appearance. Tuning the system typically involves connecting a microphone and saying "testing 1, 2, …" into the mic; listen for resonate frequencies indicating you should reduce those bands on the EQ, or dips in the spectrum indicating where frequency bands could be increased. This skill takes practice to develop. Listen closely for frequencies that might peak and turn into feedback. Play familiar music through a system so you can assess its evenness and balance. It may help you to visualize the output using a spectrum analyzer.[7] Do this while playing a constant white noise signal through the system and positioning a microphone near the desk to pick up to the sound. This will help to visually reveal any significant peaks and troughs in the frequency spectrum, which can then be compensated for by adjusting the graphic EQ.

Next, design a channel layout. Decide which instruments or microphones will be on which channels of the mixer. Label the mixer clearly. Connect all the instruments and microphones to the stage box accordingly, testing each as you go.

With everything working, it is time for the sound check. The sound check is a time prior to the gig to have musicians on stage to iron out levels for each channel, set channel EQ and effects, and establish a baseline balance for the main and foldback monitor mixes. Again, follow a systematic approach to achieve this efficiently. If there are a number of groups performing in a concert, keep written records of the settings for each one (or save snapshots of the settings if it is a digital desk). Do sound checks in reverse order of performance so that the last group to sound check is the first group on stage. To prevent unintended sounds coming through the sound system between sound check and performance, mute the channels.

Operating the mixing console during the live show requires listening and concentration. The objective of live mixing is to achieve a well-balanced ensemble in which all parts are audible. When there is an important point of focus, such as the lead singer or an instrumental soloist, make sure that the singer or soloist can be heard clearly. When there are several inputs from one instrument, such as a drum kit, make sure there is internal consistency among those parts, as well as an overall balance with the other parts. Listen carefully for potential feedback from a microphone or for other issues that need attention. Act quickly but not abruptly to make adjustments.

Sound system setup and operation are skillful and performative acts that require technical and musical judgment. In educational settings, all students may find it useful to become competent at these skills—skills that some students will go on to master.

Recording the Gig

Given that the sound from the performance is going to the mixer for reinforcement, it might seem like an obvious step to record the gig from a copy of the main mixer outputs. However, this will result in an unbalanced recording, because in the performance space the sound reinforcement signal will combine with the live sound in the room. Therefore the main (and monitor) mixes emphasize softer instruments and vocals and contain little of the louder instruments like drums and brass instruments.

A straightforward alternative would be to set up a stereo pair of microphones near the mixing console and record the sound as the audience hears it. This can even be done by a separate team; it need not involve the sound system operator(s) at all.

Another alternative would be to do a multi-track recording of each channel for later mixing in the studio. This requires a mixing desk with sends from each channel to the recorder's audio interface; however, if the mixer is already software-based, simply record the tracks directly during the performance. In the latter case, the recorded mix may include level and other adjustments made during the performance that will need to be taken into account during the mixdown.

It can be quite educational to record a performance using all of the methods described here and have students listen to and compare the different outcomes.

Conclusion

A loudspeaker system is essential for hearing the output of electronic and digital music. Speaker systems in educational settings range from playback of an MP3 player with headphones to a live sound system for a public concert. The stages in the audio signal path of each of these may be similar in principle, but they vary greatly in sophistication depending on the level of control and complexity required. This chapter outlined many of the elements in a sound system and how they come together in operation. Even in our digital age, loudspeakers are still analog and bear a close resemblance to their earlier counterparts. In most other stages of the sound reinforcement process, digital audio technologies have become increasingly dominant. As wireless audio transmission becomes more advanced, device-to-device configurations will achieve greater flexibility, and device mobility will be enhanced. These advances in digital audio technology are beneficial, but the musical skills of listening carefully to sound timbre and ensemble balance remain as critical as any technical skills for the effective operation of sound reinforcement systems.

Reflection Questions

1. What kinds of listening setups are suggested for small groups in music classroom settings?
2. Name the components in the basic sound system's signal flow diagram.
3. What do the terms 'powered mixer' and 'powered speaker' mean?
4. In a live sound system, what is the stage box's function?
5. What type of microphone does a lead vocalist typically use on stage?
6. What is a direct input (DI) box used for?
7. Equalization (EQ) is applied to each channel and to the main mix. What is its purpose in each case?
8. What are the large and small drivers in a two-way speaker cabinet called?
9. Name the two wireless technologies used for transmitting digital audio.
10. How many speakers are required for a 5.1 surround system?

Teaching Tips

1. Keep learning goals in mind when selecting hardware for sound reinforcement systems.
2. Set up a multi-speaker audio system at school with as many speakers as can be gathered; have students experiment with mixing their own works over the system.
3. To encourage peer learning, have students work in groups of two or three when practicing the setup of a sound system.
4. To reinforce an understanding of audio signal flow, have students draw diagrams of how sound system components interconnect.
5. Use digital music playback and a virtual graphic EQ for students to hear the effects of increasing and decreasing various EQ bands.
6. Encourage students to take turns operating the mix at performance rehearsals so that each student has learning opportunities.
7. For an individual virtual mixing exercise, assign students to practice using playback of a multi-track project in a digital audio workstation (DAW), like *GarageBand*.
8. Use a wireless audio receiver connected to a set of speakers to enable students to share projects from their individual devices with the class.
9. Encourage vocalists to practice mic technique as a regular part of their vocal training to prepare them for amplified stage performance.
10. Assign a 5.1 surround mix production as an extension activity for advanced students working on a film scoring project.

Suggested Tasks for Educators

1. Familiarize yourself with the setup of various audio systems by connecting and disconnecting all components several times.
2. Using a mixing desk, add effects such as reverb and delay to a microphone signal.
3. Use equalization to improve the clarity of a mix.
4. Plan a program of ongoing personal development focused on skills in sound reinforcement system operation.
5. Locate a knowledgeable mentor who can provide technical support about using digital audio hardware and software.

Chapter Summary

Loudspeaker playback is a significant element of the experience of music technology. Sound needs to be heard, and speakers are the interface from the electronic to acoustic sound worlds. Sound systems may be used in educational settings in many forms and contexts—from personal listening using headphones or in sound studios, to small playback systems or headphone distribution for group collaborations, to live sound reinforcement for public performances. Components of sound systems are increasingly integrated; the choices are expanding and the line between analog and digital components is blurring. Significantly, the emergence of wireless audio streaming has reduced the cable clutter from audio systems and allowed mobile devices to remain unencumbered while still sharing output. Despite these advances, the basic building blocks and techniques of sound system setup and operation remain the same. These include miking acoustic performers and direct input from electronic instruments, operating the mixing console, and using digital control surfaces, applying effects and EQ, and managing main and monitor mixes for the audience and performers during a live concert. This chapter provided an overview of these topics; an educator or student may learn and absorb the details covered to gain a basic understanding of and confidence in working with a variety of sound reinforcement systems.

Notes

1. See a definition and explanation of electrical impedance and its significance to music technology here: http://whirlwindusa.com/support/tech-articles/high-and-low-impedance-signals/.
2. There is a difference between pre- and post-fader configurations for the auxiliary send. For details, consult an audio mixing text or an online resource such as http://sound.stackexchange.com/questions/14216/difference-between-pre-and-post-fade.
3. Avid *Artist Mix*, eight-fader control surface: www.avid.com/US/products/Artist-Mix.
4. *Wireless Mixer*, a MIDI fader app by Borce Trajkovski for Android devices—http://trajkovski.net/.
5. *Modular V* is a virtual analog synthesizer from Arturia that emulates the Moog modular synths of the 1960s, right down to the swaying of virtual patch leads: www.arturia.com/evolution/en/products/moogmodularv/intro.html.
6. Dolby provides an online guide to the position of speakers for various surround sound configurations: www.dolby.com/us/en/consumer/setup/connection-guide/home-theater-speaker-guide/.
7. See Chapter 8 for more details about spectrum analyzers.

ten
Electronic Music Performance

Electronic music refers to music produced using instruments such as synthesizers, samplers, computers, drum machines, guitar effects pedals, and modified electrical devices (circuit bending). The history of electronic instruments goes back over 100 years, and the range of instruments is ever expanding. Early examples include the *theremin* and the *telharmonium*. Synthesizers became available commercially in the 1960s, with one of the most notable being the *Minimoog* (seen in Figure 10.1). Synthesizers continue to play a significant role in popular and experimental music making, but today's technologies are as often virtual (software based) as they are physical.

In the 1980s, the MIDI protocol allowed electronic instruments to communicate with one another, and affordable sampling instruments emerged. Additionally, in the later decades of the twentieth century, technologies not originally intended for performance were adopted by musicians, most notably turntables and laptop computers. Computer software developments allowed for algorithmic and interactive music systems in which the machines themselves became performance partners. More recently, using apps, musicians have transformed mobile computing devices into virtual instruments.

Live electronic music in the early twenty-first century is generally aligned with musical styles broadly described as electronica or electronic dance music (EDM). Electronic music also has roots in the high-art tradition, pioneered, for example, by Karlheinz Stockhausen, Pierre Henry, and Pierre Boulez. Moreover, electronic sounds have been a prominent element of many experimental music genres. The influence of these acousmatic and electroacoustic traditions is alive and well in laptop orchestras and electronic ensembles, especially in academic contexts.

Electronic music in the dance tradition often consists of mechanically precise and sometimes complex rhythmic material. Popular versions of this music focus on how danceable material is. Producers pay careful attention to subtle timbral changes but often downplay traditional concerns with harmony, melody, and rubato phrasing. The timbral palette for electronic music is derived primarily from synthesizer sources, but may also feature vocal and/or instrumental samples, or found sounds. Musical textures

FIGURE 10.1 The *Minimoog* monophonic analog synthesizer.

are built up by layering, and a mixture of gradual and sudden changes in texture add dramatic variety. Live performance of this music involves a combination of direct gestural control and meta-level arrangement and mixing of elements. Performances may incorporate well-established interfaces such as piano and computer keyboards, emerging interfaces including mobile devices with multi-touch interfaces, or more idiosyncratic and bespoke controllers.

This chapter explores contemporary live electronic music: its technologies, its practices, and some of the educational opportunities that live electronic music presents.

Learning through Live Electronic Music

Live electronic music provides rich opportunities for music education because it is at the crossroads of many important considerations for student engagement. It connects with popular culture, providing relevance and motivation for students. Its emphasis on performance, or at least control, gives access to the embodied nature of musical experience, as opposed to the often disembodied nature of music technologies. It embraces a culture of experimentation and improvisation that provides opportunities for creative expression and stimulates an inquiring mind.

The diversity of live electronic music provides many possibilities for educational activities. For example, electronic and computer-based instruments may be used for improvised live performances including sound collages, film scores, and dance parties. Performances may include a range of gestural controllers and triggering devices, such as theremins and cheap domestic electronic keyboards. The preparation and control of synthesized, sampled, or sequenced materials typically used in live electronic music is fun, requires skill, and requires aesthetic judgment. This music is frequently improvised, making activities more immediate and accessible than composed repertoire tends to be (especially for inexperienced musicians). For the student interested in electronic engineering, there are many kit-based synthesizers and gestural controllers that can be assembled. This 'maker' aesthetic has a cachet in today's youth culture, and many students will enjoy making instruments as a part of learning music. For those interested in computing, there are real-time tools and apps that can be used for performance; programming itself can even become a performance practice through live coding.

Software synthesizers, sequencers, and modular audio patching systems enable students to construct quite sophisticated sonic materials and structures. Students can create their own patches for use in live performance, build electronic instruments for others to play, or write music using production software for live playback and manipulation. Modular synthesizers have regained popularity in recent years, and these systems range from simple devices such as the *Doepfer Dark Energy II*[1] to complex Eurorack modular systems (seen in Figure 10.2). Electronic instruments and virtual electronic music apps also add to a rich instrumental environment and stimulate music students.

FIGURE 10.2 Performance on a modular analog instrument by Jesus Lopez-Donado.[2]

While many synthesizers have a keyboard interface, many other controllers are available for electronic instruments. Some are based on acoustic instruments, such as the saxophone, drum kit, guitar, or trumpet, and others use sensors, including light beams, pressure pads, ribbon sliders, and touch screens. This diversity allows students with different technical fluencies and stylistic interests to participate meaningfully in music activities.

Electronic Instruments

This section provides more details about the most commonly used classes of electronic instruments.

Turntables

Even though CDs and then MP3 files replaced vinyl records for music distribution, DJs and turntablists continue to use turntables for electronic dance music. This performance culture has played an important role in keeping vinyl record production alive.

The mixing and scratching of vinyl as musical expression emerged from the Jamaican Dub music culture; its evolution began with individuals playing records over sound systems for street parties. It was further popularized and transformed through blending with other electronic music technologies in the United States in the latter decades of the twentieth century.

Turntable systems consist of two decks and a mixer. The mixer is used to crossfade between the decks and to make minimal timbral variations. The *Technics SL-1200* phonograph is a well-known turntable used by DJs. Turntablists using CDs or virtual decks frequently choose the Numark, Denon, and Pioneer DJ and CD players.[3] Turntables have not escaped the laptop and tablet computing revolutions, and virtual turntable software systems, such as *VirtualDJ*[4] or *djay,*[5] are widely available.

DJ mixers allow the cross-fading and control of two music sources (e.g., turntables and CD decks or MP3 players). Mixers are sturdily constructed and can withstand aggressive onstage use. They allow an individual to monitor the input and/or the output via headphones, so that one track can be cued in the headphones while the other track is being heard through the main output. See Figure 10.3 for an example of a simple two-channel DJ mixing desk.

Headphones, which may be used to cue tracks and other musical material, have become an integral component of a DJ's equipment list. Headphones used for this purpose usually have an over-the-ear design with enclosed speaker capsules that block other sounds in the room.

Synthesizers and Samplers

Synthesizers have long been the core of electronic music. While digital synthesizers largely replaced analog instruments, older analog instruments are prized, and new releases of revised older models are common. Recently released analog synthesizers include the *Prophet 12* (Dave Smith), the *Phatty* (Moog) and the *Dark Energy II*

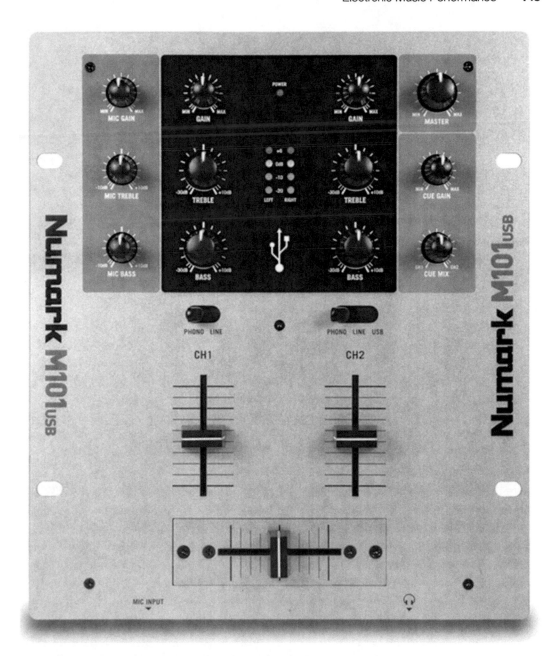

FIGURE 10.3 The *Numark M101*, a simple DJ mixer with two channels and a crossfader.

(Doepfer). Classic analog synthesizers include those made between the 1960s and the 1980s, from companies such as Arp, Korg, Moog, Oberheim, Roland, Sequential Circuits, and Yamaha.

Digital synthesizers can create a range of unique sounds, but often focus on replicating the sound and instability that gave classic analog instruments a particular warmth. This simulation process is called analog modeling. Keyboard synthesizers that feature analog modeling include the *Virus* (Access), the *Origin* (Arturia), the *Radius* (Korg), the *Nord Lead* (Nord), the *AN1x* (Yamaha), and the *V-Synth* (Roland).

FIGURE 10.4 The *Nave* synthesizer app on the iPad.

There is a wide array of software-based virtual synthesizers, often packaged with digital audio workstation (DAW) software or available as plug-ins. To be sure, any computing device can be transformed into a synthesizer with software, and there are many fine examples for mobile devices as well, including the *Animoog* and Waldorf *Nave*[6] for the iPad (seen in Figure 10.4).

Samplers are another category of instruments used in electronic music. Samplers allow the digital recording (or *sampling*) of sounds that can be edited and performed, as described in Chapter 3. Sampling instruments originally involved using short sound clips that could be looped, triggered, and arranged into larger structures. For performance purposes, samplers allow real-time control over pitch, duration and timbre of sample playback, and triggering sounds using MIDI sequencers or physical controllers. Early samplers, such as the *Fairlight CMI*, featured piano-like keyboard controllers. Keyboard samplers and rack-mounted versions without the keyboard have been produced by Alesis, Casio, E-MU Systems, Ensoniq, Fairlight, Kurzweil, New England Digital, Roland, and Yamaha, to name a few. In the 1990s, as trends shifted to sampling drum sounds, electronic instruments increasingly featured trigger pads as a performance interface. Percussion-based samplers include the *MPC* series (Akai), the *ESX-1* (Korg), and the *SP-404SX* (Roland). Today, most samplers are software-based and use the computing device's storage for the large quantities of samples that are typically preloaded or available as add-on libraries. Examples of these include *Kontakt* (Native Instruments), *ESX24* (Logic), and the *MachFive* (MOTU).

Drum Machines

Because rhythm is at the heart of electronic dance music, it is no surprise that the drum machine has played a prominent role in defining the sound and style of this musical genre. Drum machines are sequencers for percussive sounds. Like synthesizers, drum machines from the 1970s and 1980s have become classics. Like analog synthesizers, original drum machines became highly valued, and later technologies frequently emulated them. Classic drum machines include the *TR-808*—shown in Figure 10.5—and *TR-909* (Roland), the *SP-12* (E-MU), and the *LM-1* (Linn). Continued interest in classic drum machines has spurred new releases from some of the original drum machine manufacturers. Examples include the *Aira TR-8*[7] (Roland) and the *Tempest*[8] (Roger Linn and Dave Smith).

In the 1990s, drum machine capabilities were incorporated into percussion-oriented samplers like the Akai MPC series. Today, software drum machines are widely used in computer-based systems. In live performance, musicians use drum machines to loop and edit rhythm patterns on a note-by-note basis. Preset rhythms can be selected on the fly, and the timbre of the sounds can be manipulated. These features were incorporated into virtual drum machines available for mobile devices; these include the *DM1* (Fingerlab)[9] and *ReBirth* (Propellerhead)[10] for Apple's iOS, and the simply named *Drum Machine*[11] for Google's Android.

The 16-step sequencing layout of classic drum machines visually subdivides the musical measure and makes experimentation with rhythmic patterns and loops easy and intuitive. Consequently, in many educational settings, drum machines with step sequencers are some of the best access points into music technology and live electronic music. This percussion-oriented interaction with music technology has spurred a whole class of instruments featuring drum pads for performance and sequencing called pad controllers.

FIGURE 10.5 An advertisement for the original *Roland TR-808* drum machine.

Pad Controllers

Pad controllers feature a matrix of percussion pads that can be assigned many tasks. Typically, pad controllers trigger sounds or music clips, but a pad controller can also act as a multi-track step sequencer or as an unconventional keyboard for a melody or bass line; it can even trigger chord changes. This grid layout has become so ubiquitous for musical organization that there is even a doctoral thesis on the topic.[12]

Early pioneers of the matrix layout for triggering electronic sounds include drum pads such as the Octapad[13] (Roland) and the *MPC* series (Roger Linn and Akai), and less percussive oriented grid controllers like the Monome[14] and Tenori-on.[15] Contemporary pad controllers have a matrix of triggers that light up to display their status, and may include numerous additional buttons, dials, or faders. Examples include the Launchpad[16] (Novation), the QuNeo[17] (Keith McMillen), and the Push[18] (Ableton), shown in Figure 10.6.

These devices are control surfaces and typically do not have any sound-making capability; they instead trigger synthesizers and samplers on other devices via MIDI. Some synthesizers and samplers include grid controller interfaces that provide the convenience (and expense) of combining controller and audio creation in one device. Examples include the Octapad (Roland) and the MPC series (Akai).

FIGURE 10.6 The *Ableton* Push pad controller.

FIGURE 10.7 The *iMPC* interface on iPad that replicates the classic Akai MPCs from the 1990s.

As is common in today's music technology landscape, there are *virtual* pad controllers for touch screen–enabled mobile devices. The tactility of interaction makes for quite a successful transition to the touch screen format; however, the dynamic and pressure sensitivity of pads is usually lost. Examples of these apps include *Drum Pads 24* for Android and the *iMPC* for iOS (seen in Figure 10.7).

The *iMPC* and similar apps are particularly attractive for music classrooms because they include a wide range of high quality sounds, limited multi-track sequencing capabilities, and the ability to add and edit recorded samples. Apps like the *iMPC* provide more than enough functionality to be the basis of a comprehensive creative curriculum focused on electronic and contemporary music.

Controllers with a touch interface do not always incorporate a literal grid of buttons. The Korg *Kaoss Pad*, for example, is a popular controller that features an x–y pad and on-board audio and video signal processing. The *iKaossilator*, a software version, may be used with touch screen devices. The *Orphion*[19] app for iOS offers expressive performance control of percussion and string articulations. A similar touch controller with many customizable features, the *Gestrument* (gesture instrument) for iOS,[20] was developed by Jesper Nordin and is used for a wide range of musical interactions and styles. Watch the videos on the *Gestrument* web site[21] for some inspiring examples.

Instrument Controllers

MIDI controllers can emulate acoustic instrument design. Examples include MIDI keyboards, guitars, wind instruments, violins, and drum kits. These allow musicians with existing instrumental techniques to use their skills with electronic sound sources. They also provide additional incentive for students to develop instrumental performance techniques. An instrument that combines traditional and contemporary controllers—such as the M-Audio *Axiom* keyboard controller—is a popular choice in school music technology labs. Of these instrument-like controllers, electronic drum kits are understandably popular in educational contexts because their sound can be more easily managed than that of an acoustic drum kit.

Numerous apps are available that turn mobile devices into pseudo instrument controllers. Many of these are based on instrument gestures such as tapping, strumming, blowing, and sliding. The company Smule[22] was an early entrant to this market and now offers a range of music instrument apps. The transfer of skills between these and acoustic instruments is likely to be less than that between dedicated hardware controllers simply because the mobile device's form does not correspond with traditional acoustic instruments. However, virtual instrument apps can be fun and may be used to facilitate skills like rhythmic timing, pitch selection, and ensemble cooperation.

A number of sensors and electronic devices that can be used to control electronic music are taking the concept of music controllers to a new level, and will be covered next.

Sensors and Electronic Circuits

For many musicians, the search for new and interesting ways of performing makes live electronic music that much more exciting. This section looks at how some devices that were not designed for music making have been adapted for that purpose. It also explores some DIY approaches to constructing bespoke electronic musical interfaces. Many of the devices described here provide the basis for fun student projects, and can provide excellent stimulus for interdisciplinary collaborations teaching science and computing.

There is a variety of inexpensive small computing devices that can be used to connect sensors and write simple music programs. For example, the *MaKey MaKey*[23] board connects a computer to any conductive material (such as people, carrots, and aluminum foil) to create a trigger system. Tap the carrots, for instance, like a piano keyboard, and the *MaKey MaKey* sends these triggers to the computer as keystrokes. The keystrokes then start or stop a range of sounds using appropriate software. See Figure 10.8 for such a setup, or watch many example videos available online.

Similar, more flexible outcomes are possible with the *Arduino* micro controller.[24] The *Arduino* receives input from a variety of sensors and sends output to control sounds, lights, or motors. A great example of the *Arduino*'s advantages for children is the *MusicInk* project.[25] *MusicInk* uses conductive ink (and some other technologies) to turn children's drawings into playable musical instruments.

Another small and inexpensive computing device is the *Raspberry Pi*,[26] which focuses more on programming than sensor interaction, but still has interesting musical

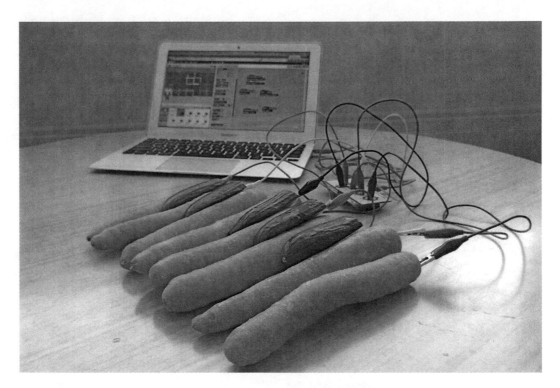

FIGURE 10.8 A 'veggie' keyboard using the *MaKey MaKey* board (inspired by Silver and Rosenbaum).

applications. One such application is the *Sonic Pi* project, which uses simple computer code to create musical compositions.[27]

A few commercial sensor-based technologies can be transformed into music controllers with appropriate software. The Xbox Kinect is a movement tracking device developed for gesture-based gameplay. There are two versions: the original, designed for the Xbox 360 game console, and a newer one for the Xbox One console. At the time of writing, music software adaptations target the original 360 version. The Kinect can be used as music controller with *Synapse* software,[28] which turns body movements into open sound control (OSC) data for mapping to music software. There is also software for connecting the Kinect 360 with the *Gestrument* app (see earlier mention).[29]

Another gesture sensor is the Leap Motion controller.[30] This small device connects via USB to a computer and can track the movements of up to 10 fingers waved above the device. Movements can be mapped to musical controls using a variety of Leap Motion apps. See Figure 10.9 for a selection of music apps available on the Leap Motion web site.

The Reactable[31] is a dedicated music controller that employs gestures. The original tabletop version allows one or more musicians to move objects (blocks) around on its tabletop screen to control sound synthesis and sequencing patterns. A version of the Reactable is also available as an iOS app. The Reactable is a complete instrument rather than a controller of other sound sources, and it highlights the diversity of the less conventional music interfaces that are available.

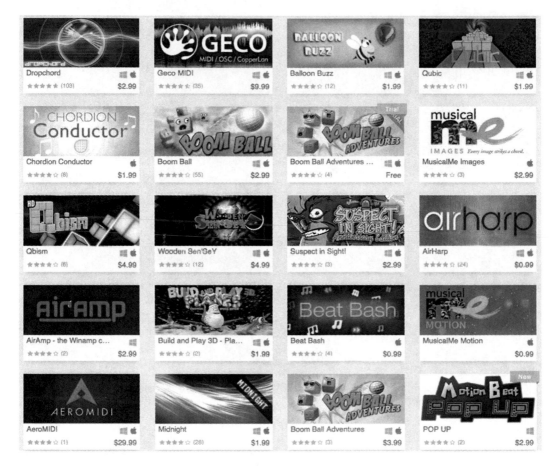

FIGURE 10.9 Some music apps for the Leap Motion controller.

Performance Software

Controllers provide a physical interface to gestural control of sound and musical structure, but it is the performance software systems they are controlling. As described in Chapter 4, DAWs are the major music software applications. These were developed for music production, not performance, and consequently use a strict linear timeline metaphor that is not conducive to live performance. In recognition of this, developers created new software with modular and nonlinear structures. These became popular for live electronic music, and include *Ableton Live, Reason, FL-Studio, AudioMulch, Max,* and *Reaktor. Ableton Live* is very popular for electronic music; its session view, seen in Figure 10.10, features a matrix of clips that can be dynamically triggered and looped. For this approach, an individual should prepare clips and their on-screen organization before the performance, and arrange their playback and manipulate their sonic output during performance.

In addition to these software that feature fixed, even if extensive, interfaces and functionalities, there are software options that allow musicians to customize their own live electronic music systems. One of the most convenient ways to design a software controller interface is

FIGURE 10.10 *Ableton Live* features a matrix of musical loops (clips) that can be adjusted in real-time.

to use visual tools such as *TouchOSC*[32] for iOS and Android. *TouchOSC* includes a range of touch screen interface widgets, including sliders, dials, x–y pads, and buttons, which can be arranged in custom layouts. Controlling these widgets generates values that are transmitted to connected devices via Open Sound Control, wireless MIDI Bridge, OS X CoreMIDI Network Sessions, or a compatible MIDI interface. This is a very flexible option for creating custom music controllers.

For the more adventurous, there are computer programming environments dedicated to electronic music making. These are extremely flexible and allow the imaginative user to build an almost endless number of electronic musical creations, but they do require some dedicated study and practice to master. These environments can be separated into two categories: visual programming languages, in which programs appear like flow charts that trace the steps in the algorithm; and text-based programming languages, which act more like conventional computer code. Below are lists of each type.

Visual programming environments:

- AudioMulch[33]
- Scratch[34]
- Pd[35]
- Max (and Max for Live)[36]

Text-based coding environments:

- Music Python[37]
- Processing and Minum or SoundCipher[38]
- SuperCollider[39]
- Extempore[40]
- Overtone[41]
- ChucK[42]

While these programming environments can be challenging to start, more advanced or inquisitive students and educators may find them appealing. Entry-level books, tutorials, and projects are available to assist the beginner. As with the sensor and electronics devices, these software tools for electronic music serve as a bridge to interdisciplinary collaborations with computing and information technology curricula.

Performance Practices

Electronic music performance practices vary in a number of ways. These include differences in musical style, the amount of gestural activity, how actions change the sound, the size and frequency of gestures, the performance context, the size of the ensemble, and the interaction with the audience. It is generally true that electronic music performance may only require minimal gestures to control parameters (in the same way that playing notes on the piano only requires small finger movements), but virtuosic performance often involves layers of energetic movement. Every artist has his or her own approach to live performance and how direct the connection is between gesture and sound. Think of the differences between a DJ who selects a new song every few minutes and a performer actively playing lines on a keyboard or adding percussive parts from a drum pad. Different approaches range from actions executed in a calm manner while sitting behind a laptop, to running maniacally onstage from device to device, adjusting, playing, and triggering frenetically.

As with acoustic instrument performance, the size of an electronic music ensemble changes the performance dynamics. In an age of automated machine music (sequencing and algorithmic processes), electronic music performances need not involve large ensembles. Typical group size is from one to four performers, and laptop orchestras have their own benefits (discussed later). Consequently, electronic music may be performed by solo musicians or small and large groups. Remember that the interaction between ensemble members adds to the performance experience, and while the sonic outcome may not vary significantly with size, the interaction and control dimensions vary a lot.

Performances can include the operation of electronic instruments, vocals, dancing, and visual display. Data projection of visual material during electronic music performance is particularly common; given that both digital sound and images can emanate from one computer, combining these in performance is not difficult.

The venues for live electronic music are many, but they rarely include the concert hall. More common for electronic music performances are nightclubs or bars, where there is a social and informal atmosphere. Large public events are also common and include rave parties and music festivals at which many different artists perform over several hours, often on several stages. Experimental music presentations are, however, usually designed for listening, not dancing, and use small spaces such as cafes, art galleries, or small theatres. In educational settings, an informal space, like a library study area or even a classroom, may be more conducive to electronic music performance than a large and echoic sports stadium.

Electronic music ensembles come in many forms. In a school setting, they can cover a rich variety of musical styles, but typically focus on electronic dance music, minimalism, and electroacoustic genres. Electronic music ensembles are often used to provide a group music making experience for students who might not otherwise experience ensemble music, such as pianists, composers, and DJs.

Electronic Music Ensembles

Electronic music ensembles have been successfully run in many education settings since (at least) the 1980s. These groups often begin with a small electronic keyboard ensemble or a group of smartphone or tablet computers users (seen in Figure 10.11), and they may include a drum machine, a beatbox, or an MPC (Music Production Controller). These devices can be augmented with various MIDI controllers to further interest students and prompt wider participation. Ensembles may include a sound mixer and one or more visual projectionists. Repertoire can include member-generated compositions, improvised jams, or works written by the ensemble director. Developing repertoire by starting with free improvisations and later refining it into more structured works can be successful too.

FIGURE 10.11 *Concussion*, an iPad ensemble, performing at Griffith University, 2012.

Changing the sound system setup is also interesting, and one way to do this is by introducing multi-speaker performances. Individuals or small groups of players could stand around the space, each with his or her own amplifier, or a person could do a sound diffusion of the ensemble's output over a multi-speaker array as part of the performance.

Laptop Orchestras

Since the mid 2000s, laptop orchestras have served several purposes. They have been a research platform for new computer music systems, a pedagogical method for involving groups of people in electronic and computer music, and a new artistic practice. The *Princeton Laptop Orchestra*, based at Princeton University, is an early example of the laptop orchestra. Affectionately known as PLOrK, it set a trend for other laptop orchestras, many of which similarly abbreviated their names.

A laptop orchestra can have 10 to 20 people, each with their own computing devices. They may be connected to a common sound system, or each player may have his or her own localized amplification. The ensemble *PowerBooks Unplugged* even uses built-in laptop speakers for amplification; their performers sit or stand in the audience for spatialization effects from their laptops during concerts. Computers in a laptop orchestra are often connected via a local network to synchronize timing, to communicate via text chat between ensemble members, and to share code snippets.

Laptop orchestras typically use one of the programming environments mentioned in the section on performance software. This allows members to customize sounds and musical structures in many ways. Laptop orchestras encourage group participation, and, in educational settings, they encourage students to learn the programming language and algorithmic music techniques. The ability to share the work of sound making among performers makes laptop orchestras ideal for beginners and as pedagogical tools.

Mixed Ensembles of Electronic and Acoustic Instruments

Ensembles of electronic and acoustic instruments have a long heritage. They include rock and jazz bands with electronic instruments and rhythm sections, and art ensembles using traditional and experimental instruments. The electronic instrument's versatility in such ensembles usually means there can be many viable configurations. Percussion and electronics is a particularly effective ensemble mix, both timbrally and visually. Examples of percussion and electronic combinations are Speak Percussion's collaborations on the works *City Jungle, Cradles*, and *Transducer*.[43]

Issues to be considered in mixed ensembles include tuning, balance, and sound spatialization. Electronic instruments are always out of tune (or always in tune, depending on your view), because they are usually set to mathematically perfect equal temperament, and not even the acoustic piano sticks to those rules. It may be necessary to set electronic instruments to be stretch tuned—sharper in the higher registers and flatter in the lower registers—so that they are in tune with the acoustic instruments.

When amplified, electronic instruments should be able to balance their volume within any ensemble mix. However, attention is often required to control volume levels, which can vary between sounds and between works and sections of works. Although velocity sensitivity will go a long way to controlling the volume, a musician should control individual volumes by hand slider, foot pedal, or other controller when necessary.

Without careful attention to sound quality and speaker position, amplification may cause mixed ensembles to sound spatially incohesive. Often it is useful for each electronic instrument to have its own small powered speaker next to it on stage. Another alternative is to mike the acoustic instruments, bringing them into the amplified space. Speaker location needs to be considered so that (1) the speakers can be located near the instrument that is producing the amplified sound, or, alternatively, (2) the acoustic and electronic sounds appear to be transmitted from the same (loudspeaker) locations. Reverb is common on modern electronic devices and needs to be used with restraint in a mixed ensemble; in most cases, live performance is best with little or no reverb, so that acoustic and electronic instruments sound in the same space.

Live Coding

Live coding is a creative practice that entails the writing and editing of computer code as an integral part of the performance. Live coding is predominantly a musical practice, but people can also live code graphics, video, or any other digital form. It is typical for live coders to project their screen, so the audience can follow along as the work is created and developed (seen in Figure 10.12).

While live coding is clearly performative, the fact that the code describes musical algorithms (processes) means that it combines elements of composition and performance. Think of live coding as an on-the-fly algorithmic composition. The code is the score for the work, which is written and executed during the performance. Because the score (code) is edited to transform the music and vary the arrangement during performance, the code that remains at the end is not the complete score, but rather the remnants. This material transience of the code-score reflects the improvisational nature of the live coding (typing) practice. For an example, watch Andrew Sorensen's *A Study in Keith* performance, which is a live coding improvisation inspired by Keith Jarrett's jazz piano improvisations.[44] Also, watch Stephen Ramsay's interesting commentary on this work in his presentation to the Critical Code Studies Working Group in 2010.[45]

Live coding activities require a software platform that supports audio output and the dynamic compiling and running of code. Many of the programming environments listed toward the end of the section on performance software (discussed earlier) can be used for live coding. However, these are often noncommercial and have limited documentation, which makes live coding somewhat difficult to access for educational purposes. On the other hand, as a platform for combining technical, compositional, and improvisational skills, live coding provides rich opportunities for students to develop skills in many areas. There are some accessible approaches to this practice—especially using the *Scratch* environment[46]—but, by and large, live coding is considered a virtuosic pursuit and is something for students to be inspired by and to aspire to.

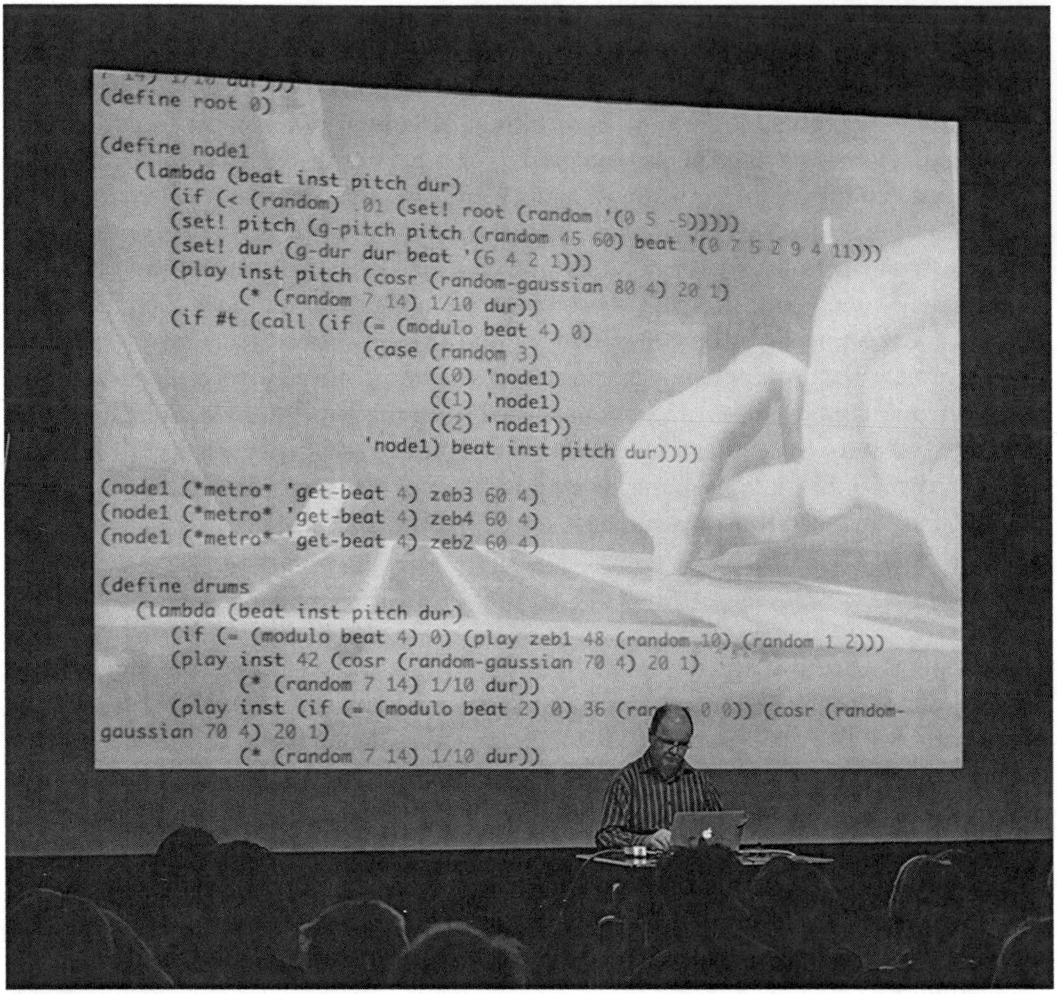

FIGURE 10.12 Andrew R. Brown (the author) performing at the Live Code Festival 2013 in Karlsruhe.[47]

Conclusion

Electronic music and instruments have a heritage going back over 100 years and have developed rapidly over the past half century. As electronic and digital technologies have become smaller and more powerful, the ways they can be incorporated into live performance have multiplied. Musicians in the electroacoustic, rock, pop, and dance music cultures have embraced live electronic music in different ways; and the impact of the Internet, music file sharing, wireless communications, continued miniaturization, and increasing computation power seems to ensure that live electronic music will provide even more surprises and opportunities in the future. Music technologies have enormous potential when treated as instruments, and it is important that educators see them as such, and not simply as tools. Electronic music performance can be an avenue for creative exploration of sound and a vehicle for musical expression. It can be a solo or group activity, and the skills required can range from simple to the extremely virtuosic. Computational devices have the potential to open up a world of live music to students, but they need to learn to play these devices, not just use them.

Reflection Questions

1. What is the definition of electronic music?
2. Which musical elements do electronic musicians focus on?
3. When did electronic music begin?
4. What is turntablism?
5. Who were some of the early pioneers of electronic music?
6. What is 'step sequencing' on drum machines?
7. What is unique about a pad controller?
8. How many members are typically in a laptop orchestra?
9. A 'mixed' ensemble includes electronic instruments and what else?
10. What is live coding?

Teaching Tips

1. Have students build a theremin from a kit and perform with it.
2. Show an old silent film to encourage small group improvisations with electronic sounds.
3. In the spirit of pioneering electronic music artists such as Wendy Carlos and [Isao] Tomita, have students perform electronic versions of classical repertoire.
4. Hold a DJ festival for interested students.
5. Purchase a variety of different performance apps and create a small electronic music ensemble with mobile computing devices.
6. Use drum machines with step sequencers to introduce concepts of meter and rhythm to students.
7. Revisit the pedagogical practices of Carl Orff using simple apps on touch screen tablets instead of xylophones.
8. Create an electroacoustic ensemble (using a mixture of acoustic and electronic instruments) and have students arrange music for it.
9. Create electronic music workstations with a small mixer and speakers to encourage electronic music ensembles.
10. Locate electronic toys that make sounds and use them as the basis for an electronic composition or toy orchestra project.

Suggested Tasks for Educators

1. Explore some of the latest electronic performance equipment at a local music store.
2. With a turntable or turntable app, experience how difficult it can be to perform accurate rhythmic scratching and beat matching.

3. Listen to recordings from electronic music history to familiarize yourself with the repertoire.
4. Watch a film with an electronic music soundtrack, such as *Blade Runner*, paying particular attention to the score.
5. Create drum patterns on an app such as *ReBirth* that emulate a classic 16-step drum sequencer.

Chapter Summary

Live electronic music performance has a long history of innovation in western music. A variety of electronic music practices have emerged over time, including musique concrète, acousmatic music, electronic music, electroacoustic music, and electronic dance music. Electronic music seems to be increasingly popular, especially in dance music settings. A range of electronic and digital music technologies can be used for live performance, including tape recorders, laptop computers, turntables, drum machines, signal processors, smartphones, tablet computers, and even electronic toys. Live electronic music can be presented in formal and informal settings, and large and small venues. It can involve minimal or expansive human activity, and can be an interesting avenue for combinations of music and a range of other art forms and media. The educational potential of live electronic music stems from its cachet within youth culture, its accessibility through easy control and improvisation, and its ability to bridge popular and high-art musical ideas and conventions. Electronic and digital technologies are the most recent class of musical instruments, and they are still finding their place in music education despite their widespread use in contemporary culture. The performance possibilities for solo and ensemble settings is ever changing, and this chapter outlines many of the practices that can be taken up in educational contexts. There is great potential for live electronic and digital music making technologies in the classroom and on the stage. This chapter introduces the knowledge and ideas necessary to turn this potential into reality.

Notes

1. *Doepfer Dark Energy II*, analog modular synthesizer: www.doepfer.de/Dark_Energy_II_e. htm.
2. Photo by Paris Buttfield-Addison taken at CreateWorld 2014.
3. Reviews of some popular CD turntables can be found on the DJ Booth web site: www. djbooth.net/index/dj-equipment/reviews/C10.
4. *VirtualDJ*, DJ software and hardware: www.virtualdj.com/.
5. *djay*, virtual turntable software for OS X or iOS: www.algoriddim.com/.
6. *Nave*, a wavetable synthesizer by Waldorf for the iPad: www.waldorf-music.info/nave-overview.
7. Roland AIRA series of analog modeling synthesizers and drum machines: www.roland. co.uk/aira.
8. *Tempest*, a modern drum machine that extends an old tradition: www.davesmithinstruments.com/products/tempest/.

9. *DM1*, a virtual drum machine by Fingerlab: www.fingerlab.net/website/Fingerlab/DM1. html.

10. *ReBirth* virtual drum and bass machine software from Propellerhead: www.rebirthapp. com/.

11. *Drum Machine* app for Android by Bruce Trajkovski: http://trajkovski.net/.

12. Adney, R. (2011). *The HarmonyGrid: Music, space and performance in Grid Music Systems*. Doctoral thesis, Music and Sound Discipline, Creative Industries Faculty, Queensland University of Technology, http://eprints.qut.edu.au/46602/1/Roland_Adeney_Thesis.pdf.

13. Roland Octapad was an eight-pad percussion MIDI controller designed to be played with drumsticks: http://en.wikipedia.org/wiki/Roland_Octapad.

14. Monome, an early grid controller interface: http://monome.org/.

15. Tenori-on, a grid based sequencer designed by Toshio Iwai and manufactured by Yamaha: http://en.wikipedia.org/wiki/Tenori-on.

16. Launchpad controller from Novation is a popular and inexpensive device: http://us.novationmusic. com/midi-controllers-digital-dj/launchpad.

17. QuNeo pad controller from Keith McMillen Instruments provides expressive and flexible controllers: www.keithmcmillen.com/QuNeo/.

18. Push from Ableton brings the matrix interface of the company's Live software into the hardware domain: www.ableton.com/en/push/.

19. *Orphion*, instrument app for iOS: https://itunes.apple.com/au/app/orphion/id495465097?mt = 8. A video demo is here: www.orphion.de.

20. *Gestrument*, gesture instrument app controller for iOS: https://itunes.apple.com/se/app/ gestrument/id576235482?mt=8.

21. *Gestrument* app web site: www.gestrument.com.

22. Smule have a range of apps to turn a mobile computing device into a musical instrument: www.smule.com/apps.

23. *MaKey MaKey* kit and information: www.makeymakey.com/.

24. *Arduino*, small and inexpensive computer system: http://arduino.cc/.

25. *MusicInk* project description and video on the Arduino blog: http://blog.arduino. cc/2013/04/23/musicink-learn-the-music-play/.

26. *Raspberry Pi*, computer: www.raspberrypi.org/.

27. *Sonic Pi*, information available about this project at these sites—www.cl.cam.ac.uk/projects/ raspberrypi/sonicpi/index.html and www.raspberrypi.org/archives/4906.

28. *Synapse*, software for the Xbox Kinect: http://synapsekinect.tumblr.com/.

29. Connect the Kinect to the *Gestrument* software using software linked to here: www.gestrument.com/more_info/.

30. Leap Motion controller: www.leapmotion.com/.

31. Reactable: www.reactable.com/.

32. *TouchOSC*, software from Hexler: http://hexler.net/software/touchosc.

33. *AudioMulch*: www.audiomulch.com.

34. *Scratch*: http://scratch.mit.edu.

35. *Pd (Pure Data)*: http://puredata.info.

36. *Max*: http://cycling74.com/products/max/.

37. Music Python has a textbook co-written by this author: www.crcpress.com/product/ isbn/9781439867914.

38. Processing is mainly oriented toward visuals, but includes a built-in audio library called minim and an extension developed by this author called *SoundCipher*: http://processing.org.

39. *SuperCollider*: http://supercollider.sourceforge.net.

40. *Extempore*: http://extempore.moso.com.au.

41 *Overtone*: http://overtone.github.io.

42. *ChucK*: http://chuck.cs.princeton.edu.
43. Speak Percussion performances with electronics—City Jungle http://youtu.be/-wGv64TYD-I —Cradles http://youtu.be/gRyUS4PkN5M —Transducer http://youtu.be/74q3ZP2x6-E.
44. *A Study in Keith* live coding performance by Andrew Sorensen: http://vimeo.com/2433947.
45. "Algorithms are Thoughts, Chainsaws are Tools." Stephen Ramsay: http://vimeo.com/9790850.
46. Live coding in *Scratch*, Eric Rosenbaum—http://youtu.be/rDyo4p1qLuE, Alex Ruthmann—http://youtu.be/nEkzaL80M6Y.
47. Photo by Daniel Bollinger taken at Live Code Festival 2013: http://imwi.hfm.eu/livecode/2013/.

eleven
Machine Accompaniment

Machine accompaniment involves the use of interactive systems that play along with human performers. Systems such as *SmartMusic*[1] have resonated with instrumental and vocal instructors and have provided an increasingly robust method of assisting student practice. Interactive music systems have also been used to develop new human-machine performance practices, especially in improvisational and new music contexts. The influence of digital systems on music extends to networked performances, where people and machines are linked via local and intent networks for collaborative interactions. This chapter will provide an overview of these systems and the ways in which they can be used to enhance music instruction.

Interactive performance with computing systems can be a useful learning experience and can scaffold a learner's performance. Auto-accompaniment and interactive music systems are based on machine listening and performance technologies designed for the specific purpose of accompanying or partnering human performance. Software such as *SmartMusic* from MakerMusic and *Essential Elements Interactive*[2] from Hal Leonard provide prepared accompaniments to follow the student soloist. Although the auto-accompaniment software systems let students take the lead, playing along with them still requires musical sensitivity and allows students to hear how their part fits into the overall ensemble. The analytical and reflective activity this promotes can improve the learner's understanding of ensemble playing and help him or her appreciate the complexity of musical interactions. Even greater freedom of interaction and control are provided by improvisational interactive music systems.

These are often based on bespoke software that is not publicly available, such as *Voyager*[3] by George Lewis or the author's own *CIM*[4] software. But, as will be discussed later, there are off-the-shelf options for exploring interactive music performance, many of which are inexpensive apps for mobile devices.

Non-interactive musical accompaniments can also be created by software such as *Band-in-a-Box*[5] from PG Music. There are, of course, many prerecorded play-along tracks that are either commercially available or created by the teacher. This chapter will focus on interactive systems and will make little further reference to these non-interactive alternatives.

As well as being vehicles for supporting performance, interactive music systems can open up opportunities for composition. In fact it is quite common these days for live electronic music performances to be improvisational and for digital devices to play a somewhat active role in them through algorithmic processes. The algorithmic nature of interactive systems requires musicians to have skills of composition, sound design, and software development if these systems are developed from scratch. Software environments such as *Pd*[6] and *Max*[7] can provide scaffolding for these activities. However, for most student musicians, their entrée into human-machine music interaction is via commercial auto-accompaniment systems that play along with them while they are performing known repertoire.

Auto-accompaniment Software

Auto-accompaniment systems put the user in a position of control—not unlike that of a conductor or soloist—where the performer dictates the music's tempo and phrasing, while additional parts are played by the software. These systems provide opportunities for the less skilled musician to experience control of some of the expressive characteristics of highly complex music. They can provide a rewarding experience where students hear their performance in context and as part of a more complex musical whole. Such experiences can help musicians develop a sense of autonomy, self-confidence, and musicality.

Commercial auto-accompaniment systems include *SmartMusic, Essential Elements Interactive,* and *Home Concert Xtreme.* They all provide core auto accompaniment features but vary in repertoire availability and extensibility. *SmartMusic,* currently the major player in this market, has an extensive and exclusive music library, while *Essential Elements Interactive* provides support for Hal Leonard's method books, and *Home Concert Xtreme* allows performances with any material in MIDI file format. These systems, to varying degrees, have become platforms that supplement their accompaniment capabilities with additional features that act as rehearsal tools or music tutors. The larger systems also function as learning management systems by supporting the storage of performance data and communication between stakeholders. Increasingly, these systems provide apps for many different devices (as shown in Figure 11.1) allowing for their use at school, in the teaching studio, and at home.

Auto-accompaniment software allows the musician to play along with music displayed on screen. Typically the user can adjust the tempo to allow for practice at slower speeds or for playing technical exercises at various tempi. Music can be transposed to support a variety of instruments or for practicing pieces or exercises in any key. Using its knowledge of the music to be played, the auto-accompaniment software keeps track of the musician's performance via microphone input and plays an accompanying part (or parts), in time, using virtual instruments. The system can match the performer's tempo and dynamic expression and, because the software can follow the music, it also manages automatic page turning or score scrolling.

The software can track performance in several different ways. It might play the accompaniment in short sections and wait for performers to play notes before continuing. It

FIGURE 11.1 *SmartMusic* play-along view on the iPad.

might track the performers' tempo and play along, adjusting its own tempo as required, ensuring that the performance is continuous. In this mode the software can also track the musician's progress through the piece and jump to a new location if the performer skips around the score. Also, the software might play the accompaniment at a fixed tempo without listening to performers, expecting them to keep up.

Auto-accompaniment software can achieve this performer tracking because it 'knows' the music that is to be played. It can compare what it hears with the score to make an assessment about pace and location. It is therefore critical that repertoire is available in a format that suits the system. Most systems use a proprietary file format where files are sold separately or included in a subscription package. Alternatively, scores might be available as part of a printed (or electronic) music book, purchased with the software. In many cases the style of accompaniment can be varied for added interest.

As well as for performing musical pieces, auto-accompaniment systems are useful for technical practice, aural recognition, or sight-reading exercises. Before selecting an auto-accompaniment system, it is important to check the available repertoire. Often the library of provided material can be supplemented with user-created material. The *SmartMusic* system does this via export from *Finale*, the company's music publishing software, and *Home Concert Xtreme* imports MIDI files, created in appropriate digital audio workstation (DAW) software or downloaded from many online sources.

These systems usually record performances so they can be played back for reflection and review, archived, or shared. If this facility is not built into the software, then it is a simple matter for students to use digital devices to make their own recordings, which can then be viewed, stored, or shared. As well as capturing data, some auto-accompaniment systems can save scores, recordings and usage data in a portfolio, stored in the cloud. This is a useful method for sharing data between students, teachers, and parents and for documenting student development.

Because the software is actively tracking human performance it can provide relevant feedback. Typically, it does this by showing correct and incorrect pitches and rhythms on the digital score. The software might also assess other performance features, including consistency of tempo, dynamic variability, and intonation.

Machine Listening and Response

A computer music system used for interactive performance needs to listen and to perform. In order to listen, the computer receives input from human performer(s), usually in the form of MIDI data or an audio signal. One of the important aspects of machine listening is the decision about which aspects of the performance to monitor. MIDI signals send gestural information about notes pressed—including pitch, volume, and timing—as well as the movement of continuous controllers such as sliders and dials, and of switches such as foot pedals, triggers, or drum pads. Using MIDI input, the software directly monitors performance gestures. Input can also be from an audio source, typically a microphone. Audio signals provide direct access to the sound; abstract information, about pitch and timing, for example, is obtained by analyzing those signals, in a process that is similar to the human process of 'perception' or 'understanding.' As the computer monitors the performance it might need to infer performance parameters—a potential source of error. Where knowledge of pitch and rhythm is not critical, the computer will respond directly to the signal's other features, such as volume or frequency spectrum.

Interactive music software might listen for events that trigger a response, such as playing a particular pitch, or it might look for patterns in the data, such as a specific phrase or an increase in the average volume of a performance. The computer might respond by playing an answering theme or harmonization, or make a corresponding change in its own volume level or an increase in textural density.

A prominent researcher into interactive music systems, Robert Rowe, defines three methods by which a computer responds to data from a performer: with music that is sequenced, transformative, or generative.[8] Sequenced musical responses are preset or prerecorded and do not change from one performance to the next. They are useful where each music performance is similar or where a more predictable response is necessary, such as in auto-accompaniment software. Prepared sequenced responses can be of any length and complexity.

A transformative response utilizes the human input (or an analysis of it) to form the response. A simple example would be the playing back of a performed phrase that has been transposed or elongated. Transformative responses are quite common and musically satisfying, because imitation and repetition form the basis of much compositional music and improvisation. Interactive music systems that employ this technique extensively include *The Continuator* by François Pachet and *CIM* by this author and his colleagues[9] (an interface for CIM is shown in Figure 11.2). The use of a transformative approach for

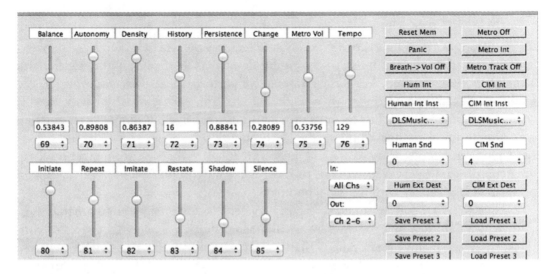

FIGURE 11.2 The interface for version 3 of the *CIM* software.

stimulating musical creativity in young people is well documented in Pachet's research.[10] Such responses also give the listener the impression of a dialogue between musician and computer. Even if this dialogue is quite superficial, comparable to the ELIZA computer conversation program from the 1960s,[11] it can be surprisingly interesting.

Generating transformations of data relies on compositional devices that have been used in many musical genres, such as reversal, repetition, and counterpoint. Computational techniques for musical transformations, including Markov processes[12] and genetic algorithms,[13] are also widely used. Methods of transforming the data can be classified into several categories: (1) constraining, which includes processes such as filtering, limiting, thinning, quantizing, and compressing; (2) transforming, which includes delaying, transposing, scaling, reversing, and gating; and (3) extending, which includes repeating, elaborating, harmonizing, or evolving. Interactive performance systems allow these musical and mathematical ideas to be explored in an active way.

Interactive music software might generate a response composed by the computer. Generated responses are variable to some degree but constrained to produce a similar outcome each time. The computer might, for example, generate a pulsed percussive performance based on a probabilistic selection of rhythms and sounds. The automatic drummer plug-ins in many DAWs use this kind of process. Generative methods can be based on mathematical formulae, such as fractal theory, or on rules from serial techniques or evolutionary variation. Music can also be generated by structuring fragments (cells or motives), which are either stored prior to performance, taken from the performance data, or generated from basic principles. These fragments might also be transformed in various ways, including those mentioned above. A generated response will often take into account the input data—a good example is the *GenJam* system created by Al Biles[14]—or it might simply produce material, within constraints, that provides a stimulus for a live performer to work with.

Most practical interactive performance systems will utilize a combination of sequenced, transformative, and generative responses to suit the predictability and aesthetic preferences of the musician.

Human Input

Playing along with an interactive music system requires the use of an interface between performer and computer. Input to the digital device can be from an audio signal via a microphone or pickup. For simple interactive performances with audio input, the audio signal can be passed directly to digital effects processors, which provide delays, reverb, and other effects. Effects units provide an inexpensive but immediately exciting way of entering the world of interactive performance. For many years, electric guitarists have used simple delay or looping pedals to enhance their performance. Building up a complex musical layer with one or more delay units is an effective way to extend performance practices with music technology.

A pitch to MIDI converter can be used to convert the audio signal into a MIDI message, which can then be processed by a MIDI-based music package. Examples of converter hardware include the Sonuus G2M[15] and B2M. However, pitch to MIDI converters can be unreliable at times and work better with some instruments than others. An alternative is to choose from a range of dedicated MIDI controllers (see Chapter 10). They are designed specifically to interface with computer systems and their designs are often based on acoustic instruments—in the form of synthesizer keyboards, wind controllers, such as those from Yamaha and AKAI, violins from Cantini,[16] or percussion controllers, ranging from the MalletKat MIDI Xylophone[17] to various electronic drum pads. Less conventional controllers include various Data Glove devices, such as the Inition X-IST Data Glove,[18] video-based motion tracking systems, like the Xbox Kinect with *Synapse* software,[19] and infrared controllers, like the *D-Beam* used on some Roland products.

Performance Partnerships

When interacting with smart software, the computer can become a collaborator or assistant during a live performance. As in any other musical partnership, it takes time to learn how to work with an interactive music system and how to control the musical outcome successfully. In such a partnership, the interactive musician can explore various degrees of control over the algorithmic nature of the software. The system's behavior might range from order to chaos and from prepared playback to random interjection. The musical challenge lies in finding a space between order and disorder where there is predictability yet challenge, and a degree of organization that provides coherence yet maintains interest. In the end, what is aesthetically pleasing will vary from person to person, from piece to piece, between styles, and over time.

Interactive performance involves a balance of responsibility and control. A system's creator must decide which aspects of the music will be controllable by the performer(s) and which by the computer. The system must also have constraints within which the interactive performance takes place. All technologies have built-in constraints; for example, the set pitch limitations of the piano and the polyphony limitations of the flute. Digital devices have limitations of speed and processing power: limitations on polyphony, timbral complexity, and speed of interactive response. In addition, computing devices are programmable and therefore provide greater variety in the way they can respond to performance. So, while the division of labor between acoustic instrument and players is relatively fixed, that between the performer and the interactive music system might vary considerably. As a result, exploring the musical opportunities of a performance partnership between human being and machine can be very rewarding.

Interactive Music Systems

The term *interactive music* might seem like a statement of the obvious, of course music is interactive. So what is meant by interactive music with digital technologies? Interactive music systems rely on a computer reacting like a human collaborator, in real time. In performances using interactive music systems, the computer acts as a semi-autonomous entity carrying out a series of operations that might be as simple as a trigger or as complex as an automatic adaptation to a performer's actions. Performances with interactive music systems occupy the space between a one-to-one direct physical relationship, typical of acoustic performance, and the playing along with preset accompaniment, Karaoke-style. Often these performances include elements of improvisation, from both human being and machine. This form of interactive improvisation with algorithmic systems is considered by Roger Dean to be one of the most fascinating possibilities of human-computer interaction, permitting a musical practice he describes as "hyperimprovisation."[20]

There are numerous interactive music systems, usually designed for use in particular compositions or a small set of works. Their creators tend to be researchers from the computer music community and include Laurie Spiegel, Joel Chadabe, Max Mathews, Roger Dannenberg, Barry Vercoe, Robert Rowe, Todd Winkler, Richard Teitelbaum, Jean-Claude Risset, Todd Machover, David Wessel, George Lewis, and Cort Lippe.

Other forms of interactive performance might use multiple technologies involving audio, video, and lighting—as employed by Laurie Anderson, for example; they might be as simple as the use of a digital delay device and sample triggering, as in the performances of Linsey Pollak.

Music produced by interactive music systems is as diverse as the musicians who create it. It can be complex and challenging or simple and accessible. Whatever the case, many musicians are attracted by the combination of performance excitement, compositional control, and technological intrigue.

While building an interactive music system is an interesting challenge, it is likely to be beyond the scope of many school music programs. Therefore, a good place to start exploring this field is with software-based interactive music environments. A variety of more experimental interactions are possible with products such as *Spongefork*[21] and *Musolomo*,[22] which allow the user to synthesize and manipulate sounds using the computer keyboard and mouse as controllers.

The advent of touch devices—including smartphones and tablets—has facilitated an explosion of interactive music apps. Rather than requiring traditional music performance as input, they need only simple touch gestures to trigger and control musical processes, which makes them accessible and fun. Despite being simple to use, they demonstrate the balance between human and machine agency in generating a musical outcome that is typical of interactive music systems. Below is a list of iPad apps that provide accessible interactive music experiences.

- *PatternMusic*—builds and controls looped sequences.
- *RjDj*—manipulates prepared musical 'worlds'.
- *SYnC SYnTHE*—creates loops and tones with a node-like interface (see Figure 11.3).

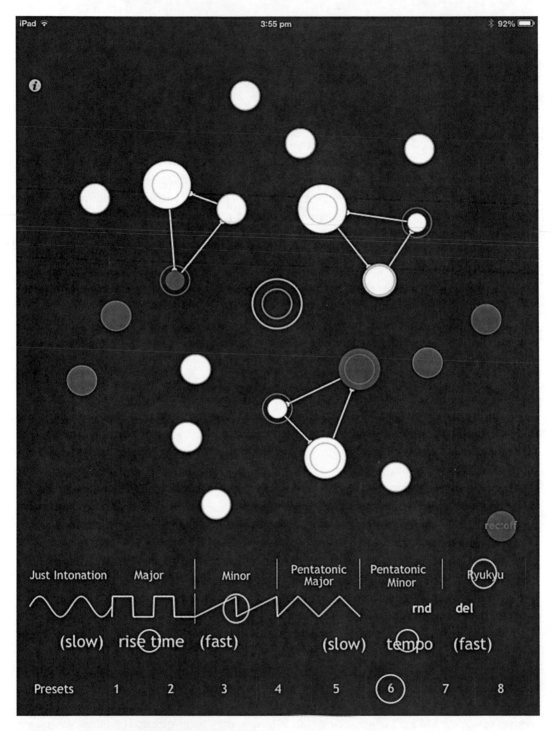

FIGURE 11.3 The *SYnC SYnTHE* app on iPad.

- *Sounddrop*—creates obstacles for 'balls' to bounce around triggering sounds in a physics world.
- *Otomata*—controls the number and behavior of simple 'robots' that sound on collision with the environment and each other.
- *eDrops*—manipulates ambient musical layers and continuously falling sound objects.

Dedicated interactive composing software systems, such as *M* by Cycling '74[23] (shown in Figure 11.4) and *Nodal*[24] by CEMA Research, provide easy-to-use visual interfaces that can be used in performance to create interactive music that develops and evolves. The *M* software allows the user to construct loop-based sequences from MIDI input that can be transformed and played back via a MIDI synthesizer.

Other interface controls enable parameters or sections to be changed in real-time. A 'conductor' area of *M* can be used to control two variables at once as the mouse is dragged across the conductor grid. More sophisticated environments, which allow the user to graphically build interactive performance systems include *AudioMulch*,[25] *Symbolic Composer*,[26] *Pd*, and *Max*. There are several computer music languages, such as *Supercollider*[27] and *Extempore*,[28] that combine the power of general-purpose programming languages with libraries of music-related functions. These can be used to program sophisticated interactive music systems. These are not for the technologically faint of heart.

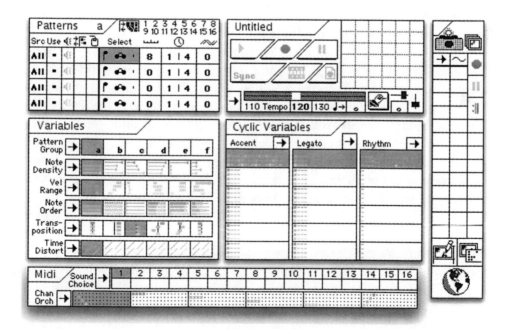

FIGURE 11.4 The interface for *M*, an interactive MIDI-based software application.

Networked Performance

As the speed and reliability of computer networks have increased, so have interactive music performances between local machines and across the Internet. The Internet is becoming another venue for performance or collaboration. Despite formidable technical challenges there were many pioneering achievements in networked music making in the twentieth century. In the mid- to late 1970s *The League of Automated Music Composers*—a group formed in California—performed works created on computers connected over a network, each influencing the others' musical output. In the early 1990s, some members of this group formed *The Hub* and continued this work with more reliable MIDI-based networks. Another pioneering Internet-based interactive music project is William Duckworth's *Cathedral* (1997),[29] which includes a variety of interactive activities from webcasts to music games.

Networked improvisation is an interactive music activity where people jam over a network connection. The connection might be local, between two computers in one room; or global, via an Internet connection to another geographic location. Software such as the author's *jam2jam*[30] simplifies network improvisation by using generative musical processes to assist in making the music. Adjusting parameters on *jam2jam* controls the generative music processes, and these meta-level control changes are sent over the network to keep the various jamming nodes coordinated. More sophisticated systems enable interactive performance over the Internet by streaming MIDI or audio data between locations. These systems can be awkward to coordinate and synchronize because of latency introduced by the variability and delays in data transfer over the Internet. There are a number of local network synchronization and audio streaming protocols for mobile devices that allow for networked performances on these devices. Protocols for iOS including *Wireless Sync-Start Technology* (WIST) developed by Korg,[31] *Open Sound Control* (OSC),[32] and Apple's *Airplay*, communicate over Bluetooth. Apps that use these protocols to allow easy networking on several local devices are Korg's *iKaosillator*, Akai's *iMPC*, and Apple's *GarageBand* for the iPad.

Another approach to networked performance is to set up audio streams between remote sites so that musicians can hear each other and play as if they were in the same location. The technical concept, that is, customizing an Internet connection for low-latency operation, can be difficult, and delays between sites are almost inevitable. Nevertheless, the approach has resulted in many successful performances. A good example is the video of the telematic performance in 2011 of *Deep Tones for Peace* by Mark Dresser and colleagues.[33] Networked performances have been conducted using a range of technologies, from simple video conferencing to specialized software like *JackTrip*.[34] A few commercial systems, such as *eJamming*[35] or *Online Jam Sessions*,[36] provide end-to-end solutions for network performances suitable for educational environments.

Conclusion

Machine accompaniment can be used to support traditional instrumental learning and exploratory musical practices. Auto-accompaniment software can greatly assist performance students with their practice and learning of repertoire. By providing backing music that keeps pace with the student performance, these systems provide a stimulating interactive environment for learning an instrument. Interactive music systems take similar technologies and transform them into new modes of performance collaboration between human beings and machines. Computer networks can be used to mediate human–human and human–machine performances, as either local or remote networked performances. At present, most commercial interactive systems are focused on adaptive accompaniment for instrumentalists following known repertoire, while systems that aim for a stronger sense of partnership and improvisational interaction between performers and digital devices are somewhat experimental. For use in schools, there are accessible interactive music software apps, particularly those developed for mobile devices with touch screens, such as smartphones and tablet computers. Networked jamming can be managed between remote sites using online services such as *eJamming*.

Reflection Questions

1. How does machine accompaniment differ from a play-along audio track?
2. In what ways can auto-accompaniment systems scaffold learners' actions?
3. What does the *SmartMusic* software do?
4. Why is an interactive music system performance seen as a musical collaboration between musician and machine?
5. What musical features does machine listening software 'listen' for?
6. Describe the differences between sequenced, transformative, or generative music.
7. Name three interactive music apps for the iPad.
8. What does a pitch to MIDI converter do and why might you need one?
9. What is the difference between the *jam2jam* and *M* software applications?
10. What is meant by the term 'network improvisation'?

Teaching Tips

1. Have instrumental students use an auto-accompaniment software system for scales and other technical exercises, as well as for repertoire practice.
2. Create customized pieces and accompaniment for your auto-accompaniment software of choice.
3. Have students keep a portfolio of their practice sessions with an auto-accompaniment system, as a way of monitoring their progress when learning a new piece.
4. Have students begin interactive activities with apps for their mobile devices.
5. Use an algorithmic computer music application, like *Band-in-a-Box*, to provide a backing track for student performances.
6. Have students listen to the musical responses of an interactive music system to stimulate a discussion on the bounds and conventions of musical styles.
7. Set a research assignment for students to locate, investigate, and critique an interactive or network music performance.
8. Challenge senior students to explore an environment used by professional interactive musicians, such as *AudioMulch* or *Max*.

9. Have students experiment with remote performances using a video chat service such as Skype or Google Hangouts.
10. Make links with another institution and engage in a network performance over the Internet using *eJamming*.

Suggested Tasks for Educators

1. Ask for a demo of an auto-accompaniment system; you might be surprised how well the systems follow a live performance.
2. Test the limits of an auto-accompaniment system by dramatically varying tempo and skipping about the score.
3. Look up, and listen to, the interactive works of those people from the computer music community named in this chapter.
4. Download and watch the videos of *The Continuator* application being used by young children to see the excitement that interactive music can bring.
5. Use the free trial period of the *eJamming* service to experiment with networked performances.

Chapter Summary

As digital machines get 'smarter' they move beyond functioning as a tool or instrument and take on roles as accompanists and musical collaborators. Auto-accompaniment software such as *SmartMusic* is the most obvious application of these technologies in music education. This type of software can support beginner instrumentalists as they learn repertoire and practice technical tasks—adapting its accompaniment by listening to the soloist and offering critique based on what it 'hears'. Interactive music systems build on the same technologies to create semi-autonomous musical collaborators. These systems go beyond playback of repertoire to generate algorithmic music that responds to input from a human performer in real time. Interaction with a computer music system can be via a microphone that picks up acoustic sounds, by sending data from a MIDI controller, or by using a mouse or finger to control a graphical interface. Interactive music can be as simple as a person controlling an algorithmic music process, or it can be as complex as a system that, in real time, analyzes a human performance and generates appropriate music in response. Networked performances extend the concept of human–human and human–machine musical partnerships by synchronizing performances over the Internet. While interactive and networked music systems can be very complex, some easy-to-use options are available, including *M* and *eJamming* for computers and a range of apps for iOS and Android mobile devices. Because interaction is a key ingredient in music making, it makes sense that interacting with a responsive computer music system provides a rich area for investigations into new musical experiences.

Notes

1. *SmartMusic*, auto accompaniment software: www.smartmusic.com/.
2. *Essential Elements Interactive*, play-along software from Hal Leonard: www.essentialelementsinteractive.com/.

3. Information on the *Voyager* software and recordings of some performances with it at http://modisti.com/news/?p = 19310.

4. Examples of performances with the *CIM* software: www.youtube.com/cimsresearch.

5. *Band-in-a-Box*, software for generating musical backing tracks from chord progressions, includes popular and jazz styles: www.pgmusic.com/.

6. *Pd (Pure Data)*, a visual programming environment with many music-specific building blocks: http://puredata.info/.

7. *Max*, a visual programming language with good support for music, sound, visual media, and interaction: http://cycling74.com/products/max/.

8. Rowe, R. (1993). *Interactive music systems: Machine listening and composing*. Cambridge, MA: MIT Press.

9. Brown, A. R., Gifford, T., & Voltz, B. (2013). Controlling Interactive Music Performance (CIM). In M. L. Maher, T. Veale, R. Saunders, & O. Bown (Eds.), *Proceedings of the fourth international conference on computational creativity* (p. 221). Sydney: Association for Computational Creativity.

10. Pachet, François. (2002). *The continuator: Musical interaction with style*. Paper presented at the International Computer Music Conference, Göteborg, Sweden.

11. Details of the ELIZA natural language processing program can be found here: http://en.wikipedia.org/wiki/ELIZA.

12. Markov process: http://en.wikipedia.org/wiki/Markov_process.

13. Genetic algorithm: http://en.wikipedia.org/wiki/Genetic_algorithm.

14. Biles, J. A. (1994). *GenJam: A genetic algorithm for generating jazz solos*. Paper presented at the International Computer Music Conference, San Francisco: ICMA.

15. Sonuus G2M, guitar to MIDI converter: www.sonuus.com/products_g2m_app.html.

16. Cantini, MIDI violin, www.cantinielectricviolins.com/2/.

17. MalletKat, MIDI xylophone, www.alternatemode.com/malletkat.shtml.

18. Inition, X-IST Data Glove, http://inition.co.uk/3D-Technologies/x-ist-data-glove.

19. *Synapse*, software for the Xbox Kinect, http://synapsekinect.tumblr.com/.

20. Dean, R. (2003). *Hyperimprovisation: Computer-interactive sound improvisation*. Middleton: A-R Editions, p. xxiii.

21. *Spongefork*, interactive music software for Mac OS: http://spongefork.com/.

22. *Musolomo*, interactive music software for Mac OS: http://plasq.com/products/musolomo.

23. *M*, by Cycling 74: http://cycling74.com/products/m/.

24. *Nodal* software: www.csse.monash.edu.au/~cema/nodal/.

25. *AudioMulch*: www.audiomulch.com.

26. *Symbolic Composer*: www.symboliccomposer.com/.

27. *Supercollider*: http://supercollider.sourceforge.net/.

28. *Extempore*: http://extempore.moso.com.au/.

29. *Cathedral*, web-based interactive work by Bill Duckworth: http://cathedral.monroestreet.com/index.php.

30. *jam2jam*, collaborative audio visual performance software: http://jam2jam.com.

31. WIST, information and applications: www.korguser.net/wist/.

32. *Open Sound Control*, information and specifications: http://opensoundcontrol.org/.

33. *Deep Tones for Peace*, networked performance; video of the making and performance: http://youtu.be/KlRo-EmM_j4.

34. *JackTrip*: https://ccrma.stanford.edu/groups/soundwire/software/jacktrip/.

35. *eJamming*, interactive networked audio for remote performance: http://ejamming.com/.

36. *Online Jam Sessions*, interactive networked audio for remote performance: http://onlinejamsessions.com/

section IV
Reflection

twelve

The Internet, Music Scholarship, and Commentary

Investigation of and reflection on musical history and practice is a vital part of a complete music education. Music scholarship includes musicology, which has a history of being very document-centric, and also embraces practice-based reflective activities.[1] Using the Internet, music scholarship and critique can encompass even more. This chapter explores the Internet's role in revitalizing these activities in a contemporary context. There are many research sources, including books, journals, people, and places, that can be used for music research. There are many online forums, blogs, and social media communities for discussing and commenting on music. This chapter focuses on the sources and practices the Internet has made possible.

Music education discussions often focus on musical praxis, experience, expression, and aesthetic awareness, which generally involve personal or interpersonal skills. However, contextual understanding remains important for complete musicianship, and music research plays an important part in expanding a musician's contextual awareness. If there was any hesitation in admitting the importance of music research in school and college music programs, the Internet provides resources that proves that this hesitation was unfounded.

Scholarship in the Music Curriculum

In the Internet age, the old method of investigation—long hours spent poring over dusty old books or music manuscripts in order to find some obscure fact—has been replaced by the new method of searching online sites full of colorful graphics, sound bites, and video segments. In fact, surfing the Internet is more like watching television with a remote control in one hand than like tedious academic work. In addition to web surfing, Internet research can also include investigation via email and social media dialogue. It may even involve the game-like intrigue of seeking out a vital source or fact. Ultimately, it can bring together a student's intellect, performance skills, sense of narrative structure, and visualization abilities toward the creation of a media-rich project. "Writing about music is like dancing about architecture"[2]—which is why using multiple media in music research and reporting is so valuable for a student's education.

Investigation and critique should be proudly added to production and presentation as cornerstones of music education. To that end, this chapter explores the opportunities and pitfalls of music scholarship and communication on the Internet. Included are some technological and methodological concerns, considerations of censorship and copyright,[3] and possibilities for student-created digital media documents as reports.

Scholarship Opportunities on the Internet

The sources of online information are steadily increasing, and many materials are now only available online. Among these are many reputable online music sources, including traditional references such as the *Encyclopedia Britannica* and *Grove Music*, which require a subscription to use. But the Internet opens up many new information sources. Educational institutions that make materials developed for their own students available online provide useful resources, as do music companies sharing information about their wares, various professional and amateur associations, academic journals, community resources such as *Wikipedia* (as seen in Figure 12.1), and sites created by music enthusiasts.

Searching Online

The major tools for Internet research are search engines, including Google, Bing, Yahoo, and Yandex. Using these in an effective manner requires one to select appropriate keywords that clearly identify the topic without being too broad. Querying techniques such as the use of AND, OR, site: and "quoting phrases" can greatly improve the accuracy of search results. Specialized searches such as *Google Scholar*,[4] which indexes academic articles, or *Google Books*[5] can limit the types of documents to those more relevant to music research. The digital archive *Wayback Machine*[6] indexes sites that may no longer be online and can be useful for finding information on musical styles or ensembles no

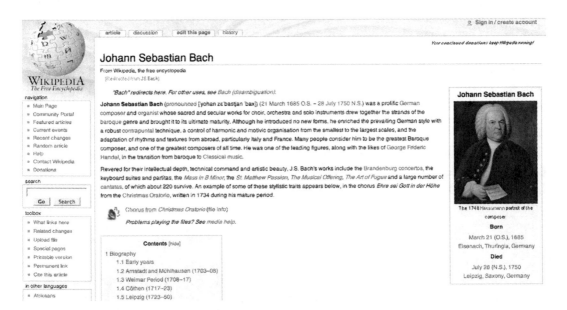

FIGURE 12.1 A portion of the *Wikipedia* entry on J. S. Bach.

longer active. Finally, *Creative Commons Search*[7] provides access to materials preauthorized for reuse, including audio, images, video, and text.

Most academic journals have online catalogues. The catalogues display the title and abstract of academic articles, and many have full document downloads available (often requiring a subscription). Many academics provide prepress versions of articles on their institutions' web sites; search for these if you already know the title of an article.

Internet Surfing Tips

As with most technologies, the Internet's strength is also its major flaw: it contains *a lot* of information. It can be frustrating to sift through the classifieds for secondhand Bach-brand trumpets when searching for facts about J.S. Bach's compositions for trumpet. Searching can also be time consuming, not only because of inefficient search techniques, but as a result of slow Internet access speeds and the resultant long waits for requested information. Below are some tips to make Internet searching more productive.

- Tip 1: Do some background research in traditional media to identify precise informational needs before searching the web.
- Tip 2: Use explicit search keywords.
- Tip 3: Use a variety of search engines and aggregate the results.
- Tip 4: Save interesting sites for later examination; use online time for searching, not viewing.
- Tip 5: Keep records of useful sites to speed up subsequent search sessions.
- Tip 6: Follow secondary links and references from useful sites to avoid searching from scratch every time.
- Tip 7: Use online discussion groups and social media to crowdsource recommendations for information sources.

Discerning 'Good' Information

Information available via the Internet represents as wide a range of quality as it does content. With more traditional forms of publication such as books, CDs, and films, high production costs and publisher curation usually provided a degree of quality control. Publishing a web page is very easy and inexpensive by comparison. It is therefore important to judge the reliability of the source and check the accuracy of the content.

The source's reputation can provide a degree of confidence about the likely accuracy of its content. For example, is a 12-year-old fan's site about The Chemical Brothers' music as reliable as the web site of a university professor in contemporary music? Usually not. But the Smithsonian Institution's science history information should be as trustworthy as Stanford University's tutorials on sound synthesis.

When the author or publication details are not known, one should triangulate sources, check information against common sense, and deliberately seek conflicting information for quality control. To avoid overreliance on Internet sources, when possible, one should cross-check information with sources in other media.

Internet sources can also vary in the level of detail they provide; content ranges from the superficial to the complex. Finding sources with appropriate levels of sophistication and detail can be challenging for music research activities in schools. One solution to this can be to accumulate a library of 'suitable' links as starting locations for project studies. As part of each research project, students and staff can contribute more items to the list.

Online Forms and Data Collection

Inquiry is not only about reading other people's ideas; it is also about gathering data and generating one's own conclusions. The Internet can be used to gather data using e-mail, social media, and web surveys. Online forms are widely used in Internet commerce to gather personal details or feedback, but they can also be used for gathering research data. Use this approach for worldwide responses to a survey.

A simple method for setting up a survey is to use a blog site that allows visitors to comment on blog entries. Post each question as a separate blog post, and let visitors respond to the questions as comments. This is easy for students to set up with free blog tools such as *Wordpress* and *Blogger*, as seen in Figure 12.2.

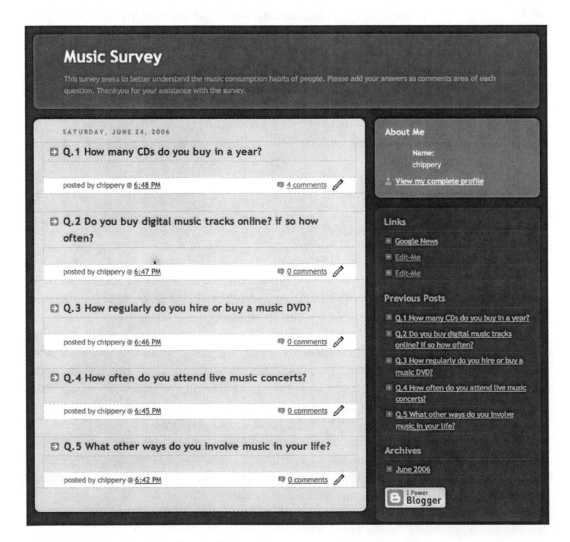

FIGURE 12.2 An example of an online music survey created using a blog.

Another approach is to use dedicated survey tools, such as *SurveyMonkey*[8] and *Google Forms*.[9] These services allow an individual to create and administer online surveys. Send a link to participants and collate response data into a table or spreadsheet. Some data analysis tools may be available online, but data can be exported and analyzed offline too.

Collaborative Projects

The Internet's communication capabilities have given rise to another mode of musical research, the online collaborative project. *Noteflight*[10] online notation service, *Ohm Studio*[11] online sound recording and mixing service, and others like these allow students to exchange compositional ideas by swapping music files and logging into shared online music production spaces. Network jamming software such as *jam2jam* and *eJamming*[12] enable group improvisational sessions over the Internet. These tools, combined with social media and messaging services, can be used for collaborative music research through their support of the communication and exchange of data, materials, and reporting documents.

Collaboration can be a linear process in which drafts of one document are moved back and forth between researchers, or an asynchronous process in which each student works on a different aspect of the project. A more interactive approach can incorporate real-time collaborative document editing with programs such as *Google Docs*, Microsoft's *Office Online*, Apple's *Pages*, and *SubEthaEdit*. Cooperative projects require students to articulate ideas as they communicate, provide a setting in which to engage with musical terminology and enhance student understanding.

Subtle changes in vocabulary make significant differences in search effectiveness. Using the Internet for music research requires students to sift through irrelevancies to find the information they need to know. Additionally, sharing these projects emphasizes the need for students to clearly articulate their questions and answers.

Online Music Commentary

People love to talk about music. Online communications have vastly amplified this, as they have done for all forms of dialogue and written expression. These network effects have not been without consequence in influencing musical culture either, as Carl Wilson observed: "Online music blogs and discussion forums sped up the circulation of such trends of opinion."[13] To see evidence of the popularity of music-related discussions, just search 'music' on *Twitter* or *Tumblr*, or look at the number of comments on music videos hosted on *YouTube*.

It might be tempting to dismiss this online commentary as ill-informed gossip. It may even be possible to question the value of talking about music at all because, one might suggest, music expresses itself. However, there is a long history of music criticism and many volumes have been written about music and its internal workings, its meaning, its social functions, and more. Talking about music is also a very pragmatic and commonplace matter for musicians, as Gillian Wills points out: "Whatever aspect of music philosophers, poets and idealists like to pontificate about, professional musicians routinely talk about and interrogate music's meaning."[14]

The vast repositories of music commentary online are a rich resource for music scholarship. They can provide insights into musical trends or the reasons for musical preferences, and they facilitate engagement with the analysis and critique of others. The range of sources is vast, from social network chatter to formal music reviews in online newspapers and from fan discussions on forums like *Reddit* to debates among academics in online journals.

Perhaps even more important for students developing their music scholarship than access to the written commentary of others is the opportunity the Internet provides for them to participate in dialog about music. After all, "learning through interaction and participation is all-important within the online community."[15] At a small scale, online discussion forums can be established where participants in music courses could share experiences and knowledge and conduct debate. Online forums are successfully used as part of most online learning deliveries. On a broader scale, students can engage with community-based or public online networks to seek opinions, ask for information, and test ideas as part of their musical enquiries.

Internet Content Restrictions

Issues of information appropriateness and censorship always surround new media, and the Internet is no exception. One of the duties of care for educators is to ensure that learning materials are appropriate and the online environment is safe for students. Supervising Internet sessions and pre-identifying 'suitable' sites will generally be helpful in this regard, but students need to be educated in what is appropriate Internet use. Reasonable steps to protect students include a combination of regulation and education.

Every government has regulations and guidelines about using Internet and mobile technologies with children. In the United States, a law aimed at restricting pornographic content on the Internet was introduced in 1996 called the Communications Decency Act (CDA).[16] Due to constitutional concerns, it has not yet come into full effect. In 2000, a more focused bill, the Children's Internet Protection Act (CIPA) was passed, which requires schools in the United States to use Internet filtering and other means to protect children from harmful Internet content.[17] In Australia, the Australian Communications and Media Authority (ACMA) is responsible for content regulation of mass media, including television, computer games, and the Internet. It has a co-regulatory scheme established under Schedule 5 of the Broadcasting Services Act 1992, with some revisions made in the early 2000s that include a code of practice and the authority to investigate complaints.[18] The Australian government provides information about safe Internet and mobile device use for children, teachers, and parents at its *Cybersmart* site.[19] In the United States, the slightly alarmingly named United States Computer Emergency Readiness Team provides tips for "Keeping Kids Safe Online,"[20] and the United Kingdom provides a similar service called *KidSmart*.[21] As part of the Digital Agenda for Europe, the European Commission in 2007 and 2012 released principles and frameworks for mobile device and Internet usage for children. These measures include age-appropriate privacy settings, parental controls, takedown provisions, and awareness-raising campaigns.[22] Based on these guidelines, member states have implemented their own legislation and/or codes of conduct.[23]

In addition to raising student awareness and staff supervision, education providers can limit access through black- or white-listing inappropriate or appropriate sites. A combination of reasonable protective measures and teacher, parent, and student responsibility should allow Internet research to be a positive learning experience that is no more harmful than using other media.

Copyright

The digital processes that create easy access to music materials over the Internet also enable easy copying and sharing of media. Copies of digital media may be, moreover, identical to the originals. Such ease of access and copying prompts the need to raise awareness of copyright responsibilities to avoid illegal (even if well-meant) activity. The digitization of all media means that picture, text, sound, or video data on the Internet is treated equally in relation to copyright law.

Copyright relates to making copies, so it is worth understanding what constitutes a digital copy. Technically, viewing an Internet site on a computer involves making a copy of the data in the memory of the host computer. However, in most countries the law does not consider holding data in computer memory as a breach of copyright. Copying occurs if the information is saved to permanent storage, printed out, or recorded onto another medium. But the question of what can and cannot be copied does not have a straightforward answer.

Generally, copying media is not permitted without the copyright owner's permission. Some copying, such as backing up legally purchased media, may be permissible. If there are no restrictions, such as password protection to access information on the Internet, then there is assumed to be an implicit agreement for use (but not copying) of that information. If there are any notices restricting use or claiming copyright, then normal offline copyright provisions apply. E-mail documents and information posted to Internet forums or social media sites are also covered by copyright law; the copyright remains with the author unless the End User License Agreement (EULA) for the Internet service states otherwise (which it often does). In most cases, to reuse online material requires the author's permission. As with books, short text quotations can be used if appropriately cited (see below), but the use of audio or video segments is not as clear-cut.

Often scholarship will include gathering original data, for example, through a questionnaire. When collecting data for projects, it is good practice to seek an agreement from the participants for the use of the data at the beginning of the project.

To avoid the complications of constantly having to seek permission from copyright holders, work can be covered by a Creative Commons license[24]—an alternative to conventional copyright. An increasing amount of material on the Internet is being covered by Creative Commons licenses. Such material can include text in blogs, audio files, and videos. A major advantage of these licenses—as opposed to traditional copyright—is that the author can explicitly allow limited use from the start. This means that it is not necessary to contact the author to know if the material can be used—the license makes it clear under what conditions someone can (or cannot) use the work. All Creative Commons licenses require attribution to the original author if the work is used. They may optionally allow noncommercial or commercial use and/or allow the material to be used in derivative works (such as remixes). With services like the *Creative Commons Search* engine, it is possible to locate images, music, video, and text that can legally be used for a research project or presentation, especially for noncommercial purposes like education.

Referencing

Beyond the legal requirement for attribution in Creative Commons licenses, it is an important academic principle that the source of information and ideas is attributed. References, or citations, are used to credit people for their work.

Citation of electronic documents exists to acknowledge the source of information and ideas and to allow a reader to check the sources. Therefore, the citation should include the author and document details, date, and place of (electronic) availability. If no date of publication is available, which is quite common online, then the date of access can be used.

There are a number of formatting styles for presenting citations. Typically there is an abbreviation within the document—for example, (Johnson 1997)—and a full citation in the reference section at the end of the document. The *Publication Manual of the American Psychological Association* (APA) provides the following format for referencing online sources:[25]

> Johnson, D. (1997). The History of the Flute [On-line]. Retrieved from http://www.abcd.org.au/music/flute.html

The methods of referencing within an electronic research report can vary. Standard processes for printed documents, as seen above, can be applied; or, for a slight variation, convert each in-text reference to a hyperlink either to the full citation at the end of the report or—if the reference is to an electronic source—to the external site.

Reporting Findings as Digital Documents

While accessing the Internet for information can be exciting and useful, creating reports as media-rich documents such as web pages and other digital publishing outcomes is equally important. As discussed in Chapter 8, this practice empowers students by letting them not only read Internet sources but also write them. An obvious advantage of a web-based report format is that the report can then contain embedded examples of performances, including video and sound recordings. These can complement text and images. Another advantage is that web documents can have hyperlinks to other sections and/or documents.

Narrative vs. Hypertext

Web documents provide a narrative flow of information interrupted by hypertext links: active connections to another location on the web page or Internet. The basic structure of each web page is a linear narrative from top to bottom, with links pointing to connections with additional or supporting information.

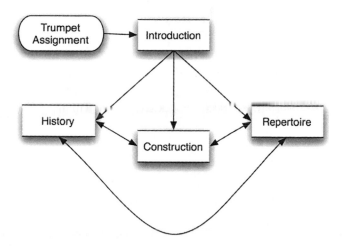

FIGURE 12.3 A mind-map or flowchart can be directly converted to a hypertext document, maintaining the rich interconnections of information.

A hypertext link (typically highlighted) redirects the user to a different document or different section of the same document. From an educational standpoint, hypertext links in a research report encourage students to see connections between information and topics. See Figure 12.3 for an example of this kind of structural organization. A student's use of hypertext links can expose the ways they understand the nonlinear organizational structure of the material and can provide educators with an opportunity to gain insight into the thinking and understanding of the student.

Sound and Video on the Internet

One of the Internet's greatest assets for the music researcher is the wide range of available sound recordings and videos of music. However, the use of sound and video on the Internet is not as standardized as the use of text, and there are a number of issues relating to quality and accessibility that need to be considered.

Sound and video can be accessed over the Internet in two main ways; files can be *downloaded* to the user's machine before playback, or they can be *streamed* to the user's machine in chunks and played back as they arrive. Sound and video playback on web pages requires extensions to web browsers called plug-ins. Audio and video plug-ins are included with the browsers, but from time to time some software, such as Adobe Flash Player, may need to be updated.

Sound and video files can be uploaded to online services such as *SoundCloud* and *YouTube* and later embedded into web-based research reports. As the user accesses the content, the media will stream to the browser from these services.

Empowerment Over Knowledge

As students create in a medium, they gain an understanding not only of the content, but of the medium itself. When students prepare research reports as web documents, they become increasingly critical of the web sites they explore. As they become aware of the strengths, limitations, and tricks of creating web documents, they can 'read' other's documents more directly and quickly. They become aware of technical issues too, such as the difference in quality between various audio and video formats, the design layout and the informational balance between text, graphics, and sound. Through creating web sites, students will hopefully see the importance of site structure and use of links, and they will develop the ability to discriminate between good content and good presentation.

Conclusion

Scholarship and critique in music education has been given a new lease on life thanks to the Internet, because it provides a valuable platform for communication, a rich data source, and an outstanding presentation vehicle. Internet-based activities can make investigation an appealing partner of production and presentation in the curriculum. The Internet also provides a means of global communication for data collection, collaboration, and presentation. Appropriate care needs to be taken that children's use of the Internet is productive and safe. Material collected from the Internet needs to be validated for accuracy and its use is subject to some legal restrictions and academic conventions for attribution. Web-based reporting involves sound, video, and interaction, not just text and images. The Internet is a two-way street that helps integrate the school and the world. When used for investigation and publication, the Internet can be both a window to the world and a global stage.

Reflection Questions

1. How has the Internet changed music research practices?
2. How does the Internet make music research more appealing?
3. What opportunities for music learning has peer-to-peer collaboration over the Internet made possible?
4. What are some tools for creating online surveys?
5. What are the barriers to students accessing the Internet in schools? How can they be overcome?
6. What types of referencing practices are appropriate at different levels of schooling?
7. What is the difference between streaming and downloading audio?
8. What does *hypertext* mean?
9. What are the benefits to students of using web documents for research reports?
10. Why is it important that students be able to write and read web documents?

Teaching Tips

1. Guide students through a tutorial on advanced Internet searching techniques.
2. Have students learn how to create forms for online surveys.
3. Encourage students to join Internet discussion groups on music topics that interest them.
4. Make posters outlining the Internet surfing tips suggested here and post them near computer terminals in the music room.

5. To ensure research validity, require students to triangulate their sources in research assignments.
6. Discuss with students how to judge information quality and facilitate student discussions on the topic.
7. Invite a guest speaker to talk about Creative Commons licenses and how they affect musicians.
8. Assign students to create research reports as web documents that include links to external reference sources.
9. Provide workshops in audio and video recording and digitizing so students can embed their own media in research reports.
10. Include discussion about the links between information within a research topic. Use hypertext links as a way of revealing these connections in a project report.

Suggested Tasks for Educators

1. Find out which online journal databases your library subscribes to and see how many music journals are included in those databases.
2. Learn about search engines' advanced search options to improve your Internet searches.
3. Design a collaborative music research project to connect several schools using Internet services.
4. Explore a network jamming service. What are its strengths and weaknesses?
5. Consider which Creative Commons licenses you would recommend to students.

Chapter Summary

Research and reflection on musical activities is a vital part of a complete music education. Discussions of music education often center on musical praxis, experience, expression, and aesthetic awareness. However, contextual understanding remains important, and the Internet has revitalized this contextual understanding. Music research now involves wide-ranging access to information about the broader musical content, its context, and the people involved. Research activities have traditionally included analysis, history, musicology, and sociology, but can also include music-making practices. The use of audio and video materials for both inquiry and reporting serve to draw musical practices into music research. The Internet, as an information conduit, and the computer, as a tool for analysis and production, are revitalizing music research. The Internet provides a wealth of information, but requires that this information be validated for accuracy and reliability. Material from the Internet is, like from traditional media, subject to copyright restrictions. The use of Creative Commons licenses can provide greater clarity about the reuse of materials. All materials and sources should be acknowledged in research reports in keeping with academic standards and fairness. This chapter outlines these issues and explores ways the Internet is used for research and reporting and some of the issues that arise as a result.

Notes

1. The term *research* is used here to mean inquiry. The importance of novelty and originality is a somewhat controversial part of research's definition. For more of the author's perspective on the issue, see the following: www.explodingart.com/arb/Andrew_R._Brown/Blog/Entries/2012/7/18_Small-r_and_Big-R_research.html; A. R. Brown & A. C. Sorensen (2009), Integrating creative practice and research in the digital media arts. In H. Smith & R. Dean (Eds.), *Practice-led research, research-led practice in the creative arts*. Edinburgh: Edinburgh University Press, pp. 153–165.
2. A saying attributed to Martin Mull in the 1970s: http://quoteinvestigator.com/2010/11/08/writing-about-music/.
3. Concerning intellectual property matters in this chapter, note that details presented here are subject to variation between jurisdictions and changes over time.
4. *Google Scholar*: http://scholar.google.com.
5. *Google Books*: http://books.google.com/.
6. The *Wayback Machine*, Internet archive search: http://archive.org/web/.
7. *Creative Commons Search*: http://search.creativecommons.org/.
8. *SurveyMonkey*, online survey and questionnaire tool: www.surveymonkey.com/.
9. *Google Forms*, online survey tools: www.google.com/google-d-s/createforms.html.
10. *Noteflight*, online notation that facilitates sharing of scores: www.noteflight.com/.
11. *Ohm Studio*, online digital audio workstation software for distributed and collaborative projects: www.ohmstudio.com/.
12. *eJamming*, online music performance service: http://ejamming.com/.
13. Wilson, C. (2014). *Let's talk about love: Why other people have such bad taste*. London: Bloomsbury, p. 14.
14. Wills, G. (2012). Ah, music. A magic beyond all we do here! In A. R. Brown (Ed.), *Sound musicianship: Understanding the crafts of music* (pp. 289–299). Newcastle upon Tyne: Cambridge Scholars, p. 289.
15. Kenny, A. (2013). "The next level": Investigating teaching and learning within an Irish traditional music online community. *Research Studies in Music Education, 35*(2), 239–253.
16. Access to the CDA act: http://transition.fcc.gov/telecom.html.
17. Wikipedia entry on CIPA: http://en.wikipedia.org/wiki/Children%27s_Internet_Protection_Act.
18. Information of ABA internet codes and standards of conduct: www.acma.gov.au/~/media/Content%20Classification/Regulation/pdf/Internet%20Industry%20Codes%20of%20Practice%202005.PDF, www.acma.gov.au/webwr/aba/contentreg/codes/internet/documents/iia_code_2002.pdf.
19. *Cybersmart* provides information that empowers children to be safe online: www.cybersmart.gov.au/.
20. Keeping Kids Safe Online, tips for Internet security and safety: www.us-cert.gov/ncas/tips/ST05-002.
21. *KidSmart*, information to promote safe Internet use by children: www.kidsmart.org.uk/.
22. Overview of the European Commission's "better Internet for kids" policies: http://ec.europa.eu/digital-agenda/self-regulation-better-internet-kids.
23. European safe mobile use measures: www.gsma.com/gsmaeurope/safer-mobile-use/national-measures/.
24. Information about Creative Commons licenses: https://creativecommons.org/licenses/.
25. American Psychological Association. (1994). *Publication Manual of the American Psychological Association*. Fourth ed. Washington: APA, p. 218. www.apastyle.org/.

thirteen
Learning Online

Advances in online technologies and greater access to them have resulted in rapidly increasing opportunities for learning. Online learning services are available from providers across the world and are becoming a part of most school, college, and university offerings. Digital media learning materials and services can be delivered via apps on mobile devices. Some of these apps include online connectivity; others are self-contained. In many ways, online services and mobile apps provide similar functionality. In particular, they are available on demand and just-in-time. Mobile apps are so pervasive in contemporary culture that Howard Gardner, the well-renowned education researcher, and his colleagues call young people today the "App Generation":

> It's our argument that young people growing up in our time are not only immersed in apps: they've come to think of the world as an ensemble of apps, to see their lives as a string of ordered apps, or perhaps, in many cases, a single, extended, cradle-to-grave app.[1]

In this chapter the term *online learning* will be used to refer to the use of both web-based and app-based technologies in the delivery of educational services. Online learning involves the delivery of part or the whole of a course of study via the Internet. It includes the use of communications technologies to facilitate online learning communities of peers and educators. It also allows teachers and learners to extend the geographic and temporal limits of educational engagement. The increasing use of Internet-based mobile technologies supports interaction with teaching materials—not just reception of information—and enables communication among learning communities in any location and at any time.

These developments have impacts for traditional schooling and lifelong learning alike. They have made online learning a mainstream concern for education in the twenty-first century. This chapter surveys online learning practices; discusses their benefits and limitations; and explores significant issues relating to online music teaching, and how creativity and performance skills are managed where face-to-face contact is limited or absent.

Teaching music is a challenge for online education because of its reliance on embodied skills in many areas. Therefore it is not surprising that online courses in music have focused on music appreciation and aural awareness, music history and theory, music technology skills and, occasionally, on composition and arranging. Except in a few cases of necessity for remote students, the teaching of performance studies has usually been conducted face-to-face. This has not prevented a flood of online instrumental tuition videos but these have typically focused on the beginner musician. The use of live video conferencing is the most common form of performance teaching over the Internet. Despite the cautious uptake in music education, online learning has in recent years moved ahead more quickly in other disciplines.

Until the popularization of the massive open online courses (MOOCs) in the late 2000s, mainstream education had not been particularly quick to embrace online learning strategies. Prior to the 1990s, the infrastructure and economic drivers were not really adequate, and neither was there a compelling educational reason for them to be so; there was (and still is) plenty of room for innovation in face-to-face teaching. In the mid 1990s, the WebQuest format was initiated where teachers set inquiry-based tasks and students are directed toward online information sources to complete the task.[2] Prior to widespread Internet connectivity, distance education was possible via a range of methods including radio and TV broadcasts, two-way radio, posting of printed course materials, instructional software, video conferences, and itinerant teachers.

There was a different pattern in large companies, such as IBM, where online training was more quickly adopted. For them the cost efficiencies of electronic training for thousands of globally distributed staff were significant compared with on-site meetings or external seminars. As network infrastructure and Internet bandwidth have increased, so has the take-up of online learning strategies in educational institutions. It is now recognized that the benefits of online learning, including easy information access and peer interaction, can enhance the learning for online and campus-based students.[3] The extent to which online learning can, or should, be a substitute for face-to-face, or campus-based, education is still being explored.

Online learning has its jargon, so some definitions of key terms are worth establishing. The term *online learning* is used here to refer to the use of Internet technologies or mobile apps to deliver or support education. *Distance learning* refers to situations where students and teachers are geographically separated and can rarely meet face-to-face. The term *flexible delivery* means that students have choices about how they can access information; this usually involves making resources available at different times or in multiple spaces, and allowing students to undertake study when it suits them. The term *blended learning* refers to practices that combine in-person and online learning. A particular style of blended learning is the *flipped classroom*, where lecture-style delivery is done online and outside of class time—often via videos or readings—and class time is spent on practical work and interaction with peers and the teacher. A great resource for preparing curated video materials for flipped classroom delivery is TED-Ed. As well as linking to videos from *TED.com* and *YouTube*, a lesson can include introductory text, links to additional resources, short-answer questions, and a discussion forum.[4]

Online Learning Technologies

There is a range of online learning technologies and new variations are appearing all the time. Each type of technology supports particular learning activities. This section canvasses various learning activities and provides an overview of the tools and the types of functionality provided by online technologies.

Information Sharing

There is an extended history of the technological distribution of educational materials. Formats have included radio, audiotapes, videos, CD-ROMs, and broadcast TV (Open University). Online learning technologies continue this trend by making information available through web sites, streaming of audio visual content, file downloads (including eBooks, PDFs, and podcasting), and the use of content management systems (CMS) and mobile apps. Teachers and students can use messaging services and social media networks to share links to media and reviews or commentaries related to these media, and as a platform for discussions surrounding them.

Interactive Apps

Web sites and mobile apps are interactive technologies that can deliver navigable content, simulations and microworlds, educational games, and more. Interactivity allows engagement with content beyond consumption and facilitates the 'gamification' of learning through the setting of goals, the offering of rewards, and the monitoring of achievement. For example, there are many music apps for mobile devices that quiz users on music-related information; an example is *Music Tutor*, shown in Figure 13.1, which drills staff pitch recognition. There are also skill-based rhythm games that require users to tap in time. Both offer incentives through stepped levels of difficulty, high scores, and badges. Online music games, such as those by Music Games International,[5] combine challenge and fun to draw users into the world of music.

Digital Media Content Creation

As well as *receiving* information, students also *create* information using various online tools. For example, blogs for creating online journals and digital portfolios, web page authoring tools, and web-based media content creation tools. The latter allow creation of visual images, music passages, character animations and so on. A variety of applications in this category were explored in Chapter 8.

Online Communication

The Internet provides many ways to send messages within a learning community, including discussion forums, e-mail lists, messaging services, and social media platforms such as *Facebook*, *Twitter*, *Google+*, and more. Many online learning platforms provide dedicated discussion boards and organize classes into small peer support groups, which

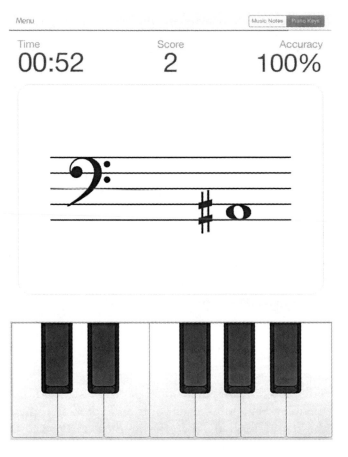

FIGURE 13.1 A screenshot from *Music Tutor* by jSplash for the iPad.

allow people to build meaningful interactions and avoid being swamped by the potentially large number of communications in large online courses. Peer interaction and discussion not only help those who have questions, but assist those who learn by teaching as they offer answers.

Online Collaboration

Many communication tools can also be used for collaboration, facilitated by messaging, file sharing, and synchronous media editing. Cloud based storage services, such as *Dropbox*, *Google Drive*, or Microsoft's *OneDrive*, can assist with file sharing. Collaborative writing technologies include wikis and web-based document editors like *Google Docs* or *Office Online*. Collaborations can benefit from real-time video discussions with tools such as *Skype*, *FaceTime*, or Google *Hangouts*. Various instant messaging clients allow immediate transmission of text and images between group members. Collaborative drawing tools like *CoSketch*[6] or *Twiddla*[7] provide a shared whiteboard for sketching ideas and taking notes; these can visually augment voice or messaging chat sessions.

The Rock Our World project has been using digital file sharing as the basis for creative collaboration among schools since 2004.[8] A group of students in one school create a drum clip in *GarageBand* and pass that on to the next school, which can be anywhere in the world, where students add a second track and pass on the session to a third school, and so on. Finally the *GarageBand* session finds its way back to the students that initiated it. Along the way, students communicate with each other about the music through live video chats. The Rock Our World web site includes information about becoming involved and teaching resources to support the project. The project has also released a mobile app to support the taking and sharing of photo images that make people smile.

Assessment and Learning Management

Online courses, like others, require administration. There is a range of platforms that support online courses. They provide assistance with listing and advertising, enrollment, serving course materials, monitoring participation, automated or peer reviewed assessment, and more. Online assessment practices face challenges that include identity verification and managing scale. Approaches to solving them are both technical (e.g., identity checks and automated grading), and social (e.g., peer feedback and assessment).

Online resources are often designed to achieve more efficiently or conveniently those tasks which are already part of music education programs, including tasks such as peer group discussions, collaborative work groups, access to recordings and videos about music, and storage of work and ideas. The advantage of online tools is that they extend the capacity for engagement to occur in a greater range of places and times. By breaking down the barriers of time and space, online and mobile technologies provide an opportunity to rethink methods of delivering music education. Areas ripe for reconsideration in light of online learning are the scheduling of lessons, the regularity of interaction, the duration of sessions, class sizes, and participant demographics. One form of course delivery, which was built to exploit these opportunities, and which has captured the imagination of learners and educators in recent years is the MOOC.

The Rise of MOOCs

The term MOOC was coined in 2008[9] and gained prominence several years later with some high-profile course offerings. In 2011, for instance, three such courses from Stanford University each achieved enrollments of more than 100,000 and attracted the attention of educators. So, what are some of the properties of MOOCs and why are they so popular?

MOOCs use the Internet to deliver course materials: videos, podcasts, readings, interactive web apps, and tests. Access can be self-paced or dictated by a scheduled delivery of content. Materials are typically packaged into bite-sized chunks and information is delivered, often as short videos, in a modular way with content viewing followed by tasks and tests. This modularity allows students to traverse the content graph in a way that interests them or best suits them. Research into MOOCs has found that frequent interruption for retrieval tasks and tests is effective,[10] and that modularized delivery helps to sustain engagement.

MOOCs are designed to be scalable, to be *massive*. They leverage the ubiquity and infrastructure of the Internet to achieve this scale. While it is possible simply to access educational materials online, MOOCs structure content and activities into a course. They typically have a start and end time that keeps participants focused on similar topics; this assists the cohesion of peer interaction. Providing deadlines for accessing materials and submitting assignments provides targets and motivation, just as these strategies do in other educational situations.

MOOCs are generally *open* access and many courses are often free of charge or low cost, which goes a long way to explain their popularity. Course durations can vary from 2 to 12 weeks. Shorter courses might be designed as teasers for conventional courses. Longer MOOCs might be taught in conjunction with conventional courses and provide enrichment for students enrolled in on-campus degree programs.

These *online* courses include web-based forums to help build a learning community and provide peer support and feedback. Technologies used for communications can range from e-mail lists to social networks, web-based forums, blogs, or specialized learning management systems. Students in close geographic proximity or with similar interests can set up study groups for either face-to-face or online meet-ups.

Common methods of assessment in MOOCs are machine-graded multiple-choice quizzes or tests, and peer-reviewed assignments. Delivery platforms include systems for computer-corrected multiple-choice or short-answer questions, but for longer-form writing or subjective value judgments, peer grading can be effective[11] and is used to manage larger cohorts. Students are encouraged to learn from their peer-marking activities as much as from receiving feedback on their own work.

Formalized MOOC providers in America include *Udacity*, *Corsera*, and *edX*, and in Europe, *FutureLearn*, *Iversity*, *Alison*, and *Eliademy*. These providers offer a range of free and paid courses with varying degrees of formalized accreditation, from badges and certificates of participation through to complete undergraduate and graduate degrees. MOOCs have been closely associated with university courses but providers that cater to a more general audience include *Kahn Academy*, *CodeAcademy*, *Lynda.com*, and *YouTube for Schools*.[12] These services share many MOOC features, including scalable delivery, peer interaction, online testing, and achievement certificates.

MOOC platforms offer online courses in many subject areas, and at the time of writing there were a growing number of music courses, including:

- *Introduction to Programming for Musicians and Digital Artists*[13]—first offered in 2013 on Coursera and run in conjunction with an on-campus delivery.
- *Exploring Beethoven's Piano Sonatas*[14]—a short musicology course offered on Coursera; an image from its front page is shown in Figure 13.2.
- *Play With Your Music*[15]—a short introduction to music production that uses free web-based music technologies in its delivery. It is offered through the Peer2Peer University platform.
- *An Introduction to Music Theory*[16]—one of a number of music theory MOOCs; offered on the institution's self-hosted MOOC site.
- *Critical listening for studio production*[17]—an introduction to aural awareness, focused on the needs of electronic musicians and record producers and available on the FutureLearn platform.

FIGURE 13.2 The opening page for the *Coursera* delivery of a music MOOC.

There will certainly be a steady flow of new music MOOCs. Music educators who want to use a MOOC in their teaching will need to decide whether they will create their own courses or use an existing one. As an aid to keeping up to date with the latest MOOC offerings the *Mooc-List* site provides a reasonably comprehensive coverage.[18]

Learning at a Distance

Online learning has both benefits and disadvantages. Accessing an education via the Internet can overcome many logistical issues that stand in the way. Benefits include side-stepping geographic remoteness; allowing study at times and places that suit students; and provided course costs are kept low, the removal of economic barriers to study. The flexibility of online learning promises to reengage adult learners and perhaps to deliver the much-anticipated benefits of lifelong learning.

As mentioned earlier, a feature of MOOCs is online peer interaction, which also has its positives and negatives. The possibility of many people participating in online learning communities creates opportunity for new and productive relationships among learners. However, the technologically mediated nature of digital communications means that these relationships might not be as rich as in-person interactions. While participation in online learning is high, completion rates are very low. This could be a real problem or it might simply be a property of the minimal commitment associated with low costs and modest certification. There is a risk that students will not be sufficiently engaged to realize some of the benefits of an online learning community. Motivation (or lack of it) is a particularly crucial determinant of student success or failure in online learning.

There is some debate about the types and depth of knowledge that can be successfully mastered using online learning. For example, online learning might not be appropriate for elite training in music performance, but there are still many opportunities for the online delivery of music education. This debate is addressed by the philosopher Hubert Dreyfus, well known for his commentaries on the extent and limits of computational technologies.

In *On the Internet*,[19] Dreyfus discusses the impact of shifting from face-to-face contact to online learning. The book outlines stages of education in which different skills are learned in specific ways and provides a critique of the importance of embodied or emotional knowledge at each of these stages. Dreyfus argues that the semi-detached nature of online education makes the transference of some advanced understandings difficult. Given the heavy reliance on physical involvement and emotional commitment in musical activities, Dreyfus's observations are pertinent to decisions about how best to use Internet technologies to support music education. He suggests seven stages through which a student progresses to become an authority in the domain:

1. Novice—features and rules of the domain are provided for the person to acquire and follow.
2. Advanced Beginner—the person learns maxims that contextualize general rules in a specific context that he/she experiences and which are based on a variety of examples.
3. Competence—the person develops plans or perspectives that make sense of and prioritize an otherwise overwhelming number of rules and maxims.
4. Proficiency—the person develops intuition through involvement, which replaces reasoned responses.
5. Expertise—the person is able to make more subtle and refined discriminations allowing an immediate and intuitive response leading to the development of a personal style.
6. Mastery—the person develops his or her own style and innovative abilities.
7. Practical Wisdom—the person develops a sense of cultural awareness that allows him or her to act appropriately within the given domain at any time.

Dreyfus argues that online education alone can only be successful in the first three stages, and that face-to-face interaction is required to advance learning beyond those stages. Involvement, he suggests, is learned through modeling of intellectual and emotional engagement with the domain provided by the teacher or other mentors. Emotional engagement is developed in situations where the students take risks in situations that matter to them, such as in public performance and master classes with respected figures. Beyond stage three, Dreyfus suggests that some form of face-to-face apprenticeship is required, within which the student will pick up ineffable clues about the domain and how to navigate it in the complexities of real world situations. For stages six and seven he suggests that multiple apprenticeships with more than one teacher or mentor are required for students to gain sufficient diversity of perspective.

Online learning can provide many opportunities for enhanced interaction and access to information for students in music programs but, while developing online courses and materials, it is worth keeping in mind Dreyfus's comments about the disembodiment of mediated communications. It is also important to consider that in the time since Dreyfus made these comments the richness and the immediacy of online communications have increased substantially; this is likely to ameliorate some of the concerns about the richness of online interactions. Further, the multiplicity of domain mentoring and modeling he cites as crucial to the attainment of wisdom might well be enhanced by online social networking.

Designing for Online Learning

Given that online learning materials often have to operate in the absence (or reduction) of face-to-face contact, the designer of learning materials for these contexts needs to respond appropriately. The author and Bradley Voltz developed a series of elements for the design of online learning materials with just such a context in mind; these design elements are presented below.[20] They arose after years of experience in creating and evaluating online learning resources designed for a wide range of age levels and curriculum areas, with a particular emphasis on music education.

The design phase is critical in the development of learning materials. Educational design work combines elements of lesson planning, instructional design, creative writing, visualization, software specification, and the development of digital media. At the design stage it is also important to take account of the technologies available for delivery. The design strategies presented here require such consideration. However, good designs can often be independent of the technology platform with which they are built or delivered and considerable knowledge, based on previous teaching experiences, can be brought to bear on the development of online learning.

There are six elements of an online learning design, which address many of the issues involved with material development and help to keep the focus of the educational experience on effective learning outcomes. These six elements are the activities, the scenario, feedback, delivery, context, and the impact of the resource. These design elements provide a framework within which educational designers can work and careful attention to them can minimize the gap between the educational goals and the experience of students who are using the online learning resource.

Here is a brief overview of the six elements for designing effective online learning resources:

- Activities—the design should include student tasks that will provide a rich and diverse experience. Providing multiple perspectives and experiences of a topic is more likely than a single type of activity to lead students to the desired educational outcomes.
- Scenario—a situation or story, which situates the tasks in a meaningful relationship to the students and the real world, should be developed and communicated.
- Feedback—it is important to include timely and frequent reaction to or commentary on student actions. This helps them to reflect on their work and to turn experience into understanding.
- Delivery—the design should consider, and work with, the opportunities and limitations of the technical means of production and the types of interaction they enable.

- Context—the design should accommodate and complement other material and human resources that are likely to be available to the student. An online mediated experience can always be part of a broader learning context.
- Impact—designers should anticipate the likely effects, even beyond educational outcomes, of the activities on staff, students, and the environment. These effects include potential psychological, cultural, ethical, and physical impacts.

These elements of effective instructional design can be used within a variety of design approaches, but a participatory design method is especially appropriate to education. In participatory design, the users—in this case students—are involved throughout the design process to inform decision making and to offer critique as the design progresses.

When using these elements of effective instructional design, it is important to remain aware that technology can amplify the strengths and weaknesses of activities and delivery systems. Because of this, the design phase is critical in ensuring that students will experience all of the intended ideas and interactions, rather than only those that are ready at hand. Planning the use of online learning technologies in this way should allow them to have a positive impact on students and to amplify their musicality.

Conclusion

When used effectively, online learning technologies can extend the reach of great educators and facilitate increased student participation. There are times when access and circumstances mean that online learning techniques are the primary method for students to access music education. However, for most students, online learning resources will enrich face-to-face musical interactions. The benefits of online technologies for education include their use of media-rich documents and resources, the ability for students to engage with material when it suits them, and to benefit from communications with a peer learning community. The challenges of online learning include keeping a focus on developing musical intelligence and avoiding the risk of letting increased information *about* music (quantity) replace the experience of *making* music (quality). It is also important to ensure that students accessing online learning are not limited to entry-level musical skill development because of the lack of face-to-face interaction through which they can learn much more than we can tell.

Reflection Questions

1. What does the acronym MOOC stand for?
2. How might peer-to-peer communications be supported by online learning technologies?
3. Why was big business an early adopter of online learning?
4. What aspects of music education are especially challenging to deliver with online learning?
5. What are the strengths of e-learning technologies?
6. List Hubert Dreyfus's seven stages of learning.
7. Why does Dreyfus think online learning has restricted educational prospects?
8. What are the six elements of effective online learning design suggested by Brown and Voltz?

9. What is the difference between the Scenario and Context design elements?
10. How might online learning challenge or augment the traditional organization and structure of schooling?

Teaching Tips

1. Use a flipped classroom model to maximize lesson time on practical tasks and have theoretical information delivered online.
2. Employ online forums and social media groups to share knowledge among peers in order to encourage greater debate about topics.
3. Have students post work online for others to comment on. Use this both as a method of formative assessment and as feedback.
4. Use rich media materials online to minimize the distancing effect of mediated communication.
5. Have students use a blog as a portfolio tool to store and reflect on their digital work.
6. Use interactive music games as an extension activity for students who finish other work early.
7. Use online collaborative writing tools for group report writing.
8. Enhance the education of remote students by increasing the electronic links between them.
9. Augment learning opportunities in campus-based courses by integrating materials from a MOOC.
10. Lead a class discussion to increase student awareness of online learning opportunities and restrictions.

Suggested Tasks for Educators

1. Do an audit of the online learning technologies you currently use.
2. List the skills you consider essential for your students to acquire and then imagine how they might be taught using online learning technologies.
3. Audit a music MOOC to gain further insight into the experience and operations of these online courses.
4. Use the online learning design elements as a guide to designing new online learning resources.
5. Investigate several online education service providers and assess their suitability for use in your teaching context.

Chapter Summary

One of the major impacts of Internet technologies on education is their use as delivery platforms for educational materials and as communication platforms for staff and students. The use of contemporary technologies, including the Internet and mobile apps, for teaching is called online learning. These technologies are used for distance education, where students are not able to attend regular music lessons, as a support for conventional teaching methods in flipped classrooms, and as an alternative to traditional modes of instruction. A popular type of course delivered using these technologies is described as a massive open online course (MOOC). Advantages of this kind of delivery include on-demand and just-in-time access to learning materials, self-paced learning, increased access and participation in education, and support for peer learning communities. Online learning involves mediated communication between people, and this disembodied nature of online learning experiences imposes some limitations on what can be taught using them. Designing online learning experiences for students needs to take these pros and cons into account. Effective design of online learning considers the activities being undertaken, creates scenarios within which those tasks make sense, makes effective and frequent use of feedback to students, and tries to augment existing resources within the students' learning environment. Online learning is an important platform for education but is not a panacea. In terms of aiding the development of musical intelligence, which is a particularly experience-based endeavor, online learning can provide rich media experiences and interactions that are an improvement on text-based materials, but are not a replacement for face-to-face musical encounters.

Notes

1. Gardner, H., & Davis, K. (2013). *The app generation: How today's youth navigate identity, intimacy, and imagination in a digital world.* New Haven: Yale University Press, p. 6.
2. WebQuest site: http://webquest.org.
3. Fowler, G. A. (2013). An early report card on MOOCs. *Online.wsj.com.* Retrieved March 4, 2014, from http://on.wsj.com/1eDknup.
4. TED-Ed, online lessons using selected video resources: http://ed.ted.com/.
5. Web-based music games by Music Games International: www.musicgames.net/musicgames_nopop.htm.
6. *CoSketch*, multiuser online whiteboard: http://cosketch.com/.
7. *Twiddla*, web-based collaborative whiteboard: http://www.twiddla.com/.
8. Rock Our World, collaborative music and video production via file sharing: www.rockourworld.org/.
9. MOOC origins detailed in the Wikipedia entry at http://en.wikipedia.org/wiki/Massive_open_online_course.
10. Karpicke, J. D., & Blunt, J. R. (2011). Retrieval practice produces more learning than elaborative studying with concept mapping. *Science, 331*(6018), 772–775.
11. Peer assessment research: Lebler, D. (2008). Popular music pedagogy: Peer learning in practice. *Music Education Research, 10*(2), 193–213; Sadler, P. M., & Good, E. (2006). The impact of self-and peer-grading on student learning. *Educational Assessment, 11*(1), 1–31.
12. *YouTube for Schools*: www.youtube.com/schools.
13. *Introduction to Programming for Musicians and Artists*: www.coursera.org/course/chuck101.
14. *Exploring Beethoven's Piano Sonatas*: www.coursera.org/course/beethovensonatas.
15. *Play With Your Music*: www.playwithyourmusic.org/.
16. *An Introduction to Music Theory*: http://lms.bhtafe.edu.au/mooc/course/index.php.
17. *Critical Listening for Studio Production*: www.futurelearn.com/courses/critical-listening-for-studio-production.
18. *Mooc-List* site, which includes a tag to search for music MOOCs: www.mooc-list.com/tags/music.
19. Dreyfus, H. L. (2001). *On the Internet.* New York: Routledge.
20. Brown, A. R., & Voltz, B. (2005). Elements of effective e-learning design. *International Review of Research in Open and Distance Learning, 6*(1). Retrieved from www.irrodl.org/index.php/irrodl/article/view/217/300.

fourteen
Assessment

Music learning assessment is concerned with what students know and can do. This chapter focuses on how music technologies can help with assessing students' musical intelligence. So what is meant by *assessment* and *musical intelligence*? David Elliott, in his book *Music Matters*, distinguishes between evaluation and assessment. He understands assessment as 'constructive feedback'[1] and evaluation as 'grading.' This chapter, on the other hand, considers assessment as relating to both feedback and grading. At the same time, this chapter affirms Elliott's main point that the primary purpose of assessment is to "articulate feedback to students about the quality of their growing musicianship"[2] with the ultimate aim that students, by developing their ability to self-assess their musical achievements, become autonomous learners. Music educator and researcher Don Lebler eloquently expands on this idea, writing:

> Assessment of learning occurs when a student's understanding of curriculum content is measured and this is the traditional role of assessment. Assessment for learning occurs when the goal is to identify areas in which more work may be needed. Assessment as learning involves students in the act of assessment as active participants and this involvement is intended to produce learning in itself.[3]

Even though the overall purpose of assessment is to improve a student's learning, it is also useful to acknowledge that assessment processes need to provide value to other music education stakeholders: teachers, parents, school authorities, and the community. Assessment can also be used to help students and teachers understand what areas of knowledge and skill to prioritize going forward. Assessment can additionally help teachers monitor the effectiveness of their teaching practices and identify where they might be improved. Assessment results can inform parents and administrators of student achievement and progress and suggest how these relate to specified standards or targets. Assessment targets can also be used to motivate the student to reach particular goals and achievements. These and other issues of assessment in music education are the focus of ongoing research and discussion, and interested educators are encouraged to engage through activities such as the annual International Symposium on Assessment in Music Education.[4]

Before discussing the role of music technologies in the assessment of music learning in detail, it is useful to outline more clearly what we are trying to assess.

What and How to Assess

Music is a form of human intelligence. Psychologist Howard Gardner developed the idea that musical intelligence is a series of universal multiple intelligences.[5] It seems that almost every human culture on the planet has developed a musical practice, even if at times these are closely linked to dance, religion, or another cultural expression. Understanding *what* musical intelligence is represents the first step to knowing *how* to assess it, and Gardner provides a useful overview.

Musical intelligence involves musical thinking and imagination. It is the ability to hear music in one's head, and/or identify and reproduce the most critical elements of music, which, in Gardner's research, are pitch and rhythm, followed closely by timbre and structure. Direct assessment of imagination is a nearly impossible task, but evidence of imagination can be observed through actions and artifacts.

Although musical thinking is important, music is not only a cognitive skill. Music making is gestural and embodied, either directly (in production) or indirectly (during imagination). Therefore, music in performance, production, and other modes of expression are key gesture-based indicators of musical intelligence and can be used for assessment.

As well as producing music, musical intelligence involves interpreting, understanding, analyzing, and appreciating music and sound made by others. Musical intelligence involves understanding the expressive intentions of others, the meaningfulness of creative acts, and the functions of music in cultural settings.

It is also revealing to identify how music differs from other cognitive processes. Gardner suggests that there is evidence that even though music shares some semantic structural features with language, the two are different. Music shares similar features with dance and other kinesthetic intelligences in its gestural tendencies. And it is like mathematics in its fascination with patterns and elegant organization—although unlike mathematics, it is not about purely abstract structures. Music is concerned with sonic organization and is broadly related to geometry and spatial intelligences. Thus, when assessing musical intelligence, it is important to ensure that methods are not in effect testing other intelligences. For example, when assigning written tests that require linguistic skills or theory tests that require mathematical skills, it is important to distinguish which intelligences are really being tested.

Musical intelligence is a complex phenomenon involving imagination, gesture, and emotion. It is possible to develop tests and criteria for each aspect of musicianship; however, given their interrelatedness, music learning assessment should generally involve demonstrations of complete musical activities and outcomes, not isolated tasks or exercises abstracted from their musical contexts. Realistic or complete activities are sometimes described as *authentic tasks*. There is, however, a danger in assuming that authentic means music performance only. Given the wide acceptance that nonper-formance tasks—including critiquing, composing, recording, instrument making, and analysis—also require musical intelligence, a wide range of authentic assessment tasks become possible.

Musical intelligence also relates to aesthetics. Music is expressive and often springs from or provokes emotion. This suggests that music learning assessment should focus not only on rudimentary skills, but also on the appreciation and creation of expressive music. Musical intelligence is also developmental and the use of both *formative* and *summative* assessment provides for ongoing feedback on learning progress and infor-mation about the accomplishment of learning goals. Formative assessment activities should be done regularly throughout the course and many involve formal or informal processes. Summative assessment tasks are undertaken at the conclusion of modules or courses and are usually formal processes.

Because music making is bound by cultural and stylistic norms and conventions, interpersonal and sociocultural intelligences also play a role in holistic musical prac-tices. Having the knowledge and control to work within and beyond these conventions is an important measure of a mature musical intelligence. Because musical skills and abilities can vary between cultures and musical genres, assessment criteria need to be sensitive to diversity.

To keep assessment equitable and consistent it should measure student achievement against stated criteria. Use of criteria and learning goals also assists the teacher and student to have clear targets toward which they are working. Criteria can be measured in a number of ways, as a checklist, rating scale, or rubric. Learning achievements, or competencies, can be ticked off a checklist when achieved. A more subtle measure is performance against a rating scale, which has the advantage of allowing for forma-tive progress measures that can indicate progress toward the goal. A rubric provides descriptions for several levels of achievement (e.g., developing, proficient, mastery) for each criteria, and so provide the most informative feedback to the student about what is expected and what has or has not been achieved.

Finally, this section turns its attention to what data to use as material for assess-ment and grading. Complete musical tasks can exist in many forms—as performances, scores, recordings, or media-rich documents. Many of these forms can be stored digi-tally, with live performances the most problematic in this regard. Still, video and audio documentation of performances can be revisited and used for assessment. Assessment technologies generate data too. Computer systems can be handy for storing written comments and digitized explanatory examples, diagrams, and numerical scores. The next section explores in more detail how computers can be used to generate and manage assessment data, and their further utility in assessing music learning.

Assessment with Computers

Starting at the end of the music assessment process, computing technologies are often used at the final stages for collating grades and writing reports. But they can also be used throughout the learning process to document activities and provide feedback and learn-ing support. In particular, music technologies are useful during production processes for capturing work and reflecting on it. Increasingly, messaging and social media technologies facilitate communication between peers, assessors, and administrators. Databases can store information about assessment items, while project documentation and commentary provide data for reflection and assessment. In some well-defined areas, computing systems can be used to make automated judgments about student competence, knowledge, or skill. These algorithmic assessments are used in online music theory tests and software measurements of performance, and their results can become pieces of assessment data for the teacher to take into account.

Production and Response

Evaluation is an iterative and ongoing process, done throughout a musical work's development. Given that music technologies are used in a work's production, as detailed in previous chapters, they are well suited to assist with ongoing assessment and evaluation. The most obvious uses of music technologies are for documentation of and reflection on works in progress. Music technologies can be used, for example, to save files, record documentation, and articulate reflections.

An important consideration when assessing work produced using music technologies is the potential influence of the technology itself. All technologies influence the activities they are used for, and computational technologies do so powerfully. For example, if a student uses software like *GarageBand* to create a popular song, the teacher should be aware that the program includes musical clips in various styles that can be recombined to form an arrangement. Different expectations are required when the song is written using a publishing package such as *Sibelius*, which has little in the way of preloaded material. It is important for an assessor to sort out the differences between the musical affordances provided by the software and the user's creative application of them. To assist in distinguishing the tool's influence from the student's technique, consider having students provide drafts at various stages, as well as screen shots, to determine how they are using software tools. A student's written explanation of the process and critique of the outcome can also be helpful when assessing intention and action. It usually becomes clear with such documentation to what extent users are in control of their processes and are making musical, rather than simply technical, decisions.

Screen capture software, which captures a video with audio of what's on the computer, can be useful both for students to record their computer-based activities and for teachers to record their feedback. A good use of screen capture software is to use it to capture a teacher's review and feedback. The teacher can view student work on screen and record their interactions on the screen along with their verbal comments using the computer's built-in microphone. The video file can be sent to the student as feedback. This process can work for music production tasks, written work, or even a video of a student performance.

Communication

Computers are used often for communication. Communication methods include e-mail, social networks, discussion forums, and web sites. These tools can be used to easily disseminate assessment information. For example, posting assessment requirements and criteria online makes them publicly accessible and easy to comment on. E-mail and messaging services can be used to inform students and instructors about assessment schedules and to gather reviews or comments. Cloud-based storage services like *Dropbox* can be used to collate or distribute assessment items and work examples. Apps can be used to maintain records of submitted work, grades, and comments. When these records accumulate over time, they can provide benchmarks for assessing student work.

The potential of online forums for collaboration and feedback is enormous, and massive open online courses (MOOCs) have taken advantage of this potential. Just as feedback and peer review are productive in music classes and ensembles, discussion forums expand students' access to a range of different views and opinions. Online discussions allow participants all over the world to work asynchronously. Forums can also be used for peer review, letting members of a group comment on each other's work. These tools are especially useful for commenters, who can link to or embed other musical material as examples to back up their statements. E-mail lists also lend themselves well to group communications; questions or links to draft works can be e-mailed to the list for input. Additionally, most discussion forums and blog sites maintain threads that consolidate conversations, providing a history of feedback and discussion that can inform the developing work and later be reviewed for grading.

Electronic communication can support discussions between assessors and the comparison and alignment (moderation) of results. It is increasingly common for Internet video conferencing to be used for these purposes—a particularly practical tool for connecting those in remote communities and for convening assessors across an entire state or country.

Self-Assessment and Peer Assessment

Self-assessment and peer assessment are increasingly important in contemporary music education, which pursues ever more flexible and interactive approaches to learning. In recent years there has been increased recognition of informal learning, which involves tutoring and review between peers, but which has previously been unacknowledged because it existed outside formal education processes. A leading writer about informal learning in music education, Lucy Green, sums up the place of assessment in informal learning this way:

> In short, assessment is ongoing throughout the informal music learning process and is the total responsibility of the learners themselves ... Voices are being raised higher and higher at the present time in calls for a reconsideration of musical ability, away from the narrow definitions which tend to be associated with assessment models derived from formal music education towards broader, more open definitions, often associated with traditional, vernacular, popular and other 'world' music learning practices.[6]

As a way of supporting self-assessment and peer assessment, it is useful to provide criteria for making insightful judgments about musical work. A good place to start is with a framework based on the elemental categories outlined by George Pratt,[7] the aesthetic criteria proposed by Bennett Reimer,[8] or the dimensions of musical assessment

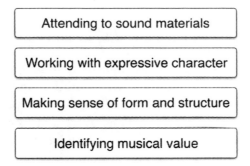

FIGURE 14.1 Reflective criteria based on Keith Swanwick's dimensions of musical assessment.

proposed by Keith Swanwick, seen in Figure 14.1.[9] These frameworks provide structure for reflection and commentary, and help learners develop their critical faculties as part of the process of developing their own musicianship and that of their friends.

As works are being produced, it can be quite helpful for assessment (and creative) purposes for students to keep draft copies of their work. Many expert musicians do this as a matter of course, so that if they take a developmental path that proves unproductive, they can go back to a previous version and try another way. As an assessment tool, the ability to look at the decisions made in the production of a musical work can reveal a good deal about thought processes and musical thinking. This information can reveal areas where understanding is well developed or underdeveloped, and which practices proved effective or unproductive. Saving a copy of a project at regular intervals can facilitate this; taking screenshots or periodically recording audio examples can be useful strategies as well. Students can be required or encouraged to record their progress until the practice becomes habitual, as it is for many experienced musicians.

Another popular tool for self-assessment is keeping a written journal, in which students record their thoughts and descriptions of processes in a regular and structured way. Journals assist students to consolidate ideas and they encourage conscious reflection about the progress of projects. The utility and importance of media documentation and written reflection supports a well-known, and very true, statement by the psychologist Mihaly Csikszentmihalyi that "activity and reflection should ideally complement and support each other. Action by itself is blind, and reflection impotent."[10]

Peer assessment has become an important component of online learning and MOOCs in particular, as discussed in Chapter 13. In these programs, which are often supported by Internet-based learning management systems that facilitate sharing and commenting on materials, groups of students regularly study together and critique each other's work.

Information Management

Assessment has administrative, as well as pedagogical, dimensions. Music assessments, especially in digital form, can generate a significant amount of data. Assessment materials include photos, audio and video, software-based project files, collections of text communications, and journal reflections. The organization of this data is a task computers are useful for. At the heart of any information organization process is a database where information is stored and indexed. More formally, this type of application is called a content management system (CMS), in which data is stored on a server (in the cloud) and accessed via a web-based user interface and/or a stand-alone mobile app.

CMSs store files and data, and any authorized person can add to, edit, or view the data. They allow an administrator to set different levels of user privileges; in a simple case, this allows students to add work, peers to comment, teachers to add grades, and parents to view students' progress. Some CMSs are tied to other database systems such as school timetable scheduling and grade submission systems; these systems, such as *Blackboard*,[11] are often called learning management systems (LMS).

Electronic Portfolios

There are many ways CMSs can be used, but a few popular approaches stand out. When used primarily as storage and reviewing areas, CMSs are commonly referred to as electronic or digital portfolios. With an ePortfolio, students typically add and organize their work within the CMS, and teachers and parents can view and review the work. Music activities lend themselves particularly well to ePortfolios because of the ease of storing digital media that ePortfolios provide. A variety of views (audio, photos, commentary, scores) can be created for the work in the CMS, allowing different presentations for assessment and exhibition purposes or for use as an online resume, and can often be viewable from mobile devices. Research into the use of ePortfolios in arts education has produced the following lesson for their effective use:[12]

- Students must maintain their creative integrity and input into the selection of the ePortfolio content.
- The onus is on teachers to equip the students with skills and abilities that will enable them to produce an ePortfolio of quality.
- The fundamental right of the user to withdraw the work at any time or restrict access is a primary rule of thumb.
- All participants should be aware of the limitations, functions, and purpose of the ePortfolio process so that the assessment process does not limit the artistic product and making experience.

Blog-like CMSs store data in chronological order and are quite adequate for most ePortfolio needs. Mainstream blog tools are great for this, and include *WordPress*[13] and *Blogger*.[14] For a simple data trail of student work, a simple blog tool is quite sufficient. CMSs often include user forums that allow discussions and commentary on relevant topics. The flexibility of access to CMSs (via any Internet-enabled device) facilitates asynchronous interaction among students outside class time.

Learning Management Systems

Beyond blog tools, more serious and fully featured learning management systems (LMS) include *Moodle*,[15] *DotCMS*,[16] *Ingeniux*,[17] *Drupal*,[18] *Campus Suite*,[19] *OmniUpdate*,[20]

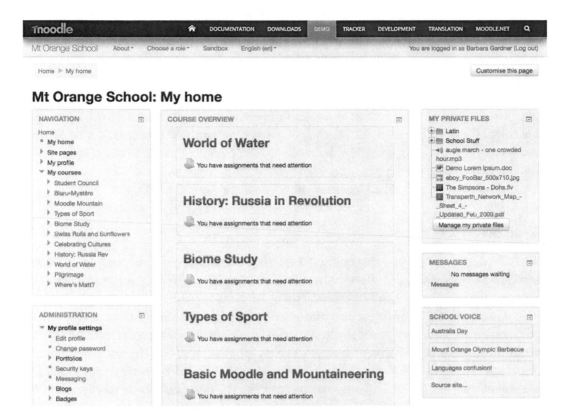

FIGURE 14.2 The student home page of a *Moodle* LMS site.

and *Jadu*.[21] A popular open-source LMS for education is *Moodle*; see Figure 14.2 for a screenshot. *Moodle* features online course materials, assignment submissions, forums, chat, and ePortfolio facilities.

There are a number of advantages to using an LMS to accumulate and review student work. These include the ability to maintain a data trail starting with initial assignment requirements, to drafts and plans, to the final work, reflections on it, and eventual evaluation or grade. This process of documentation leads to accountability and reflection on the student's part, and improves the transparency of assessment processes. As reflective self-evaluation is encouraged, the ability to self-monitor progress becomes empowering for the student; and positive self-esteem can also be developed through a student's online showcase of his or her outcomes and achievements.

Ownership and Access

Having assessment data, either digital works or comments and grades, stored in databases in the cloud or in other storage media begs a question about the governance of and access to that information. Assuming that the data is on a server controlled by a school or other educational authority, then the responsibility for maintenance and data backup is clearly with that authority, and would be part of any normal information technology governance regime. If, however, a music teacher administers the database independently, he or she would need to ensure the safekeeping of that data. Safekeeping includes making backups and taking the appropriate steps to secure data and prevent unwanted access. These issues of data safety and access are solvable, but to ensure reliability they require some attention when computer assessment systems are first set up and from time to time thereafter.

Data access policies need to be established for all online student materials. It is usual for students to access and edit their own materials, and additionally for students to make selected works available for viewing by their peers, family, or friends. Teachers and parents often have 'rights' to view student work and to add comments about it. There may also be a public web site that features selected works. When establishing online governance processes, consider the types of information that can be stored, what can be made publicly available, the needs for attribution and acknowledgment, and institutional branding. These will need to align with relevant local regulations and laws.

Automated Assessment

Automated assessment by computer used to be a feature of what was called computer-assisted instruction (CAI), which presented information and tested student understanding through simple multiple-choice tests. In this century, automated assessment is most commonly found in MOOCs, which use various machine-learning techniques to manage the grading of large numbers of assignments.

Automated tests—ones in which a computer makes assessments about a student's performance based on interactive tests—are quite common in areas of the curriculum where correct and incorrect answers are available. In particular, they are frequently used for aural and musicianship testing, as, for example, in the *Auralia*, *Musition*, and *Music Ace*[22] software packages. These types of tests became popular in the 1980s and 1990s and are still quite common. For computer programs, testing for simple correct or incorrect responses is not complex; currently systems that correct more contextual and complex tasks—such as *Harmonia*, seen in Figure 14.3, which corrects part writing and part counterpoint exercises—are becoming more widespread.[23]

Multiple-choice tests can be created using a variety of online tools. Of particular interest for automated correction is the use of a *Google Form* and an add-on script called *Flubaroo*.[24] The form allows the test to be taken on any device with a web browser, and *Flubaroo* will compare submitted answers to an answer key template for grading.

Auto-accompaniment systems such as *SmartMusic* (discussed in Chapter 11) provide performance feedback and evaluations. With these programs, students play repertoire on their instruments while the computer provides accompaniment that follows the soloist. The programs can provide feedback on the performance in terms of tempo stability, number of wrong notes, and expressive deviation from other performances of the same work. Feedback from such systems represents a useful supplement to instructor commentary, and students and teachers can track progress with the results of the program's statistical assessments. Furthermore, there is great interest in the audio analysis techniques used in music searching and recommendation engines. These technologies

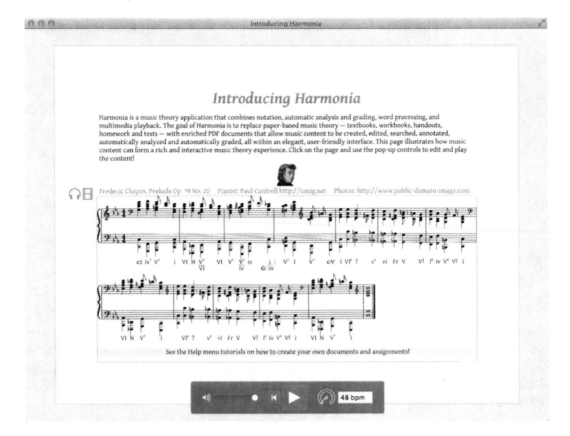

FIGURE 14.3 *Harmonia*, an interactive music theory tutor that can play back and evaluate student work.

may well contribute to further advances in automated music evaluation, and in the decades ahead, computer-based assessments of compositions and performances will likely become more effective.

Reporting

Computing devices are routinely used for writing reports on student progress and achievement. Software tools for this task can be as general as a word processor or as specific as a report template system often found as part of an LMS. Between these extremes are simple tools such as *Student Report Writer*[25] and *SMART School—Report Writer*,[26] seen in Figure 14.4, which collate a selection of prepared phrases into a paragraph for use as a written component of a report. Various database and spreadsheet programs can also be used to collate grades and/or comments. See Chapter 15 for more details on using these administrative tools.

Strategies for preparing reports include reviewing student portfolios in a CMS to confirm assessment conclusions against criteria. Moreover, instructors' regular comments on a student's online journal throughout the term represents useful formative feedback to the student and lessens the load of writing comments for reports over time.

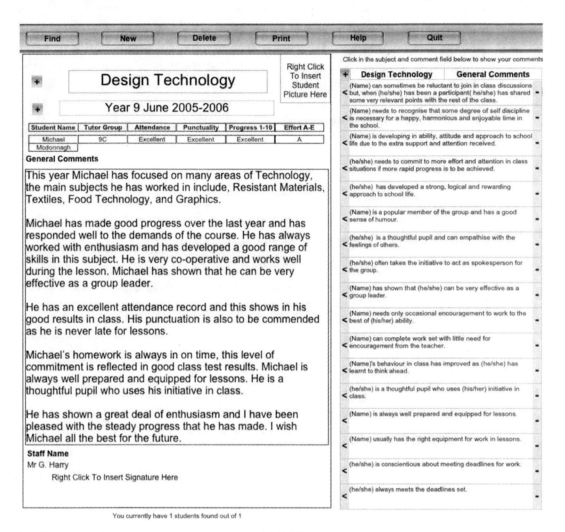

FIGURE 14.4 An example student report in *SMART School—Report Writer.*

Conclusion

Music technologies have a role in the ongoing feedback provided to students about their music education. Feedback is the essence of assessment, and it is especially useful when it is a regular part of music learning activities. Computing technologies can function as repositories for musical ideas, can help document musical progress and outcomes, and can support reflection on and review of those activities. When students have control over the documentation and reviewing processes of their musical activities, they can develop self-assessment skills that will advance their musical intelligence. Providing opportunities for peer assessment can benefit both the reviewed and the reviewer.

As mediums for electronic communication, information technologies act as links between students, teachers, parents, and the community; connect the students' musical activities to those around them; and act as conduits for valuable advice, support, and encouragement. There are a number of practical software tools that directly support assessment, including CMSs, which act as electronic portfolios, records databases, automated testing and measurement systems that can score student performance on various tasks, and word processors and spreadsheets for compiling reports and grades. While digital devices already play a significant role in music education assessment, their role seems certain to expand, as systems of communication and knowledge management increasingly use online networks and infrastructure.

Reflection Questions

1. What is assessment in music education concerned with?
2. According to David Elliott, what is the primary purpose of assessment?
3. Who are the major stakeholders in music education assessment?
4. Who coined the term musical intelligence, and what does it describe?
5. What are Keith Swanwick's dimensions of music assessment?
6. Whose works are additionally suggested as helping to inform criteria frameworks for music assessment?
7. What kinds of data can be stored electronically for review and assessment?
8. What is a CMS?
9. How can an instructor use electronic communication to improve feedback to students about their music work?
10. What types of knowledge or skill can be measured through automated computer processes?

Teaching Tips

1. Provide regular feedback to accustom students to assessment activities as part of the music learning process.
2. Set up group forums for students to discuss their music work with their classmates.
3. Provide audio and video recording facilities so that students can regularly record their work for storing, sharing, and listening.
4. Make sure that assessment criteria are culturally appropriate.
5. Encourage peer assessment as a way for students to receive more feedback and for them to develop their analytical abilities.
6. Set protocols for storage and management of student work drafts to capture information about the development of a project.
7. Establish a music ePortfolio for each student to maintain during his or her time learning music.
8. Make sure all digital storage is password protected.
9. Provide exemplar works that students can use as benchmarks for their own work.
10. Continually revisit assessment criteria in student discussions so that criteria are clear in students' minds as they work.

Suggested Tasks for Educators

1. Spend some time becoming familiar with a CMS. How do its features support assessment processes?
2. Keep an electronic journal of your own work practices to familiarize yourself with the appropriate tools and processes your students might use.
3. Review some of the research about ePortfolios to determine how they can best be used in your teaching.
4. Establish an electronic notepad to make ongoing notes about student progress that can be consulted at report-writing time.
5. Evaluate some computer-based performance accompaniment systems. How useful is the feedback they provide to students?

Chapter Summary

Assessment, which involves feedback and advice, is designed to improve student learning. In order to maximize the value of assessment, it is necessary to be clear about what musical intelligence is and how we know when students are developing it. Music technologies' capacity for capturing, presenting, and reviewing activities opens up many opportunities for feedback and assessment. Digital documentation can be stored in a content management system as an electronic portfolio, allowing student development to be more evident. Additionally, digital media technologies have changed teachers' and curriculum developers' minds about best assessment practices. For example, video assessment of performances is increasingly common, and video conferencing for moderating assessment grades is also widely used. Information technologies facilitate dialogue between students, staff, and parents about the student's musical development. Computer-based testing and measurements of student progress are becoming increasingly sophisticated and are used more widely than ever for MOOCs. Semi-automated software systems are routinely used for the preparation of student reports. Accordingly, it is clear that music technologies are playing an increasingly substantial role in the assessment of music learning.

Notes

1. Elliott, D. (1995). *Music matters: A new philosophy of music education.* Oxford: Oxford University Press, pp. 264.
2. Ibid.
3. Lebler, D. (2008). Popular music pedagogy: Peer learning in practice. *Music Education Research, 10*(2), 193–213.
4. ISAME conference information: http://reg.conferences.dce.ufl.edu/ISAME.
5. Gardner, H. (1983). *Frames of mind: The theory of multiple intelligences.* London: Heinemann.
6. Green, L. (2002). *How popular musicians learn: A way ahead for music education.* London: Ashgate, p. 210.
7. Pratt, G. (1990). *Aural awareness: Principles and practice.* Buckingham: Open University Press.

8. Reimer, B. (1970). *A philosophy of music education.* Englewood Cliffs, NJ: Prentice Hall.
9. Swanwick, K. (1999). *Teaching music musically.* London: Routledge.
10. Csikszentmihalyi, M. (1992). *Flow: The psychology of happiness.* London: Rider, p. 226.
11. *Blackboard* Learning Management Systems: http://blackboard.com/.
12. Dillon, S., & Brown, A.R. (2006). The art of ePortfolios: Insights from the creative arts experience. In A. Jafari & C. Jaufman (Eds.), *Handbook of research on ePortfolios.* Hershey, PA: Idea Group.
13. *WordPress*, blog tool: https://wordpress.org/.
14. *Blogger*, blogging service: www.blogger.com/.
15. *Moodle*: https://moodle.org/.
16. *DotCMS*: http://dotcms.com/.
17. *Ingeniux*: www.ingeniux.com/.
18. *Drupal*: https://drupal.org/.
19. *Campus Suite*: www.campussuite.com/.
20. *OmniUpdate*: http://omniupdate.com/.
21. *Jadu*: www.jadu.net/cms.
22. *Music Ace*, music theory quiz software: www.harmonicvision.com/.
23. *Harmonia*, free music theory teaching software: http://camil.music.illinois.edu/software/harmonia/. A video description is here: http://youtu.be/Eiu34nQLoTI. An article describing the underlying work is H. Taube (1999), Automatic tonal analysis: Toward the implementation of a music theory workbench, *Computer Music Journal, 23*(4):18–32.
24. *Flubaroo*, a tool for grading online multiple-choice tests: www.flubaroo.com.
25. *Student Report Writer*, by Mind Technology for the iPad: http://mindtn.com/studentReportWriter/.
26. *SMART School—Report Writer*, software to assist with writing student reports: www.report-writer.co.uk/

section V
Implementation

fifteen
Administration and Productivity

In addition to their value for learning and production, computing technologies can help teachers and students manage information to make their daily work more effective. Using a computer for administrative tasks might not be as exciting as using it for music production. However, it can have a significant impact on teacher productivity and the efficient running of a music program and is, for many teachers, their first contact with computing technologies. It is wise to be better acquainted with how technologies operate in this essential area: the business and administration of music education.

There are both benefits and pitfalls in the use of computers for educational administration and productivity. The benefits are the computer's ability to assist with data management, tracking and organization of resources, timely tracking of student progress through assessment, assistance with reflection and planning of music curricula, and as a tool for collating and reporting on activities. Some of the major pitfalls include the tendency to create too much detailed information and to direct the focus to statistics and text rather than toward musical outcomes and social benefits. The lack of flexibility in some administrative systems can also make them frustrating to navigate, and rapidly changing systems can lead to a sense of 'serial stupidity' when users, just feeling comfortable with one process, find that another has superseded it.

This chapter will explore some of the common applications and uses of computer technology for music education administration, outlining the benefits and the opportunities for increased efficiency and productivity. A fundamental understanding of digital processes might make the surface-level changes in process or appearance seem less significant.

Document Preparation

Like most other professionals, educators communicate via documents: curriculum designs, grant funding applications, worksheets, written tests, student reports, and so on. This takes up a significant part of the teacher's working life, so it is well worth getting to know the software tools that can help prepare these documents.

Word Processing

Documents are largely text-based, so it is not surprising that the word processor is the most widely used application. Throughout the history of computing, humble text editors have gone through a significant process of evolution. They were originally, and still are, used to write computer code, but now have become much more sophisticated. Text editors focus mainly on illuminating program syntax and structure, searching and modifying text, auto-completing keywords, and highlighting syntax.

Word processors have developed along a different path. Their focus is on writing prose rather than code and on the preparation of documents for reading and publishing. As a result, writing tools such as grammar and spell checkers are important, as are features connected with the appearance of text, including font types, sizes, formats (bold, italic, etc.), and layout options such as page size, margins, numbering, paragraph justification, and headers and footers. Over time, word processors have enabled the addition of graphic elements and other media. Contemporary word processors, including *Microsoft Word* and the free *LibreOffice Writer*[1] can do far more than is required by most educators, except perhaps those who want to publish their own books. Simpler programs like Microsoft's *WordPad*, Apple's *Pages*, and various note-taking apps like *Evernote*[2] (shown in Figure 15.1) are sufficient for most educators' needs. Online word processors, which run in a web browser and store documents in the cloud, are

FIGURE 15.1 A version of *Evernote* running on the iPad.

increasingly popular because they can be used for collaborative writing and to distribute documents simply by sharing a document's URL (web address). Examples of online applications are *Google Docs*[3] and *ThinkFree Online*,[4] although many of the major desktop word processors also include online companion products. As well as general-purpose word processors, specialized text-editing programs are available for particular tasks—for example, the report writing software that was reviewed in Chapter 14.

There are several options for document sharing. First, files can be distributed in a format that can be read by any word processor. The most widely readable format is a plain text file, usually denoted with a .txt extension, but the Rich Text Format (.rtf) is also widely used and maintains formatting information. Second, documents can be saved in a graphic or digital printing format—most commonly PDF—and accessed by a variety of free text readers. Third, online documents can be created either on web-based word processors or by posting them to the web using blogging software where they can be read by anyone with Internet access and the web address.

Digital Publishing

Reports and grant applications might be more acceptable in text-only format, but most documents used for teaching, including handouts, assignments, concert advertisements and programs, instructional booklets, and tests will benefit from the inclusion of graphic elements. Images can be prepared using a wide range of graphic applications, the most popular of which are Adobe's *Photoshop* and *Illustrator* or the free and open source *GIMP* software.[5] However, as with word processors, these programs have more functions than most music educators need, and a simpler graphic design program will usually suffice.

Many programs come with libraries of clip art. These prepared images provide a quick way to liven up a document or to prepare an illustration. An Internet search will reveal a number of music-related clip art sites, such as *Classroom Clipart*,[6] which have images freely available for use.

It is now a simple task to combine graphics, movies, and text into one document. Tools such as Adobe's *InDesign*, Apple *iBooks Author*,[7] and the open-source *Scribus*[8] allow sophisticated layout control and output to digital formats, including those with interactive elements. *InDesign* even allows document output as apps for mobile devices. These tools help create newsletters and marketing materials that are ready for digital distribution.

Presentation Programs

Because data projectors and larger screens are in most classrooms and lecture halls, educators often make documents for screen-based presentation—as part of a lesson, during seminars and conferences, or at fund-raising submissions, staff meetings, and public information sessions. Screen-based slideshows can include rich media such as text, images, video, or audio, and usually consist of a series of slides with information that summarizes or illustrates what is being discussed. Presentation tools include specialized programs, such as Microsoft's *PowerPoint*,[9] LibreOffice's *Impress*,[10] and Apple's *Keynote*,[11] and more general-purpose document reading applications such as

Adobe *Reader* (for viewing PDF documents) and web browsers. Most software that displays information on screen can be used for presentations, but the most useful features are the ability to include rich media elements and to move from one screen to another when required during the presentation.

To be connected with external displays or data projectors, computing devices often require adaptors that have various connectors on either end. It is important, therefore, to have the appropriate one (or several) to suit the equipment being used. It is also possible to stream visual data wirelessly from a mobile device to a stationary one (a PC or set-top box) connected to the data projector. This has the advantage of allowing the presenter to control the presentation from the mobile device, rather than having to stand near the connected device. Wireless screen sharing is also useful for students' presentations; all members of the class can connect, from wherever they are, to a large shared display and monitor speakers.

Information Management

Information for music educators can encompass class lists, students' grades, equipment inventories, staffing allocations, class timetables, and more. Computing devices can manage data in systems that range in size from those that integrate data across schools, districts, or states down to those that simply maintain individual teachers' records on personal devices. Managing data of this kind typically conflates to a few common tasks: data entry, storage, manipulation, and access. The primary software tools used to manage lists of data are spreadsheets and databases.

The Spreadsheet

Data that is primarily numerical and requires calculation is best stored and manipulated using a spreadsheet. For the music educator, tasks in this category include calculating department expenditure, tracking lesson payments, accumulating grades and percentages (shown in Figure 15.2), and maintaining attendance records. Spreadsheet

◇	A	B	C	D	E	F	G
1							
2	**SURNAME**	**NAME**	**Ass 1**	**Ass 2**	**Ass 3**	**Percent**	**Grade**
3	COMERFORD	STEPHANIE	80	77	63	74	5
4	COOPER	BRIONY	90	67	77	79	5
5	CORFIELD	JOSH	70	73	90	77	5
6	ELLIOTT	ALEISHA	73	93	80	81	6
7	FULLER	DANIEL	73	77	80	76	5
8	GALLOWAY	TIMOTHY	70	73	70	71	4
9	GENOVA	AMANDA	70	73	63	69	4
10	GRADY	TRINA	80	80	70	77	5
11	GRIFFIN	MATTHEW	83	73	80	79	5
12	GRUNDY	KATE	73	48	73	66	4
13	HANSON	SHERRALEE	90	87	77	85	7
14	HO	LEE	73	83	73	76	5

FIGURE 15.2 Assessment calculations in the spreadsheet.

may be stand-alone apps or included with office suites. Examples include *Microsoft Excel*,[12] LibreOffice *Calc*,[13] and Apple's *Numbers*.[14] Software available online, including the *Google Drive*[15] spreadsheet, also work quite well where Internet access is reliable. Versions of most of the major spreadsheet applications are available for desktop and mobile computing devices, allowing flexibility of access and editing—for example, updating attendance records directly from a mobile device in class.

A spreadsheet consists of a two-dimensional table (a sheet) of cells. The sheet consists of columns labeled A, B, C, and so on, and rows numbered 1, 2, 3, and so on. Cells are referenced by their coordinates—for example, cell B5 in Figure 15.2 contains 'Josh.' Cells can contain many types of data, including text, numbers, dates, and currency.

The real magic of a spreadsheet is that cells can also contain formulas, as the cells do in the Percent and Grade columns in Figure 15.2. Usually, the cell displays the results of the formula, but when the cell is edited the formula becomes apparent. Cells in the Percent column in the example have a formula like '=C3*0.4+D3*0.3+E3*0.3'. All spreadsheet formulae begin with an equals sign followed by math that may refer to other cell values. In this example, the weighting of the first assignment (C3) is 40% and the remaining assignments (D3 and E3) are 30% each. The Grade formula in this example converts the overall percentage to a Grade scale from 1–7, as required for the sample class. Cells with formulas update automatically with changes to the data in the cells they reference. Extrapolation from these principles can result in very sophisticated, and complex, spreadsheets. Spreadsheets are also useful for speeding up simple calculations.

The dynamic nature of calculations in a spreadsheet enables the building of numerical models that simulate situations and test hypotheses—for example, testing the effect of changing ticket fees on a concert budget, or comparing the costs of purchasing different combinations of instruments for a band. Because of this, a spreadsheet is useful for financial budgets where income or expenditure forecasts and options can be easily viewed and compared.

Given that vast amounts of numerical data are not always easy to understand at a glance, most spreadsheet applications can generate charts from the data. Figure 15.3 shows a chart of the assessment data from Figure 15.2 with the distribution of marks more clearly evident in the multiple-bar graph.

The Database

When data needs to be stored, searched, and sorted on a large scale, then databases will do the job. They are the most pervasive back-end computing tools in any business. As long as the information can be digitized, then a database can help manage it. In the context of music education, database software is useful for storing student names and addresses, maintaining inventories of equipment, tracking resource loans, keeping attendance rolls, and storing digital portfolios and 'friends of the music program' mailing lists.

Many people use spreadsheets for their database requirements. For simple lists this can suffice, but for large volumes of data that include rich media elements another solution is required. Database applications often use simplified forms to assist with data

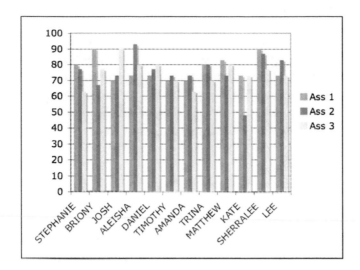

FIGURE 15.3 Graph of the assessment data from Figure 15.2.

entry; many spreadsheets don't support the use of forms, although *Microsoft Excel* does provide a 'Form' command for this purpose.

Because of their connection with business and large data sets, database software can tend toward being sophisticated and complex. However, there are relatively easy to use database applications including *TapForms*[16] for Apple platforms or *HanDBase for Education*[17] on iOS, *Data Crow*[18] for Windows, or *Google Forms*[19] online. More sophisticated database use will require applications such as *FileMaker Pro*[20] or *Firebird*,[21] or an online content management system (CMS).

Databases, like spreadsheets, consist of tables of data. In a database each row is called a *record* and each column a *field*. The data layout looks similar to a spreadsheet, but the operations on the data are more likely to be searching and matching rather than calculating. The table in Figure 15.4 shows a partial musical instrument inventory form and the resulting data table, generated using *Google Forms*. In the table, each instrument has its own record and the serial number field uniquely identifies that individual record.

Database software varies from simple flat-file databases for information such as electronic address books, to relational databases that integrate many data sources. Flat-file databases have a simple data structure that fits in a single table, whereas a relational database has a number of interrelated tables that can be interrogated—most commonly by using Structured Query Language (SQL). For example, a relational database might include a table of school musical instruments, a table of instrumental students, and a table of teachers. The relationships between students, their teachers, and the instruments they hire can be constructed and dynamically reorganized within the database, while the tables of instruments, students, and teachers can be independently maintained and modified.

Working with a database involves a process of querying, or searching, it. A query such as "How many clarinets more than five years old are in room 217?" is a typical search type. People often use databases without realizing it; a library catalogue is a database. *Google*, *Bing*, and *Yahoo* carry out searches of information databases across

Instrument Database

Instrument

Guitar

Serial Number

567-987

Purchase Date

February | 2 | 2010 | 📅

Location

Room 114

Submit

Never submit passwords through Google Forms.

▶	B	C	D	E
1	**Instrument**	**Serial Number**	**Purchase Date**	**Location**
2	Clarinet	13265	3/2/2002	Room 114
3	Clarinet	86754	8/22/2005	Room 114
4	Clarinet	34567	2/1/2001	Room 217
5	Clarinet	42365	6/24/2001	Room 217
6	Guitar	654-989	2/2/2010	Room 114
7	Guitar	567-987	2/2/2010	Room 114
8	Guitar	456-634	2/2/2010	Room 114
9	Tuba	T45672	8/5/2007	Locker 23

FIGURE 15.4 A database (a) form and (b) table for a musical instrument inventory.

the World Wide Web and can be queried by searching for key words; advanced queries allow more focused or precise searches. In principle, finding a phone number in an electronic address book is the same as searching on Google for information about drum machines, but the amount of data to be searched is vastly different and so, therefore, are the data organization, computing power, and storage space required by the database.

Learning Management Systems

CMSs, which include a database and web interface, are becoming increasingly common as a way of organizing and accessing information. Typically they are hosted in the cloud or run on a school's server (dedicated computer). As discussed in Chapter 14, there are many freely available CMSs including *Drupal*, *WordPress*, *PivotX*, *Plone*, and *Bricolage*.

A CMS can be used as an administrative tool because it can provide public or private access to information that is added to or edited from any location on the network. It is regularly used to create web sites for online newsletters, departmental blogs, students' digital portfolios, calendars of events, online tutorials, and collaborative document authoring. A CMS allows the coordination of information within one system and acts as a web-based communication tool for notifications and discussions. Several people in a music educational institution can be authorized to add or edit data in a CMS, allowing staff (or staff and students) to share the work of keeping information up to date; effectively a CMS is a database that acts as a coordinated hub for information about the music department.

A learning management system (LMS) is a CMS with additional educational features, including class schedules and records of assessment results. The LMS can deliver online learning materials to students and can use record-keeping and communication functions to track student progress and facilitate discussion between students and instructors. Like the CMS, the LMS typically provides a web interface to a database back-end and can be hosted by external providers or set up on an institution's own servers. Some popular LMS systems include *Moodle*,[22] *Online Learning and Teaching (OLAT)*,[23] *Blackboard*,[24] and *Desire2Learn*.[25]

Running the LMS is most likely to be an institution-wide project rather than an operation of a music department or individual teacher. When running, features of the institution's LMS can be used by a teacher to assist with delivering materials, storing results, and communicating with their students.

Planning and Scheduling

Managing time and projects are important aspects of educational administration. Computing technologies provide software applications that are dedicated to scheduling classes and events, keeping track of to-do lists, and managing projects; all are very helpful in the planning and running of a music education program. This section will explore some of these areas, particularly software for electronic calendars, task lists, project management, and timetabling.

Most office suites or computer operating systems include an electronic diary or calendar program to keep track of appointments and events. The standard calendar data exchange format, called *iCalendar*, allows transfer of calendar entries, including meeting requests, between software diaries. Files using this format have the .ics extension. Examples of software that support this standard include calendar apps from Apple, Google, Yahoo, and Mozilla. Microsoft's *Exchange Server* defines another protocol that is also widespread, based on its use by Microsoft's calendar and e-mail application, *Outlook*. Using one of these standards makes it much easier to distribute concert dates, assignment due dates, meetings and other events among staff and students. Online calendar systems are also available, and allow many users to access or edit a single calendar—particularly handy for ensemble rehearsal and concert schedules that need to be shared and that might require occasional updates or variations.

For instructors and students, keeping on top of tasks is a constant challenge: preparing, marking, or completing assignments; preparing for classes; rehearsing or attending events; and following up on commitments made during conversations and lessons. Software for to-do lists and note taking can support task management, especially if there is an application that syncs tasks across all devices and the cloud, including smartphones

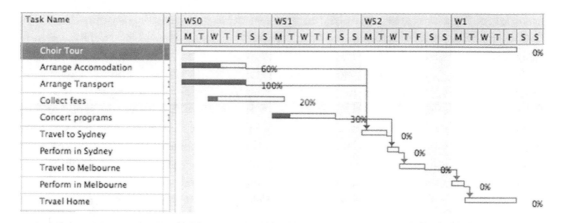

FIGURE 15.5 A Gantt chart displaying the timing and dependencies of project tasks.

and mobile and desktop computers. Applications such as *Evernote*[26] or *OneNote*[27] are popular note taking software choices and have versions available for many devices and platforms. A number of dedicated task management apps support the Getting Things Done (GTD)[28] method. This method emphasizes writing down tasks to free the mind from having to keep track of them; breaking tasks into manageable and actionable items; and regular reprioritization of tasks to ensure the most important and timely are done first. Applications that support the GTD approach include *OmniFocus*,[29] *Things*,[30] and *Remember The Milk*.[31]

Project management software can assist in planning large events and projects, including concert tours, musicals, or recording productions. Project management software, such as *Microsoft Project*,[32] Techno Grafik's *iTaskX*,[33] *Project Planner HD*[34] for iPad, or *Project Planner Free*[35] for Android, will allow users to enter the tasks and timelines for a project, visualize the timeline as a Gantt chart, as shown in Figure 15.5, and track its progress.

For the management of class scheduling tasks, including the organization of instrumental lessons, timetabling software applications include *Mimosa*[36] and *Lantiv Scheduling Studio*.[37] Automatic timetabling is never simple and it can take quite some time to achieve optimum organization, especially for complex timetables. For smaller tasks, such as scheduling instrumental lessons among a small cohort of teachers, a calendar and manual entry might be sufficient; simpler software such as *eSoft Planner*,[38] *Appointment Plus*,[39] or *Music Teacher's Helper*[40] can also assist.

Data Management

Having examined many ways in which digital technologies can be used to manage information for music teaching, it is timely to discuss managing the data itself. One of the implications of investing heavily in computer systems is that it can be disastrous if the data is lost or corrupted; so, with increased use of computing devices comes the need for increased vigilance about data management.

The most important consideration is to keep regular backups of files on a separate medium, such as an external hard drive, and also offsite, for example in cloud-based storage. Cloud storage solutions are increasingly common and are now more affordable. Files can be synchronized to many of these services, for automatic backup. Cloud syncing services include *Dropbox*,[41] *Microsoft OneDrive*,[42] *Google Drive*,[43] and Amazon *Cloud Drive*.[44]

Another thing to consider is how to manage the size of files or databases. It is usually more efficient to have several smaller files than one larger one, unless there is a need for regular cross-referencing. For example, each lesson plan should have a separate file; smaller files are more quickly searched and backed up and, if they are corrupted, less data is lost. Another way of keeping data size manageable is to archive older data and keep only recent files on hand. For example, last year's e-mails can be archived so that searching and sorting operations need only deal with the most recent and relevant information.

Printing summaries of important data—for example, student grades or project budgets—ensures that if computer data is lost there is physical backup in a filing cabinet. This need only be done occasionally, with only the latest paper version kept on file.

Finally, it is important to make sure that files and data are well organized and clearly labeled to save the frustration of not being able to find an important item when it is most needed. Taking advantage of the 'alias' or 'shortcut' functions of the computer file system, which allows a link to a file or folder to exist in many places, ensures that a file can be located at any time, regardless of which category is searched.

Conclusion

Digital technologies are useful tools for assisting with the administrative tasks that are inevitable in professional music education. Computing systems are particularly helpful in the documentation of plans and outcomes, budgets and financial planning, and assessment and reporting. Information management handles student records, resource tracking, and the planning and management of projects and activities. A wide variety of software apps and online services can be used for these administrative tasks, and it is worth the effort to learn how to use them efficiently, saving time and frustration in the long run. It is important to keep in mind that, although digital technologies function as tools to support utilitarian, administrative tasks, this does not diminish their important role as musical mediums and musical instruments.

Reflection Questions

1. What are the benefits of using the computer as an administrative tool?
2. What are the pitfalls?
3. Describe the potential benefits of web-based documents for a teaching team.
4. Which software applications support digital publishing?
5. When might audio or video materials be necessary for administrative purposes in a music education context?
6. What are the key differences between spreadsheets and databases?
7. Define CMS and LMS.
8. When might a Gantt chart be useful?
9. Name some ways to backup digital data.
10. Name some of the cloud syncing services that are available to keep data organized.

Teaching Tips

1. Save templates of forms and letters that are used regularly.
2. Have students help with preparation of concert flyers and programs.
3. Encourage students (and staff) to be familiar with administration tools to the point where they assist rather than frustrate their work.
4. Work out how to export and import data between major administration applications so that each can be used for the tasks for which it is designed.
5. Make use of graphics programs and clip art to liven up documents.
6. Get into the habit of regularly capturing and indexing audio and video of student performances to assist in assessment and reporting.
7. Encourage the use of automated saving functions in software to avoid data loss.
8. Use CMS blogs and messaging services to help develop a sense of community among music students and staff.
9. Take computing devices into lessons so that data can be entered on the spot rather than retyped from paper-based notes.
10. Keep a paper copy of important data, in case digital files are lost.

Suggested Tasks for Educators

1. See how project management software might help organize your large music projects.
2. Explore various online document systems and decide which one best suits your needs.
3. If your institution uses an LMS, then learn how it can be made to assist your work.
4. Investigate how your word processor's page layout functions can make your documents look even more professional.
5. Compare annual enrollment and assessment data and reflect on any long-term trends.

Chapter Summary

Of the many areas of human work where the computer has had significant impact on society, one of the most profound is in information management. The data management and administrative functions of the computer might not be vastly interesting to a musician—compared with music production or performance—but efficient record keeping, lesson and project planning, budgeting, coordination with peers and so on, are vital activities for the professional music educator. The main tools of the trade include word processors, spreadsheets, databases, presentational packages, project management, and online communication tools. These are also the most widely available applications for digital devices, which guarantees that there are many related software choices. Effective use of these tools makes administration less of a chore and helps effective planning and development of the music education program.

Notes

1. *LibreOffice*, a free and open source productivity software suite: www.libreoffice.org/.
2. *Evernote*, multi-platform note taking software: http://evernote.com/.
3. *Google Docs*, online word processor: http://docs.google.com.

4. *ThinkFree*, stand-alone and online version of standard 'office' applications: www.thinkfree.com/main.jsp.

5. *GIMP*, a free but powerful image manipulation program: www.gimp.org/.

6. *Classroom Clipart*, a site with images for use in educational documents: http://classroomclipart.com/.

7. *iBooks Author*, allows the creation of rich media documents for output in the iBook format for reading on iPad or Mac: www.apple.com/ibooks-author/.

8. *Scribus*, open source desktop publishing software: www.scribus.net/canvas/Scribus.

9. *PowerPoint*, presentation software from Microsoft: http://office.microsoft.com/en-us/powerpoint/.

10. *Impress*, the presentation application in *LibreOffice*: www.libreoffice.org/discover/impress/.

11. *Keynote*, Apple's presentation software for Mac OS and iOS: www.apple.com/mac/keynote/.

12. *Excel*, the spreadsheet application in *Microsoft Office*: http://office.microsoft.com/en-us/excel/.

13. *Calc*, the spreadsheet in *LibreOffice*: www.libreoffice.org/discover/calc/.

14. *Numbers*, the spreadsheet application from Apple: for Mac OS, www.apple.com/mac/numbers/; and iOS, https://itunes.apple.com/en/app/numbers/id361304891?mt = 8.

15. *Google Drive* services include productivity apps and file storage: http://drive.google.com.

16. *TapForms*, database software for Mac OS and iOS: www.tapforms.com/.

17. *HanDBase*, database software for iOS by DHH Software: www.ddhsoftware.com/handbase_ipad.html.

18. *Data Crow*, flat file database for Windows: www.datacrow.net/.

19. *Forms*, Google's data entry tool that saves data in a spreadsheet: http://drive.google.com.

20. *FileMaker Pro*, an application for substantial database needs: www.filemaker.com/.

21. *Firebird*, an open source SQL database for multiple desktop platforms: www.firebirdsql.org/.

22. *Moodle*, learning management systems: https://moodle.org/.

23. *Online Learning and Teaching (OLAT)*, learning management system: http://www.olat.org/.

24. *Blackboard*, learning management system: http://blackboard.com.

25. *Desire2Learn*, learning management system: www.desire2learn.com/.

26. *Evernote*, multi-platform note taking software: http://evernote.com/.

27. *OneNote*, note taking software from Microsoft: http://office.microsoft.com/en-us/onenote/.

28. Getting Things Done (GDT), a task management method developed by David Allen: http://gettingthingsdone.com/.

29. *OmniFocus*, task management software: www.omnigroup.com/omnifocus.

30. *Things*, task management software: https://culturedcode.com/things/.

31. *Remember The Milk*, task management software: www.rememberthemilk.com/.

32. *Microsoft Project*, project management software for: http://office.microsoft.com/en-us/project/.

33. *iTaskX*, project management software for Mac OS: www.itaskx.com/software/en/iTaskX2_info.asp.

34. *Project Planner HD*, project management app for iPad from Peritum: www.peritum.net/projectplannerhd.html.

35. *Project Planner Free*, project management software for Android: https://play.google.com/store/apps/details?id=de.thorstensapps.ttf.

36. *Mimosa*, timetabling software: www.mimosasoftware.com/.

37. *Lantiv Scheduling Studio*, timetabling software: http://schedulingstudio.com/.

38. *eSoft Planner*, lesson scheduling software: www.esoftplanner.com/web-based-music-scheduling-software.php.

39. *Appointment Plus*, scheduling software: www.appointment-plus.com/.

40. *Music Teacher's Helper*, lesson calendar and billing software: www.musicteachershelper. com/.
41. *Dropbox*, cloud-based file storage and synchronization: www.dropbox.com/.
42. *OneDrive*, cloud-based file storage and synchronization from Microsoft: https://onedrive. live.com/.
43. *Google Drive*, cloud-based file storage and synchronization: http://drive.google.com.
44. *Cloud Drive* from Amazon, cloud-based file storage and synchronization: www.amazon. com/clouddrive/home/?_encoding=UTF8&*Version*=1&*entries*=0.

sixteen
Managing Music Technologies

For music educators the purchase of music technology equipment is usually a love or hate affair. Some relish the task and enjoy delving into the details of the latest shiny thing. Others see the process as a chore or feel overwhelmed by the jargon and just want something that works. Either way, choosing music technologies is an important consideration for music educators, whose equipment budgets never seem adequate and who have to live with the implications of their decisions for years to come. As well as making plans for purchases, they have to make decisions about the physical location of equipment, the number of devices, required additional infrastructure, and ongoing resource management. These issues are explored in this chapter.

The Opportunity-to-Learn Standards for Music Instruction were published in the United States by the National Association for Music Education (then called MENC). Using them as a base, the association also published technology standards that included some useful principles that continue to hold true.[1] Here is a summary:

1. The use of technology should be a regular and integral part of music instruction.
2. Instructional strategies should appropriately utilize the unique capabilities of technology.
3. Technology-based music performance experiences should be available to students and integrated into existing ensembles where appropriate.
4. A range of music technologies should be incorporated into student learning experiences.
5. Software and hardware selections should be based on learning goals.
6. Music classes should have the same degree of access to technology resources as other discipline areas.
7. Student learning profiles (e.g., attendance records and progress reports) should be maintained using databases and other record-keeping technologies.
8. Students should have access to the Internet for music activities such as research, communicating with peers and authorities, and developing and publishing materials.

9. Children with special needs should have the same access to technology-based music instruction as other children.
10. Technologies should be used to support distance-learning experiences where necessary or appropriate.

In this chapter we will discuss aspects of these and other guidelines that can be of help in the acquisition and management of music technologies—including devices, software, and recording equipment. The aim is that the guidelines will provide a checklist and outline a process that will instill confidence in those who find managing technologies a chore and will stimulate further interest in those who enjoy it.

Task Identification

The first step toward acquiring appropriate music technologies is defining what activities and tasks they are required to support. This might be, for example, arranging band music, scaffolding the beginning composer, recording an ensemble, researching materials for a musicology assignment, or developing aural perception. Often there will be a variety of tasks identified and they need to be prioritized. Curricular needs (things you *have* to do) or aspirations (interesting things you *want* to do) should direct the process of prioritization. At this stage, it is best to focus on outcomes rather than processes— once outcomes are clear, technologies appropriate to achieving them will become more evident. Be aware that, as discussed in the chapters in Section 1, the introduction of new technologies will open up new opportunities, so there is a coupling between changes in technology and changes in curriculum; they will influence each other. For example, the current composition course may focus on popular songs in the 'words and chords' tradition, which suggests that a music publishing system is required to generate lead sheets. However, students might be more interested in electronic dance music genres; this can be fostered by purchasing a digital sampler or groovebox. When tasks have been identified and prioritized, it is time to select the most appropriate tools for the jobs.

Choosing Equipment

What is the right technological tool for each musical job? This depends, of course, on the musical needs and the availability of equipment. A three-stage decision-making process is suggested in Figure 16.1. It begins by identifying musical intentions (as discussed earlier), then choosing software that will meet those needs, and finally selecting hardware that supports the software.

In this approach decisions are clearly driven by musical or educational requirements and technologies are subservient to them. For example, in Step 1 the *intention* is to arrange the band repertoire. In Step 2, look to the *software* and identify, from various music-publishing applications, those solutions that best fit the task. In Step 3, select the *hardware* platform that supports those short-listed solutions.

The order of *intention*, *software*, then *hardware* serves well as a rule of thumb but there are some circumstances where hardware needs should be prioritized; for example, in selecting a MIDI controller for live performance or a microphone for recording. In

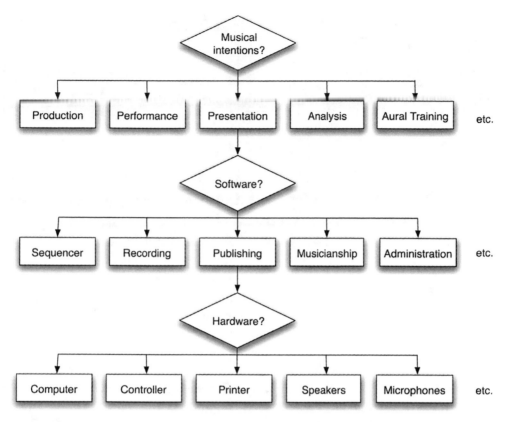

FIGURE 16.1 A decision-making process for choosing music technologies.

both these cases the hardware will make the most significant difference and can be supported adequately by many applications. When there are multiple intentions and needs—as there almost always are—then software and hardware options will be filtered by the apps and devices that service the greatest number of these or those with the highest priority. Combined with constraints on price and compatibility with previous investments the range of options narrows quite quickly.

Digital Musical Appliances

An important consideration when selecting music technology equipment is whether to purchase a dedicated device or a general-purpose device with a software solution. For example, if you are looking for a pad-oriented sampler and sequencer for live electronic music you could choose the Akai *XR20* (a dedicated device) or the Akai *iMPC* app and an Apple iPad to run it on; both solutions are similar in price and functionality. These solutions are shown side by side in Figure 16.2.

General-purpose computing devices have greater potential but often only a few of their capabilities are needed. Much less complex and more widely used are dedicated devices including MP3 players, digital music keyboards with built-in sequencers, dedicated digital multi-track mixer/recorders, electronic tuners, digital metronomes, and electronic drum machines. Donald Norman refers to these devices as *digital*

FIGURE 16.2 The Akai XR20 and the Apple iPad running the Akai *IMPC* app.

appliances; the computer is less overt and is just one component of an entire system. Norman's book *The Invisible Computer*[2] contains a detailed discussion of the differences in usability between digital appliances and personal computers.

Digital musical appliances have certain advantages: they start immediately, need little maintenance, are often portable, have handy dedicated physical controls, and usually perform a specific task very efficiently. In school settings, digital music appliances have other advantages too. The lack of configurability means they always present a consistent interface to the student, they rarely crash, and because they are good for little else but music, no other department wants to own, control, or borrow them. The disadvantage of dedicated devices is that they are rarely upgradeable and cannot be put to another task as priorities of use change. General-purpose devices, like laptops or tablet computers, have the advantage of being able to service a variety of needs with the simple loading of new apps. When versatility is required and budgets are tight, they can be an effective solution.

Desktop computing systems have traditionally been the main music technology choice but they are physically cumbersome to move, take time to setup and start up, and are complex to maintain. Tablet computers and smartphone devices have overcome most of these limitations and as a result are becoming more popular. Consider, for example, the experience of setting up a trumpet or an electric guitar; after the assembly of a few components and a short tune-up, the instrument is ready to go. Music technology devices need to be competitive with this level of convenience, and this is where mobile devices and digital appliances are attractive.

This is not a call to avoid the desktop computing device in the music classroom but rather to suggest that it is just one among many alternatives when you are selecting devices for music education.

Selecting Between Alternatives

When choosing one tool over another, you are looking for the best fit between your requirements and the relevant features the tool offers. Features should be prioritized, or weighted, and not simply counted, because some will be critical and others optional. In the potential confusion of specifications and price trade-offs it can be easy to lose track of critical requirements. To highlight the issue, consider this scenario: A soprano saxophone is required to complete a saxophone quartet line up, but there's a suggestion that a clarinet be purchased instead, because it is similar, it would be cheaper, and because there is more repertoire for clarinet than soprano saxophone. But these considerations do not meet the main purchase criterion: an instrument that can be part of a saxophone quartet. This is off-track advice—whether for purchasing acoustic instruments or music technology. To guard against this misguided advice, be clear about priorities and stick to them. If you need a music-publishing package that elegantly handles guitar tablature, don't be persuaded to purchase one that cannot do it, even if it has 20 other advantages.

Another important consideration when choosing an appropriate music technology is to select one of suitable complexity (or appropriate simplicity). This applies more to software than to hardware because many music software packages are designed for professional musicians and often include features and concepts that students will not need or, worse, find daunting or confusing. Many music software developers recognize this and produce cut down or 'lite' versions of their software, usually sufficient for educational contexts. On the other hand, be careful not to place limits on students' potential with restricted feature sets or limited tools.

This list of questions can be used as a checklist when considering the purchase of a piece of music technology:

- Does it match the prioritized needs of the situation, the curriculum, and the institutional environment?
- Does it operate at the appropriate level of complexity given the age and experience of the students?
- Have all the available options been considered?
- Is it cost effective compared with other options?
- Is it compatible with existing equipment?
- Is it durable enough for the treatment it will receive from students?
- How will it be installed and is there available space (physical or virtual) for its use and storage?
- Does it need to be portable?
- Is it safe to use in terms of electrical power requirements, weight, and so on?
- Does it suit the abilities and interests of staff and students?
- Has staff training on the equipment been arranged?
- Are additional accessories required to have it function adequately?

If you are searching for equipment, many others are likely to be doing the same, so it is sensible to work with them and share information and experiences. An Internet search will reveal discussion forums, blog posts, and product reviews that might inform your purchasing decisions.

Ancillary Equipment

Price considerations are important. The rule of thumb in budgeting for music technology systems is to spend one-third of the budget on the device, one-third on software, and one-third on auxiliary equipment. Therefore, in purchasing a stereo digital recording setup, one-third of the budget would be allocated to a computing device; one-third to digital audio workstation (DAW) software and signal processing plug-ins; and one-third to microphones, audio interface, and monitor speakers.

Ancillary equipment can alter the purchase price dramatically. Consider choosing a set of tablet computers to support a range of production, aural training, and presentation tasks. Ancillary equipment includes protective cases, software apps, charging kits, wireless speakers for decent audio playback, connectors for data projection, and wireless Internet routers to provide a local network in the classroom—not to mention furniture, music stands, and other general infrastructure. Each ancillary item plays an important role in the process of making music and has an impact on the quality of students' experiences and learning outcomes.

Physical Setup

Once purchased, music technologies need to be made available to students. Typically this involves access via physical organization in the classroom and/or procedures for booking and lending equipment for use outside the class. This section will focus on the arrangement of equipment in the teaching space.

One of the first steps in dealing with the questions of space and organization of equipment is to establish which constraints are fixed and which are flexible. Most likely, room size will be fixed, but it might be possible to distribute equipment across several rooms or make equipment transportable. Usage patterns depend upon student numbers and pedagogical constraints of habit and social expectation. For instance, the question of how many devices are required for a class is primarily a pedagogical one, not an economic one. Four different methods for organizing equipment are illustrated in Figure 16.3. *Clustered* equipment is space efficient and enables interaction among users. Equipment can be *distributed* around the space to provide several focal points for individual or small group activities. Each distributed system can be similar or varied to provide a range of facilities. The clustered or distributed 'workstation' patterns can include mixing desks, speakers, and headphone distribution amplifiers for added versatility. *Portable* or mobile equipment provides maximal flexibility for classroom organization but requires consideration of cable requirements for power and audio. Finally, the *studio* setup provides a dedicated workspace for music technology users. All of these methods support uninterrupted work in an optimal listening and operational format.

It is enlightening to examine the usage patterns for existing resources in music education and to imagine how these might be applied to music technologies. There are precedents in historical practices for differing equipment usage. For example, recorders (of the woodwind type) and textbooks are technologies that are so inexpensive that there is a set for every student—often bought by the student. Institutions frequently purchase one or two copies of more expensive or specialized books and an ensemble of handmade wooden recorders, which are shared among the class and used for advanced studies. Another example is teaching guitar in school music classes, where it is not uncommon to have a limited number of instruments—perhaps half a dozen—and on a rotation basis, to have student groups moving between playing and other activities.

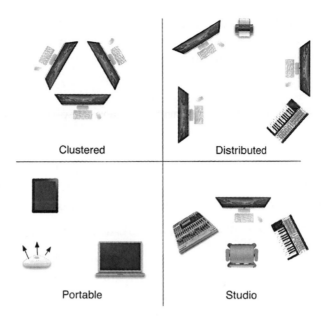

Clustered Distributed

Portable Studio

FIGURE 16.3 Some options for computer setups in educational institutions.

A third example is how to manage the limited availability of a single acoustic piano or drum kit. They are used for teacher demonstrations, and then one or two students at a time use them as part of a group of mixed instruments.[3] A final analogy can be drawn with the management of specialized acoustic instruments, such as a bass clarinet or piccolo. These are often lent, for extended periods, to students who specialize in their use and contribute to the school's musical culture by playing them in ensembles. In each of these cases it is not hard to imagine how music technology equipment can be deployed using these established pedagogical strategies.

Location and Access

As computer-based equipment is continually miniaturized, the options for its physical location are expanded. Equipment such as microphones, tablet computers, and MIDI control surfaces are very portable and can be kept in storage areas and distributed as required. Items such as synthesizers, mixing desks, monitor speakers, and laptop computers are portable (or luggable) items, which might have a home location but can be moved between teaching rooms and to performance venues as required. Fixed items include printers, data projectors, and public address systems. They need a more permanent location—ideally, as with other educational resources, in a dedicated location either in a classroom, office, storeroom, or locker—and can be booked for use in other locations as required.

In the late twentieth century, when computing devices were less widespread, it was common for an educational institution to keep all available computers in labs. Having to leave the normal music teaching spaces to do computer music making in a lab is inefficient and disconnects music technology activities from other forms of music making. Shared access to general purpose computing resources in a distant location should be avoided whenever possible. A better alternative is to have a few computers set up with appropriate MIDI and audio hardware in the music classroom. Today's students will almost always have their own computing resources at home and lab work can be done as homework.

As mobile computing devices, such as smartphones, become more ubiquitous, the growing trend is for students to bring their own devices to the music class. For educational institutions this shifts the equipment priority to providing auxiliary devices, rather than central processing units (CPU). Given that apps are relatively inexpensive, schools and colleges can augment them by providing auxiliary equipment like wireless networks, loudspeakers, control surfaces, mixing desks, microphones, and audio interfaces. The changes in the way textbooks are used provide a useful guide to this trend. Once books were expensive and the institution managed them in libraries. Now, students purchase (e)books and bring them to class. Specialized books and resources are available in teaching spaces for reference or in libraries for borrowing. The use of digital devices in education will follow a similar pattern as the cost and size of devices continue to shrink.

Ergonomics

With the increased use of any technology comes the risk of common usage ailments, including back pain, upper body muscle tension, eyestrain, and repetitive strain injuries. An important part of setting up equipment, therefore, is to pay attention to ergonomic factors, including appropriate seating with adjustable seat height and the positioning of monitors and keyboards, also adjustable for students of various heights. Long periods of repetitive work can be problematic; technology usage patterns in classes should take account of this. Occupational health and safety web sites, run by most state governments or educational authorities, offer detailed advice on appropriate ergonomic work practices.

Security and Data Storage

After spending time and energy on selecting and installing equipment, it is worth investing in security against loss or theft. Desktop equipment can be secured to furniture with locking cables that do not hinder use. Portable equipment can be housed in protective cases and placed in lockers or storerooms when not in use. Some lockers have electrical power outlets for convenient battery recharge while portable devices are being stored.

Data security is an issue when using shared devices. Common precautions against viruses and other software invasions include using and updating virus protection software, using firewalls on machines connected to the Internet, and requiring users to log in. Students should be encouraged to save and manage their own data using portable storage devices or cloud-based storage options. Teachers can minimize data loss by keeping snapshots of student work and backups of electronic resources and materials. Data should be backed up regularly and backups should be stored in a location separate from the device itself and in cloud storage, in case of fire or other incidents that could damage collocated resources.

Maintenance

An often overlooked element of setting up music technology systems is the inevitable ongoing maintenance. This includes the reimaging of computers (reloading all the software) to keep them in a stable state, given that students tend to shift, add, and delete items, seemingly at random; regular updates to software and the addition of security patches that are released from time to time; and physical maintenance, including cleaning, replacing lost leads, fixing broken items, and other minor repairs. Larger institutions have technical staff to assist with these tasks, but smaller educational programs should plan and budget for ongoing maintenance. Many computer suppliers provide maintenance contracts as a service, although they tend to be quite expensive for most educational budgets.

Professional Development

Making the most of music technology equipment requires staff to be well versed in its operation and applications. Professional development of staff can be achieved in a number of ways. Equipment manuals and video tutorials are available for private study. Educators can maintain familiarity and competence by using music technologies in their ongoing musical practice. Training sessions can be run when equipment is purchased and at regular intervals afterwards. Colleagues can gain and share knowledge in seminars, conferences, and external training courses. Knowledgeable students can be recruited to brief staff about music technologies.

The Opportunity-to-Learn Standards for Music Technology, mentioned earlier, included recommendations for professional development, which provide useful guidance and are summarized here:

1. Teachers should have easy access to online resources and services for professional and curriculum development and research.
2. A planned program of staff development should be available to provide teachers with training in applying technology in the curriculum.
3. Training should be available on a variety of levels to match the varying backgrounds and proficiencies of teachers.
4. Teachers should be supported in networking with other colleagues about the use of technology.
5. Access to technical support and mentoring, by music technology and education experts, should be available.
6. Teachers should be provided with the necessary development time for creating new curriculum materials that make effective use of music technology.
7. Teachers who receive specialized training in music technology can act as mentors for their colleagues.

Conclusion

Appropriate management of music technology resources is a key to ensuring students' learning success. When selecting equipment, keep an eye on musical and educational priorities and mold the selection and application of music technologies to meet these ends. Acquiring and managing technologies for music education can be a complex but satisfying process of matching educational needs with evolving technological capabilities. At the heart of any music technology system is the computing device and the software run on it, and either the institution or the student might provide these. Accompanying the core devices is auxiliary equipment, including audio interfaces, MIDI keyboards, visual displays, audio monitors, printers, cables, mixers, and microphones. Music technology equipment can be made accessible in a variety of ways—as permanent workstation setups, in semi-portable kits, and as bookable individual items. Keeping staff up to date with equipment usage needs to be a deliberate process. Managing music technologies for education is a considerable task, but maintaining effective music technology resources and using them well can have positive effects on the music program and so is a task well worth the educator's attention and worth doing well.

Reflection Questions

1. Why is the choice of appropriate computing equipment an important music education decision?
2. Why is task identification a critical step in selecting music technologies?
3. Name three of the principles derived from the NAfME technology standards.
4. What are the three suggested steps in the decision-making process for choosing music technologies?
5. What are the arguments for and against using digital musical appliances?
6. What are some strategies for the professional development of educators?
7. What four options for computer setups in educational institutions are outlined?
8. Given that students now bring their own devices to class, what changes can educational institutions make in their management of music technologies?
9. Why might technology lockers have electrical sockets in them?
10. What types of maintenance do digital devices require?

Teaching Tips

1. Use interested students to help instructors keep up to date with trends in computing.
2. Make sure that software and hardware are updated to reflect contemporary musical practices.
3. Always keep students focused on the musical aspects of tasks and avoid obsessions with technology for its own sake.
4. Integrate music technologies into music teaching spaces rather than separating them out into a lab.
5. Teach students the skills of selecting appropriate technologies for the musical task at hand.
6. Provide secure lockers for students who bring their own devices for use in the music program.
7. Emphasize safe computer usage practices with students.
8. Use a booking system for managing outside class use of computer music systems.
9. Utilize computer clusters to promote peer assistance.

10. Keep a file of student data CDs in the music room so that students can regularly back up their work.

Suggested Tasks for Educators

1. Make a prioritized list of your preferred learning outcomes as a basis for selecting appropriate technologies.
2. Do an audit of the music technologies you currently use and reflect on opportunities to consolidate, expand, or update these tools.
3. Compare a dedicated digital music appliance with a software-based alternative.
4. Connect with other educators who are using music technologies to compare experiences and knowledge.
5. Draw plans of four alternative classroom layouts to help stimulate non-obvious but interesting setups of music technology equipment.

Chapter Summary

The purchasing and placement of music technology equipment can be a complex task. However, in many ways it is similar to the purchase and deployment of other music resources, like instruments and musical scores. Therefore, many of the suggestions about managing music technologies will seem familiar. Because of the rate of change in computer-based technologies, each time you purchase new equipment it is wise to investigate and test all the possibilities. Steps to consider in the decision-making process are: identify the educational priorities; look for software that can support them; and select the most appropriate hardware that will run the software. Also consider digital appliances—dedicated music technology systems—as an alternative to running software on general-purpose computing devices. Having acquired equipment, you need to make decisions about locating and accessing the equipment, the ergonomics of its use, physical and data security, Internet access, ongoing maintenance, and the professional development of instructors. Even though there are many aspects to managing music technology equipment in educational settings, when these processes are well implemented they allow technologies to support music learning and to amplify musicality. Surely this is worth the effort.

Notes

1. Opportunity-to-Learn Standards for Music Technology. (1999). Published by the National Standards for Music Education. http://musiced.nafme.org/about/the-national-standards-for-arts-education-introduction/opportunity-to-learn-standards-for-music-technology/.
2. Norman, D. A. (1998). *The invisible computer: Why good products can fail, the personal computer is so complex, and information appliances are the solution.* Cambridge, MA: MIT Press.
3. Frankel, J. (2004). The one-computer music classroom. *Music Education Technology,* 2(4): 10–14.

seventeen
Integrating New Technologies

The implementation of new technologies into music education programs can have many positive effects, including stimulating the music program's renewal. However, integrating digital music technologies can disrupt established practices and challenge conventional thinking. It is important to remember, though, that the disruption new technology poses seems to be a familiar process, at least on a historical timescale. Timothy Taylor, in his book *Strange Sounds: Music, Technology and Culture*, suggests that digital technology is simply the most recent in a series of technologies, including radio and audio recording, that have disrupted existing practices: "The introduction of every major new technology, at least in the course of the twentieth century, has been accompanied by a complex mixture of wonderment and anxiety. Digital technology is no different."[1]

While the disruptive effects of digital technologies may not be unique, digital technologies provide unique opportunities. Digital skills are increasingly valued in many aspects of life. The researcher Andrea diSessa specializes in the use of computers in education and points out that understanding the computer is becoming an essential competency. DiSessa observes that "the gradual evolution to a computationally literate society guarantees we will experience changing circumstances that we would like to negotiate with skill."[2] The increasing importance of digital systems in all facets of contemporary life, from social networking to music making, underscores the need to provide students with an understanding of how digital technologies function to extend their abilities. Music education can both contribute to and benefit from this capability.

However, the anxiety about new technologies that Taylor identifies is ever present. Ongoing concerns for music educators include how to ensure that new music technologies integrate with established music activities rather than overtake them, how digital resources can be made available to students easily and equitably, how to ensure that established cultural practices are not forgotten in a headlong rush toward digital music making, and how to ensure that the value of educators is not undermined as digital technologies facilitate increased learning flexibility and student autonomy. This chapter explores many of the positive and cautionary aspects of introducing digital technologies into music education.

Technological Mediation

Young people's musical worlds are saturated with digital technologies. Especially in the area of music consumption, they use now-ubiquitous digital music players like smartphones and iPods, and have online access to recorded music through *Spotify*, *SoundCloud*, *iTunes*, and *YouTube* for music videos. In addition, social networks are the conduit for commentary and opinions about music, music recommendations, and news about musical events. These digital technologies are important mediators of musical experiences, providing young people with increased access to music and an interactive participation in musical culture.

Some of the dangers that arise as a result of the ubiquity of digital mediation of music include the potential devaluing of a particular music, even as music overall is continued to be valued. With so much music available, recorded products and artists' talents are subject to commodification. Furthermore, music competes with other digital media and activities for attention in people's lives. There is a risk that the appreciation of both the musical and sonic qualities of recorded and live music will diminish as a result. The challenge for artists today is building meaningful relationships with their audiences. The challenge for music educators is acknowledging digital mediation and helping students better understand the ways music technologies can affect musical expression, as well as how they can be used to enhance, rather than trivialize, musical experiences.

Understanding and Knowledge

Music technologies feature musical understandings embedded, in particular, in the metaphors and functionalities of the software. Educators choose one technology over another based on these predispositions in the hope that students exposed to these musical understandings and techniques will absorb them. Therefore, for educators, music technologies are not only functional, but also epistemological and pedagogical tools. Assumptions about music are encapsulated in technological designs. For example, different technologies treat music as either private or social, as individual or collaborative, as interpretive or inventive, as trivial or sophisticated, and so on. When users are exposed to these assumptions through interaction with technologies, their understandings may be influenced as a result. Music technologies' application to music education is, as with all other activities and resources, not simply about providing tools, or even about transferring ideas, but about situating the student in a musical culture.[3]

To facilitate successful integration of music technologies, it is important that technologies are comprehensible and students are motivated to use them. A technology will be comprehensible when the interface can be read easily, when the complexity of engagement is appropriate, and when the musical concepts being explored relate to and extend a student's existing knowledge.

There is a wide range of hardware and software for music production, and so it should not be difficult to find appropriate tools for students at almost any skill level or age. Sometimes tool appropriateness (or relevance) relates directly to the music genre(s) it supports; for example, audio file remixing software appeals to those interested in electronic music. At other times, appropriateness relates to the task. For example, music production software can be used to transcribe melodic dictations or to write a new pop song, but there are clear differences in the likely motivations of students doing those tasks. Although in the twenty-first century digital music technologies can be made available without much difficulty, maximizing their impact depends on careful consideration of their use.

Skills and Techniques

Since the late twentieth century, computers have been widely and explicitly used for music making in Western societies. Students are well aware that contemporary music making uses digital technologies in many forms, and they are keen to acquire the skills and techniques necessary to make the music they hear on TV and the radio, and the music they experience at concerts and download over the Internet. Even instrumentalists performing traditional repertoire are conscious of the difference that good recording production techniques and processes can make on how their work is received and judged, and they know that appropriate social media marketing can help them reach their audience.

The integration of digital music systems introduces an expanded set of musicianship skills, as discussed in Chapter 5, and a host of new performance and production techniques that can be understood, practiced, and mastered. These contemporary musicianship skills need to be integrated into the music curriculum if students are to fully explore the potential of the digital technologies they employ.

Increasing student awareness of digital processes and computing systems also has benefits beyond music education. Computational thinking is increasingly recognized as a generic competency or a new literacy.[4] Relatedly, studies of the acoustics of sound and digital signal processing can inform many areas of the music curriculum, including acoustic instrument studies, orchestration techniques, digital sound synthesis, and loudspeaker distribution. These are just some of the benefits that the integration of new technologies can have across the music program.

Integration Prompting Change

Because new music technologies require new understandings and skills, it is clear that the integration of music technologies will affect music learning. But educators are often reluctant to change their content and practices, preferring to use technologies as tools that support existing teaching methods. Unsurprisingly, this phenomenon exists beyond music education. According to the educational researcher Bridget Somekh, "much of the research on teacher's use of information and communication technology (ICT) in their teaching describes low levels of usage and minimal pedagogical change."[5] Many music educators are resistant to change because it can take time and effort to learn new skills and incorporate new teaching resources. Change can be seen as a threat to highly valued existing practices, and there is a risk that the results of change may not improve the lot of students or staff. But the ramifications of not embracing changes brought about by new music technologies must be weighed against the risks they pose. These include the wasted time and effort that result from retaining labor-intensive, tedious processes; the marginalization or increased irrelevance of music curricula that are seen as out of date; and the risk that staff and students may not benefit from new and improved processes and from the musical and educational outcomes these processes enable.

There are, of course, many ways of integrating music technologies while managing the changes these introduce. Integration by *evolution*, rather than *revolution*, is one such approach. It involves the gradual substitution of existing activities with technology-based ones.

Change as Evolution

Thinking of technological change reminds us of the rapid pace of information technology development in the twentieth century. The century also witnessed great changes in Western musical ideas; for example, in serialism and stochastic compositional methods' challenges to tonality, and the influences of non-Western musical styles such as African music in jazz, rock, hip-hop, and minimalism. Technological developments contributed to these changes. Tape recording technologies enabled musique concrète techniques, while computing technologies assisted the development of stochastic and algorithmic compositional approaches. Sound amplification technologies enabled softer voices to be heard over large ensembles, facilitating crooners such as Bob Hope and Frank Sinatra. Audio recording altered access to music and ways of making music, while distribution methods evolved from tapes and pressed vinyl to CDs, MP3 files, and Internet streaming.

The extent of these changes is immense and well beyond the scope of this chapter, but many aspects were canvassed in earlier chapters. However, it is important to understand that the parallel development of music and technology usually follows the path noted by Marshall McLuhan: a technology first imitates an older medium, and then moves on to establish itself as a new medium.[6] For example, the linear timelines of digital audio recorders were based on tape recorder metaphors, but now programs such as *Ableton Live* feature nonlinear access to audio regions. Additionally, music publishing systems such as *Sibelius* and *Finale* were based on a paper manuscript metaphor, but now include audio playback and movie synchronization functions that go beyond the metaphor. It is clear that, as with electronic mass media in McLuhan's time, the evolution of digital music technologies today begins with metaphoric imitation leading to innovative use and finally to the establishment of new metaphors.

This development process provides a template for an evolutionary approach to the integration of digital technologies into music education practices. Digital technologies can first substitute for existing practices, allowing an individual to become familiar with their tools while maintaining familiar musical content. In a second phase, instructors can take advantage of new musical practices and more flexible approaches to learning afforded by technologies for their curricula. Thus, music education practices can evolve alongside technological developments. As new metaphors are established and new techniques for music making are introduced, music learning can proceed from these revised perspectives, in an iterative process of renewal through modification.

Change as Addition

While much technological change is seen as developmental, not all change is incremental. Some technologies or musical practices are simply new. The laptop computer as a live performance instrument is one example. Although its use as an instrument inherits features from previous acoustic and electronic musical practices, the computer does not represent a development from another instrument. Similarly, consider the saxophone, which in the twentieth century was new even though it inherited features from previous woodwind and brass instruments. The saxophone found a role in new musical practices—jazz in particular—just as the laptop found a home in electronic dance music and experimental computer music.

The pressure for regular additions to music curricula are not new, but the speed of advances in the past fifty years have meant that music curricula have been under increased pressure to include more material, topics, and activities. Moreover, participatory educational theories have developed from the ideas of John Dewey, who emphasized experience over observation as a method of learning. Such participatory learning requires time for activity and reflection.[7] But participatory learning and continual additions to the music program may crowd the curriculum to such an extent that depth and quality are sacrificed if nothing else changes. This situation arises even without technologies, as educators try to accommodate changing musical cultures, increased access to information, vocationalism, and other trends. At some point, incremental curriculum bloat becomes too much, and new conceptions of curriculum structure must be substituted for old ones.

The integration of new technologies and the musical practices associated with them into music education should be seen as an opportunity to reevaluate learning objectives. These tools allow the savvy instructor to establish critical learning pathways that focus on musical intelligence rather than on the rote acquisition of skills and facts.

This requires an often challenging reassessment of what is important and essential within a music curriculum. Moving forward requires the recognition that musical intelligence is not to be equated with particular musical styles, cultures, or privileged musical contexts, but rather with the development of intuitions and abilities in any authentic context. It is best to provide rich experiences as a launching pad for musical explorations within a musical culture relevant to the student. In twenty-first-century Western countries, an appropriate launching pad is likely to involve contemporary music practices dependent upon digital technologies.

Updating Curriculum and Pedagogy

The challenges of integrating music technologies into music education practices give rise to a number of important questions. What should be in the curriculum? How should it be delivered? What effect will this have on the teacher's role?

To start, focus on how to provide *meaningful engagement* with music (using computers and/or other equipment) rather than specifying prescriptively the particular activities or tasks.[8] Chapter 1 outlines details of this approach. Likewise, turn to the music curriculum of the New South Wales Department of Education in Australia for an example of how music technologies have been encouraged in middle school music programs by the specific integration of ICTs. That curriculum provides an overview of the rationale behind it and links to useful research supporting the approach.[9] The challenge is not whether to include technology in the music curriculum, but how to best integrate it into listening, producing, performing, recording, learning, and discussion exercises.

The rapid changes in technologies and the associated expansion of musical genres and distribution methods mean that it is unlikely that a teacher will be more knowledgeable than his or her students in all respects. Consequently, the teacher's role and the student–teacher relationship may be challenged by the integration of new technologies. A technology-rich environment encourages the teacher to act as a coach to the students, assisting and guiding their learning.

Teacher as Helper

The integration of digital technologies into a music program can enable students to work at computers in self-directed ways. It can also enable them to access information via the Internet from a wide variety of sources, and to use digital tools to leverage their musicality to produce results more efficiently. This potential is most fully realized when teachers *facilitate* rather than *direct* learning activities, and when students are motivated and supported by peer networks. The teacher's role in this situation is that of a coach who facilitates, encourages, mentors, advises, and monitors student activities. At times teachers become fellow travelers with students on the learning journey, as they uncover new software features, artists, and musical uses of digital devices. Ian Brown, in his book *On Becoming a Teacher*, defines this approach as a "helper" relationship with students. He claims it is a healthy role for the teacher and is the approach most likely to lead to effective student outcomes. He summarizes his research into the ways students respond to different teacher personalities, indicating that students "believe they will most readily respond in terms of motivation or desire to learn, to a person who is 'caring,' 'considerate,' 'accepting,' 'empathetic,' 'thoughtful,' 'forgiving,' 'understanding' and 'tactful.' "[10] Being supportive facilitators is not the only way that teachers can act as music educators, but it seems to be congruent with maximizing the capacities of music technologies for student learning.

Connectivity

Digital technologies can, perhaps ironically, play a role in supporting their own integration into education through their use for communication among students, teachers, and parents. According to a 2014 report by the New Media Consortium, digital social media platforms "make it easy to share and find stories and media. In addition to interacting with the content, social media makes it easy to interact with friends and institutions that produced the content."[11]

This digital connectivity is increasingly inserting itself into music education via online resources and online courses, as discussed in some detail in Chapters 11 and 12. In 2011 Clayton Christensen, Michael Horn, and Curtis Johnson predicted an expanded role for online learning. They wrote that "online courses accounted for just 1 percent of all courses in 2007. Not much change is on the horizon if one projects linearly into the future. But when viewed from the logarithmic perspective, the data suggest that by 2019, about 50 percent of high school courses will be delivered online."[12] This suggests that the integration of digital technologies into music education will be multifaceted, affecting music production and distribution as well as access to sources of knowledge and support. With regard to the role of digital technologies for learning support, Christensen and his colleagues go on to suggest that their implementation in schools may occur in stages.

> We call the first of these stages computer-based, or online, learning. In this stage, the software will be proprietary and relatively expensive to develop … the instructional methods in this software will largely mirror the dominant type of learning method in each subject … The second phase of this disruption we term student-centric technology, in which software has been developed that can help students learn each subject in a manner that is consistent with their learning needs. Whereas computer-based learning is disruptive relative to the monolithic mode of teacher-led instruction, student-centric technology is disruptive relative to personal tutors.

A prerequisite for experiencing the full influence of these communicative effects of digital technologies is that everyone involved has liberal access to the means of communication. Typically, this implies widespread access to Internet-connected devices such as smartphones and tablet computers.

Ownership

Computers were once so expensive that only institutions or governments could afford to purchase them. Now each person may have several computing devices in their home in the form of microwaves, temperature sensors, and television sets, let alone the more obvious laptops and mobile devices. Digital devices used for music are not inexpensive, but when viewed as musical instruments, the costs are about on par with many traditional instruments. In many cases, digital devices are purchased for other purposes already, and their use for music is but one of many applications. Thus the costs of the device are amortized over its many uses, and additional software costs are not excessive.

In most educational settings, there will be a balance of institutional and personal computing devices. As outlined in Chapter 16, institutional devices can be set up permanently in music rooms or in other locations within the institution, or they can be made available to purchase or rent like other musical instruments. Device ownership by students is common (sometimes mandated) in secondary and higher education. In schools where student device ownership is the exception rather than the rule, the institution can encourage students to use their own devices in music classes by providing supportive infrastructure, including secure storage, wireless networks, and auxiliary equipment such as audio interfaces, audio monitors, and MIDI keyboards.

Funding

Funding is always a barrier to resource innovation in educational settings, and even though computing equipment is increasingly more affordable—or offset by student ownership—music technology costs are not trivial in a tight education budget. Fortunately, there is reasonable societal support for the introduction of computing technologies into schools, and so at least the argument for funding devices that have general utility, as well as musical applications, is not as difficult as it might be for other resources in the arts.

Sources of funding can exist both locally and farther afield. Most music departments have an annual operational budget; with planning, it may be possible to acquire music technology resources as part of the normal operational budget, or via a special grant from the school or institution. It is quite likely that the school's parent and community association will support technology, and a proposal to such an organization is worthwhile. Most school districts, counties, and states have development grant schemes as well. Often these are tied to specific strategic goals that the governing body has set, but it should not be difficult to find either a technological, pedagogical, or cultural angle that supports the deployment of music technology systems. Initiatives also exist in science education fields to integrate the arts and sciences; collaboration between music and science departments can give access to these. Advertisements for grant programs may appear in electronic newsletters, newspapers, or web sites, and there will often be a grants officer who can advise about programs and their requirements. There may be opportunities for philanthropic support from alumni or companies operating in the community, especially technology-focused companies looking for a feel-good cause. Be sure to investigate how equipment suppliers manage educational discounts and other support programs.

When applying for funding, it is important to have relevant documentation that supports the educational merit and technical appropriateness of the project. Such evidence is often available from music associations, equipment companies, and official music curriculum documents.

Training and Professional Development

Educators' work commitments are usually quite demanding and their time highly scheduled, so a planned staff development program is a critical part of the integration of new music technologies. Changing technologies require a process of training and support so that staff have a chance to adapt their abilities and attitudes to the new methods. New staff skills to cover may include additional skills in using the equipment, revised teaching strategies to encourage the best use of equipment, and workshops on curriculum revisions that incorporate opportunities afforded by the new technologies. As with all learning, it is useful to reinforce the new skills and knowledge by scheduling a series of professional development sessions that start before the new technologies are integrated and continue during their use. The need for such professional development is underscored by the advanced age of many music educators, for whom music technology skills development was not a part of university training. The

New Media Consortium's Horizon Report suggests that even in 2014, digital media literacy in educators is still not common:

> Despite the widespread agreement on the importance of digital media literacy, training in the supporting skills and techniques is rare in teacher education and non-existent in the preparation of faculty. As lecturers and professors begin to realize that they are limiting their students by not helping them to develop and use digital media literacy skills across the curriculum, the lack of formal training is being offset through professional development or informal learning, but we are far from seeing digital media literacy as a norm. This challenge is exacerbated by the fact that digital literacy is less about tools and more about thinking, and thus skills and standards based on tools and platforms have proven to be somewhat ephemeral.[13]

Purchasing music technology equipment should be just the splash that starts a ripple of cultural change throughout a music program and those involved with it. A staff development program is vital in ensuring that the impact of this ripple effect leads to a permanent improvement. Christensen and his colleagues highlight some opportunities and requirements of pedagogical change as follows:

> As the monolithic system of instruction shifts to a learning environment powered by student-centric technology, teachers' roles will gradually shift over time, too. The shift might not be easy, but it will be rewarding. Instead of spending most of their time delivering one-size-fits-all lessons year after year, teachers can spend much more of their time traveling from student to student to help individuals with individual problems. Teachers will act more as learning coaches and tutors to help students find the learning approach that makes the most sense for them. They will mentor and motivate them through the learning with the aid of real-time computer data on how the student is learning. This means, however, that they will need very different skills to add value in this future from the skills with which education schools are equipping them today.[14]

Depending on the extent of a school's integration of music technology and on local circumstances, a range of options for professional development become available. An existing staff member, alumnus, or even a student may be able to instruct staff on how to operate new software or hardware. Staff from retail outlets where equipment was purchased may agree to hold a session covering the installation and operation of the equipment. It may be possible for teachers from outside the music department who have experience with computing devices to talk about their pedagogical approaches or to facilitate a workshop. Staff can also enroll in a number of online courses available for particular software applications. Moreover, some associations provide training opportunities. In the United States, these include *MusicEdTech*,[15] Avid's training partners,[16] and *TI:ME*.[17] In the United Kingdom and Ireland, courses can be found through *Sound and Music*[18] and the *Music Education Directory*.[19] In Australia, the *Soundhouse Music Alliance*[20] runs short courses in music technologies for students and instructors. Other countries likely feature many similar associations and private training providers.

Conclusion

The effective integration of new music technologies into educational contexts requires the consideration of a number of factors, which include logistical issues of equipment choices, funding, location, connectivity, and security. Educational issues such as technology-related curriculum and pedagogy modifications and how to best support these through professional development must also be considered. The benefits of integrating new technologies and associated musical practices, however, are many, and include the renewal of music education programs and the resultant encouragement of educators to reassess and refine their missions and priorities. The integration of digital music systems and practices can enable more relevant, inclusive, and efficient music-making opportunities for both staff and students. An evolutionary approach to the integration of music technologies is one of a gradual, yet continual, expansion of the role of digital devices and an associated transformation of music-making practices and learning strategies. Over time, these changes will become normalized as part of the educational culture and lead to a harmonization of a student's musical experiences within and beyond the school environment. Timothy Taylor sums it up in this way: "Technology, however awe inspiring and anxiety producing it may seem to be upon its introduction to the realm of human social life, quickly becomes part of social life, naturalized into the quotidian normality as it helps people do things they have always done: communicate, create, labor, remember, experience pleasure, and, of course, make and listen to music."[21] While the pace of technological change is unlikely to slow down and the music technologies yet to be invented are difficult to predict, one thing is certain: humans will continue to strive to express themselves through sound and to apply technologies to tasks in order to amplify their musicality.

Reflection Questions

1. Why might music technologies be considered both epistemological and pedagogical tools?
2. What is 'computational literacy'?
3. What are some music technologies that are important mediators of musical experiences?
4. What is the difference between technological change as 'evolution' and change as 'addition'?
5. What do Christensen, Horn, and Johnson mean by a 'student-centric technology' approach to online learning?
6. Why is the mobility of modern digital devices important for musicians?
7. How might social networks be used to support music learning?
8. What are the advantages of music students owning their own digital devices?
9. What are the funding sources mentioned in the chapter?
10. Who can provide professional development assistance when integrating new music technologies?

Teaching Tips

1. Use the cachet of digital technologies to enhance a music program's perceived relevance to students.
2. Focus assessment in ways that allow students to use music technologies to achieve those musical outcomes.
3. Capitalize on many students' immediate sense of gratification in sound sampling and manipulation as a motivation to further music studies.
4. Select software of different complexity for students of different ages.
5. Consider how a coaching approach to teaching may lead to increased student confidence and motivation.
6. Use the connections between digital technologies and contemporary music styles to broaden the musical genres covered by the curriculum.
7. Implement computer-based tools such as publishing programs and audio editors to assign more efficient student tasks.
8. Encourage digitally savvy students to help their peers and instruct teachers.
9. Integrate digital devices into ensemble activities.
10. Encourage students to bring their digital devices to class so they may better relate classroom and home activities.

Suggested Tasks for Educators

1. Explore ways to enhance teaching practices by using more music technologies.
2. Make a list of funding sources that could be used to purchase computing technologies for the music program.
3. Locate individuals or organizations that could provide professional development in music technology.
4. Undertake a training program in music technology to increase skills and awareness.
5. Regularly visit a music store with a wide range of music technologies to keep up to date with what is available.

Chapter Summary

The integration of music technologies into music education programs can expand the horizon of opportunities for students and staff. However, as with any educational change, such integration requires planning for effective implementation. The integration of digital technologies and the music practices surrounding them can improve the relevance of a music education program. However, the effectiveness of the integration will depend on how teaching practices respond to the change. Learning activities that maximize a student's meaningful engagement with music are likely to use technology in a way that does not fixate on the equipment, but on the student's experience using it. Digital technology is changing so rapidly that it is unrealistic to expect teachers to be experts in all aspects of it, and so it is appropriate that teachers focus on coaching students and are comfortable sharing the learning journey with them. Taking an evolutionary approach to the integration of digital technologies and providing staff with professional development along the way will make the changes associated with technology integration less disruptive, and will ensure that digital technologies are used in ways that best amplify students' musicality.

Notes

1. Taylor, T.D. (2001). *Strange sounds: Music, technology and culture*. New York: Routledge, p. 201.
2. DiSessa, A. (2000). *Changing minds: Computers, learning, and literacy*. Cambridge, MA: MIT Press, p. 110.
3. The idea that technologies have a significant role to play in student learning was clearly articulated in S. Papert (1980), *Mindstorms: Children, computers, and powerful ideas*, New York: Basic Books.
4. Rushkoff, D. (2010). *Program or be programmed: Ten commands for a digital age*. New York: OR Books.
5. Somekh, B. (2008). Factors affecting teachers' pedagogical adoption of ICT. In J. Voogt & G. Knezek (Eds.), *International handbook of information technology in primary and secondary education* (vol. 20, pp. 449–460). New York: Springer, p. 449.
6. McLuhan, M. (1964). *Understanding media: The extensions of man*. London: Sphere Books.
7. Dewey, J. (1934). *Art as experience*. New York: Putnam's.
8. Brown, A.R. (2000). *Modes of compositional engagement*. Paper presented at the Interfaces: The Australasian Computer Music Conference, Brisbane, Australia.
9. Music and ICT curriculum support: NSW Department of Education, accessed April 2014. http://www.curriculumsupport.education.nsw.gov.au/secondary/creativearts/ict/music/.
10. Brown, I. (2002). *On becoming a teacher: The teachers' personality and the students' response*. Melbourne: North Essendon Therapy Centre, p. 72.
11. Johnson, L., Adams-Baker, S., Estrada, V., & Freeman, A. (2014). *NMC Horizon Report: 2014 Higher Education Edition*. Austin, Texas: New Media Consortium, p. 8.
12. Christensen, C.M., Horn, M., & Johnson, C. (2011). *Disrupting class: How disruptive innovation will change the way the world learns*. New York: McGraw-Hill.
13. Johnson, L., Adams-Baker, S., Estrada, V., & Freeman, A. (2014). *NMC Horizon Report: 2014 Higher Education Edition*. Austin, Texas: New Media Consortium, p. 22.
14. Christensen, C.M., Horn, M., & Johnson, C. (2011). *Disrupting class: How disruptive innovation will change the way the world learns*. New York: McGraw-Hill.
15. *MusicEdTech*: http://musicedtech.com/.
16. *Avid training partners*: www.avid.com/US/support/training.
17. *Technology Institute for Music Educators (TI:ME)*: www.ti-me.org/.
18. *Sound and Music*: http://soundandmusic.org/.
19. The *Music Education Directory* tracks music courses in the UK and Ireland: www.ukmusic.org/skills-academy/music-education-directory/.
20. *Soundhouse Music Alliance*: http://soundhouse.org.au/.
21. Taylor, T.D. (2001). *Strange sounds: Music, technology and culture*. New York: Routledge, p. 206.

Glossary

This glossary contains definitions of words that are frequently used in music software and tutorials about music technology. The glossary is ordered alphabetically.

Acoustics—The study of the physics of sound.

Aftertouch—Pressure adjustments applied to a MIDI keyboard while the note is sounding.

Algorithm—A step-by-step procedure for problem solving.

Amplifier—A device that increases the magnitude of a voltage or current without distorting the waveform of the signal. An amplifier takes a weak signal from a line level or mike level source and provides the necessary power level to operate loudspeakers.

Amplitude—The value of the largest sample in a signal; it corresponds to perceived loudness.

Analog signal—An electronic signal that varies along a continuous dimension.

Asynchronous—A characteristic where two or more processes run at the same time.

Attack—The beginning portion of a sound, when the musical note begins. Antonym: Release.

Binary—Base two number system, typically using values 0 and 1 only.

Bit—The smallest unit of computer data, capable of being in one of two states, 0 or 1.

Blog—A method of web-based publishing consisting of text and rich media entries, often listed in reverse chronological order. Sometimes called a weblog.

Buffer—A temporary storage area in memory.

Byte—A computer data amount equal to eight bits. A MIDI message is usually three bytes long, and a single audio sample is usually two bytes (16 bits) in size.

Clipping—Amplifier overload or signal processing increases above a maximum level, resulting in a form of distortion.

Compression—Reduction of the effective gain of an amplifier at one signal level with respect to the gain at another signal level.

Controller—A device that lets you enter or change events in a computer or other digital device. Examples: synthesizer, wind controller, mouse, computer keyboard. A MIDI controller is a controller that 'speaks' the MIDI language.

Continuous controller—Refers to non-note MIDI information where values change on a linear scale rather than simply have two states, on and off. For example, volume, pitch bending, modulation (vibrato). These parameters can change continuously over time and allow electronically generated music to sound more expressive.

CPU—Central processing unit, the chip that is the 'brains' of the computer. Sometimes used to refer to the computer's 'box' in which the CPU is housed.

Cycle—One repetition of a periodic waveform.

Digital Signal Processor (DSP)—A device, often a chip, that has a special set of functions designed for speedy processing of video or audio data.

Distortion—A variation in a signal, sometimes undesirable.

Envelope—The changes in a sound over time. For example, amplitude envelope is the change in loudness over the duration of a note: attack, sustain, decay, release.

Equalization—The selective adjustment of volume at a specific frequency.

Filter—An electronic device that permits certain frequencies to pass while stopping others.

Fourier transform—A procedure for changing a time domain representation (waveform) into a frequency domain representation (spectrum).

Frequency—The number of vibrations or oscillations per second. Measured in cycles or Hertz.

Frequency Modulation (FM)—The altering of the pitch of one signal by the pitch of another. Small amounts create vibrato while large amounts create new timbres.

General MIDI—A standard that specifies (among other things) what types of sounds will be in synthesizer patch locations 1–127.

Glitch—Interruption in the audio stream, usually unwanted.

Grain—A very small sound fragment.

GUI—Graphical user interface.

Hard drive—A memory storage device now common to all computers. Its memory is listed in megabytes (MB) or gigabytes (GB).

Microtonal—The use of notes closer than a semitone in pitch.

MIDI—Musical Instrument Digital Interface. It is a standard language that lets instruments, devices, software, and hardware from different manufacturers communicate fluently.

Mixer—A device which adds different audio signals together.

Modulation—The effecting of one signal by another. For example, vibrato is caused by regular modulation (variation) of pitch.

Morphology—The study of forms and structure. In music, how audio spectra change over time and through space.

Musique concrète—A form of musical composition made from a collage of recorded sounds.

Mute—A button or command to turn off specified tracks.

Network—A collection of computing devices connected so that they can share information and peripherals.

Network jamming—Performing music using a computer with others via local or Internet connections.

Noise—Unwanted sound.

Oscillator—A device for generating a periodic waveform.

Overtone—A spectral component of a sound; by itself, a sine wave of a particular frequency.

Pad—A long sustained 'washy' chord with a lush texture often played on a synthesizer.

Panning—Refers to moving an audio signal left or right in the stereo spectrum.

Partial—A spectral component of a sound; by itself, a sine wave of a particular frequency.

Patch or **Preset**—A synthesizer sound or software setting that is stored in computer memory.

Plug-in—A computer program that can add functionality to another. In music software, plug-ins are often synthesizers and effects processors used by host music applications.

Podcast—Refers to both the content and means of distributing multimedia files such as audio programs or videos over the Internet for playback on portable devices or personal computers.

Quantize—A process of rounding values. Typically used in MIDI sequencers to 'fix' rhythmic inaccuracies in a musical track. Quantizing 'rounds off' musical notes to the nearest eighth note, sixteenth note, and so forth as specified by the user.

RAM—Random access memory. Computer memory that can be used over and over.

Real-time—Occurring so fast that a delay is imperceptible.

Reverb—The reflecting and echoing of sounds in a space.

ROM—Read only memory. Computer memory or storage that cannot be erased and reused.

Sample rate—The speed (frequency) at which measurements of an audio signal are taken when converting to a digital waveform.

Sample resolution—The degree of accuracy with which samples are measured when converting to a digital waveform.

Sampler—A type of synthesizer which derives its sounds from recording actual sounds (instruments or nonmusical sounds).

Sequencer—A piece of hardware or software that allows you to record multiple tracks of music one on top of the other while listening to what was recorded previously.

Signal—A temporal phenomenon that carries information, such as an electrical current or digital stream of numbers.

Sound event—A sonic occurrence that occurs in a particular place during a particular time interval.

Sound module—A sound making device (synthesizer) that does not have an integral controller and must be controlled remotely.

Sound object—An acoustical event. Treated as a phenomenological sound formation referentially independent of its source.

Soundscape—The sonic environment, either as an actual environment or abstract sonic construction/montage.

Spectrum—The representation of a signal in terms of its frequency components.

Synthesis—The generation of a sound from mathematical principles or electronic processes.

Synthesizer—A programmable device that generates (synthesizes) sound.

Track—Digital Audio Workstations borrowed this term from multi-track recording studios, referring to tape tracks. A track is one of a number of locations where a musical part can be recorded and played back.

Velocity—Velocity is the MIDI way of determining how hard a note is pressed on the keyboard controller.

Waveform—A pattern of sound pressure variations over time, often represented as a series of digital sample values in a computer.

Wavetable—An area of computer memory that stores waveform values.

WYSIWYG—"What You See Is What You Get"; what is displayed on the computer monitor is what the printed output will look like.

This glossary owes a debt to several resources including:

- Dodge, C., & Jerse, T. A. (1997). *Computer music*. New York: Schirmer Books.
- Schafer, R. M. (1977). *The soundscape: Our sonic environment and the tuning of the world*. New York: Knopf.

Index